CREOLE GUMBO
AND
ALL THAT JAZZ

CREOLE GUMBO

AND
ALL THAT JAZZ

A NEW ORLEANS
SEAFOOD COOKBOOK
HOWARD MITCHAM

Pelican Publishing Company

Gretna 1999

First published by Addison-Wesley Publishing Company, Inc., 1978
Published by arrangement with the author by Pelican Publishing
    Company, Inc., 1992

Pelican edition, 1992
Second printing, 1997
Third printing, 1999

*The word "Pelican" and the depiction of a pelican are trademarks
of Pelican Publishing Company, Inc., and are registered in the
U.S. Patent and Trademark Office.*

Library of Congress Cataloging-in-Publication Data

Mitcham, Howard.
    Creole gumbo and all that jazz: a New Orleans seafood
cookbook/Howard Mitcham.—Pelican ed.
        p. cm.
    Originally published: Reading, Mass.: Addison-Wesley, © 1978.
    Includes bibliographical references and index.
    ISBN 0-88289-870-1
        1. Cookery (Seafood) 2. Cookery, American—Louisiana style.
I. Title.
[TX747.M54   1992]
641.6'92—dc20

                                        91-26188
                                            CIP

Manufactured in the United States of America
Published by Pelican Publishing Company, Inc.
1000 Burmaster Street, Gretna, Louisiana 70053

To all the cooks, past and present, public and private, who have contributed to the glorious art of seafood cookery in New Orleans.

To my friend Kid Thomas, great jazzman and trumpet player. And to all the other musicians, black and white, living and dead, who have contributed to the invention, development, dissemination, and preservation of what we know as Traditional New Orleans Jazz.

To certain individuals who have labored strenuously to preserve Traditional New Orleans Jazz and to keep it alive, vibrant, and healthy: Barbara Reed, William Russell, Richard Allen, Alan Jaffe, and Al Rose.

Photo by Johnny Donnels

Preface

It's a brazen thing for me to bring forth another Creole cookbook when there are already about forty good ones on the market. However, most of them are general books that cover the whole field of Creole and Cajun cuisine from soup to nuts. I have long felt that there was need for a Creole cookbook devoted exclusively to seafood cookery. When you begin to think about it, the great Creole and Cajun dishes that you remember best are often seafood in some form—shrimp, crabs, oysters, and saltwater fishes. Southern Louisiana is one of the most bountiful seafood areas in the world, rivaling Portugal, Spain, France, and Italy. And the heights to which the Creole and Cajun cooks have brought the art of preparing these gifts of the sea are unsurpassed by any single country's national cuisine, even that of la belle France, the mother of the art of cookery.

Creole-Cajun seafood cookery has long had a need for a cookbook in which the classic seafood items can shine alone in all their glory. With trepidation I have attempted to take on this job myself, and let me tell you, brothers and sisters, it was no mean task. It has taken over twenty-five years of study, thought, meditation, and kitchen practice, and now I find that I've just scratched the surface. It would take several lifetimes to master the art in its entirety.

I definitely am not writing for the Creoles and Cajuns themselves, who know all the answers already. Good cooking has become so ingrained in them that it is now intuition. Every Cajun housewife down on the bayou, every Creole grande dame in New Orleans, every cook in every restaurant, black or white, male or female, will be able to find plenty of flaws in this book. No two of these cooks ever do any one thing just alike or, for that matter, exactly the same way twice. It's this diversity, this perpetual creative ferment that keeps Creole cuisine alive and vibrant, the most vigorous school of cookery in America today.

A recipe is a poor dead thing, just printed letters on paper. It's the cook who takes the cold dead formula and twists and shapes it who is the true culinary artist. This type of cook measures things in the palm of the hand instead of with teaspoons and tablespoons. Quantities are vague: "a little, some more, enough." Asked how long to cook it: "till it's done."

Many peoples have made their contribution to Creole cuisine—the French, the Spanish, Indians, blacks, and a variety of representatives from the islands of the West Indies and Caribbean. The blacks especially have made a great contribution to the art and helped to preserve it. In the past many a New Orleans restaurant, in an effort to prove itself hoity-toity and very recherché, imported a famous chef from France, a real maître of the art, who spent long hours in the kitchen lecturing to his black staff on the intricacies and subtleties of haute cuisine. As soon as he turned his back, they'd go back to doing it the way they'd always done it—make the roux a very dark brown and burn the onions just a little bit to bring out their flavor. Often the grand chef threw up his hands in despair and went back to France. That's why Creole cookery has survived; its black practitioners are its backbone.

Anytime the Creole city cookery began to get tired, jaded, and effete, it would always receive a strong infusion of new ideas from the Cajuns down on the bayous, in the swamps, and on the prairies. Their husky country cooking, rich and rambunctious, blended into and gave life to the gentler methods of the city. Many of the famous dishes served in great New Orleans restaurants today are Cajun in origin. The two cooking systems, Creole (city) and Cajun (country), have become so intermingled that it's sometimes difficult to tell them apart, and this is as it should be. They're a happy amalgam.

All these converging influences have made New Orleans the most cosmopolitan and sophisticated seafood center in the world today. Paris, Marseilles, Lisbon, Rome, Athens, and all the rest must step down. That's why tourists and visitors from all over the world stream into New Orleans by the millions. They want to sample the Creole cuisine whose fame has spread so far and wide. As far back as 1856, William Makepeace Thackeray wrote: "In New Orleans you can eat a bouillabaisse than which a better was never eaten in Marseilles."

And many of the food-conscious visitors who come to New Orleans want to learn the mysteries of Creole cookery so they can practice "do it yourself" when they get back home. It is for these worthy souls that I've written this Creole seafood cookbook. I want to apostle-ize and spread the gospel far and wide.

One of the beliefs I want to dispel is that this great cookery is difficult and complex. It may have a mystique, but there's no real mystery to it once you've learned the basic ground rules. Thoreau said, "Simplify, simplify," and the great Escoffier himself said, "The greatest dishes are very simple dishes." With these ideals in mind, I have tried to bring Creole seafood cookery down to earth so that anyone anywhere can both practice the art and enjoy consuming the product.

All this seafood and all that jazz! As everybody knows, jazz was born right here in New Orleans, and now it has spread everywhere as one of America's greatest contributions to the culture of the whole world. To provide some spice and to teach outsiders a little about the colorful origins of this great music, I'm scattering tidbits of jazz history and lyrics of old jazz songs throughout this book. (Call it *lagniappe,* to use a lively New Orleans word. Pronounced lan-yap, it means "a little something extra." When a Cajun child was sent to the grocery store, the grocer always came through with a piece of candy or some other extra goody. The custom spread to the Creoles of New Orleans and other parts of Louisiana.) And so the book is dedicated to New Orleans seafood and New Orleans jazz. An old Creole proverb can aptly apply to either of them: "C'est bon comme la vie"—It's as good as life itself.

This is more than a mere cookbook. It's an autobiographical chronicle of my long love affair with New Orleans, the fun I've had cooking, eating, dancing, drinking, carousing, and loving in "the city that care forgot." Hoping you are the same,

New Orleans,　　　　　　　　　　　　　　yr. obt. svt.
January, 1978　　　　　　　　　　　Howard Mitcham

Acknowledgments

My profound thanks are due all the cooks, chefs, housewives, and restaurant owners who have furnished their treasured recipes for this book. Almost all the recipes have been kitchen tested in my "laboratory." Some of them have been modified only slightly, but others have been subjected to drastic revision. Because some of these recipes are very old and have been passed down through several generations, they have had to be reshaped to conform to modern measurements and cooking methods.

I am indebted to the Louisiana Wildlife and Fisheries Commission and to its employees who made all of its facilities available to me: J. Burton Angelle, director; Marian "Pie" Pendley, executive assistant; McFadden Duffy, public relations specialist; and Bob Dennie, editor of the Commission's excellent magazine *The Louisiana Conservationist*, who furnished many fine photographs from the magazine's files. Special thanks are due to "Pie" Pendley, who supplied me with many Cajun recipes from her great food column in the magazine and allowed me to twist them around and "embroider" them as I saw fit. When that lady brings out her own Cajun cookbook, it's going to be a humdinger. And what an appropriate name for a good cook—"Pie."

Thanks are due to the Special Collections Division (Archives) of the Howard-Tilton Memorial Library, Tulane University, for the use of old drawings and photos in their collection, and to assistant Bill Meneray, who helped me dig them out of the files. I am also indebted to the Library of the Louisiana State Museum for drawings and photos and to the librarians, Rose M. Lambert and Mary Julie Barrios, who helped me find them. Photographer Betsy Harnden, with her documentary camera, performed the tedious job of photographing the items from both libraries.

Richard Allen, curator, and Kay Wicker and Evelyn Rinnert, assistants, of the William Ransom Hogan Memorial Jazz Archives of Tulane Library furnished much help. Dick furnished history, and the girls helped me ferret out old jazz lyrics. Bob Cass transcribed dozens of old blues lyrics from his extensive antique record collection, and I have used several of these. Les Muscott, well-known jazz banjoist, and his wife, Barbara, furnished lyrics and historical information, as did "T-Bone Scotty" Hill of the French Market Jazz Band.

Most of the jazz lyrics printed in this book are copyrighted, and one of my most indispensable and hard-working helpers was Mrs. Mary T. Dyer, who sought out the copyright owners for me—a not easy task, considering how many dozens of letters of enquiry had to be sent and phone calls made. But it wasn't a thankless task, because I'm thanking her here and now.

Thanks are due to Bob Greenwood, scholar and chief bibliographer of the Tulane Library, who read the manuscript and offered helpful suggestions. Roy "Red" Mouton, a bonafide Cajun, offered information on the background of the Cajuns. Gilbert Fortier and his wife, Maggi, offered information on the Creoles, as well as recipes and illustrations from the Fortier collection. Gypsy Lou Webb patiently typed the manuscript, and Darlene Doherty, my secretary and Girl Friday, performed dozens of chores. Francisco McBride, Duane Raven, Jr., Roscoe Misselhorn, Kenneth Burke, and Emily Davis contributed their drawings with no other compensation than my effusive gratitude.

For faithful kitchen helpers, testers, and guinea pigs who have consistently aided in the preparation, cooking, tasting, and consumption of many of the recipes given in this book, I offer my profound thanks; among that number are Buell and Kathy Williams, Meda Colvin, Darlene Doherty, John, Joan, and Lurana Donnels, Allison Muscott, Armour Ratcliff, Herb Hornstra, Connie and Lois Regan, W. Gray Smith, Brian Oviedo, Jimmy Mitcham, Ulrica Mitcham, George Jones, Barbara, R. J., and Ron Donnamario, Julia, Rachel, and Bobby Turan, Artie Mitcham, Allie Nash, Conni Corll, and Mid and Vi Lester.

H. M.

Contents

Chapter 1

The Melting Pot

New Orleans has long been one of the most cosmopolitan melting pots in the world. There are few cities anywhere that have absorbed so many diverse cultures and none at all that could have done it with better grace. The ambience of New Orleans is like its most famous dish—a real living pot of gumbo, a potpourri, one hell of a stew. Thus it is no hollow accolade when enthusiasts dub New Orleans "America's Most Interesting City." And since it does everything with flair, gusto, and an irrepressible joie de vivre, it has pretty well earned that other distinctive title that people often give it—"The City That Care Forgot." For a closer understanding of this phenomenon, perhaps you'd like to . . .

MEET THE CREOLES

What is a Creole? Nobody seems to know. There are different kinds of Creoles, and each claims to be the real thing. It's a subject worth a little investigation. Webster's dictionary says a Creole is "a person of European descent born especially in the West Indies or Spanish America; a white person descended from early French or Spanish settlers of the U.S. Gulf states. . . ."

Let us peer into the shadowy background. Two aristocratic Canadian brothers, Pierre le Moyne, Sieur d'Iberville, and Jean Baptiste le Moyne, Sieur de Bienville, were given the job of establishing the colony of Louisiana, an

Earliest known view of New Orleans, drawn in 1719,
shortly after Bienville had established the colony.
(Courtesy of Louisiana State Museum)

New Orleans scene, drawn in 1735 by A. DeBatz.
Indians have come to the riverfront to trade with Bienville's settlers.

immense territory that had been claimed for France by La Salle in the 1600s. Iberville founded the first settlement at Biloxi in 1699, and Mobile was founded in 1704. However, the visionary younger brother, Bienville, was sure that the Mississippi River would someday become one of the greatest commercial arteries in the world, and he resolved to establish on the river a city that would be the capital of the new empire. Accordingly he founded New Orleans in 1719.

With twenty colonists and a small group of soldiers, he cleared out the canebrakes and forests on the site of his city, and he had his engineer, de Pauger, lay out the streets. The area was roughly a parallelogram divided into sixtysix square blocks, about 300 feet on a side. The blocks were divided into lots measuring about 60 feet by 120 feet. The present Vieux Carré (Old Square), or French Quarter, as it is more popularly known, is laid out exactly as de Pauger planned it. The provincial capital was moved from Biloxi to New Orleans in 1722, and Bienville was appointed Royal Governor. The poor man had a really tough job on his hands. The early years of the colony were fraught with disaster—floods, famines, disease, and a rough and rowdy population totally disinclined to the idea of hard work.

At first there were no women in the colony, and Bienville wrote desperately to Paris, "Send me wives for my Canadians, they are running in the woods after Indian girls." The French government accordingly swept out La Salpetrier House of Correction in Paris and shipped to the colony eighty-eight "correction girls" under the care of three Ursuline nuns. Thoughtfully a midwife was sent along with the group, a Madame Dolville, whose nickname was "Sans Regret."

The king of France gave the franchise for developing the new colony to the notorious John Law and his Mississippi Company, which created the famous "Mississippi Bubble." They advertised Louisiana as a paradise on earth, with gold and silver mines all over the place and extensive pearl fisheries waiting to be developed. The government set about vigorously helping the Company obtain colonists. According to historian Albert Phelps:

The government went boldly to the task of ransacking the jails, brothels, and hospitals. Disorderly soldiers, black sheep of distinguished families, paupers, prostitutes, political suspects, friendless strangers, unsophisticated peasants straying into Paris, all were kidnapped, herded, and shipped under guard to fill the emptiness of Louisiana. To those who would emigrate voluntarily the Company offered free land, free provisions, free transportation to the colony and from New Orleans to the situation of their grants. Wealth and eternal prosperity were guaranteed to them and their heirs forever. [*]

Although most of the immigrants were vagabonds and criminals, the Company did obtain a few good citizens. In 1721, some 125 Germans came over and settled on the west bank of the river twenty miles above the town. Their skill at growing vegetables and other foodstuffs saved the town from the constant threat of famine. In later years they became completely Creole-ized, adopting French names and the French language.

[*] *Louisiana*, Albert Phelps, New York, 1905. The Creoles themselves take Phelps's writings with a grain of salt since he was prone to exaggeration.

Ah, and then there were the *filles de cassette*, or casket girls, who were sent to populate the colony. These were chaste young ladies of excellent character chosen from good middle-class families, skilled in the duties of housewives. Before leaving France, each girl received from the company a little chest, or casket, containing a coat, shirts, skirts, underwear, and other articles of clothing. The girls were closely supervised by the Ursuline nuns, who doled them out to the eagerly waiting males. As one official wrote back to France, "This merchandise was soon disposed of, so great was the want of the country." The first group of twenty girls arrived in 1728, and they kept coming at intervals until 1751. Almost every aristocratic Creole family tree in New Orleans includes a casket girl in its upper branches. Apparently the "correction girls," in spite of their midwife, were all sterile, because not one of the family trees mentions them.

In the later years of Governor Bienville's reign, a "Petticoat Rebellion" signaled the origin of what we now know as Creole cuisine. A group of about fifty young wives marched on the governor's mansion, carrying the weapons of their craft in their hands. They vigorously pounded frying pans with metal spoons and caused quite a hubbub. They protested to the governor that they were tired of a diet of corn meal mush and that something had to be done to improve the food situation. Fortunately the governor had the solution to the problem right under his own roof. His housekeeper, a Madame Langlois, had been truckin' around with the Choctaw Indians and had learned from the squaws many of their cooking secrets: how to make lye hominy and grits; how to use powdered sassafras (filé) and make gumbo; how to make corn bread, cook rice, and make jambalaya; how to cook fish, crabs, shrimp, crawfish, and wild game. Bienville put the petticoat rebels under the charge of Madame Langlois, who opened a cooking class and taught them all these bright new ideas. And on that note Creole cookery was off to a rousing start.

By 1743 the social life and customs of the Creoles had begun to emerge. The Marquis de Vaudreuil, who was governor, set the pace. He led the royal high life with banquets, balls, parades, and displays of pomp and circumstance, trying to imitate the French court at Versailles. The governor and his aristocratic assistants brought their cooks with them from France. Trained in the methods of classic French cuisine, they were forced by shortages and necessity to adopt the methods of Madame Langlois. And the burgeoning art got another shot in the arm.

Next came the Spanish. In the Seven Years War France was thoroughly defeated, and by the Treaty of Paris in 1763 she ceded to England all of Canada and Nova Scotia and all her possessions east of the Mississippi. The French king was an artful dodger, however, and to save Louisiana, he gave the colony to the King of Spain on November 3, 1762, three months before the signing of the Treaty of Paris. Those Bourbon monarchs stuck together. But it was such a hot potato that Spain waited for seven years before taking over formal control in 1769. Louisiana was a thriving Spanish colony until 1800, when it was ceded back to France, ending a thirty-eight-year period of growth.

The few Spanish who came to Louisiana were absorbed by the earlier French settlers, but they gave the new race and society its name. *Criollo*, the Spanish word, was transformed by the French into *Creole*, and as noun and adjective it came to signify just about everything that came from Louisiana. There were white Creoles, black Creoles, Creoles of mixed blood, Creole horses, Creole onions, Creole tomatoes, and of course, Creole cookery. The Spanish contributed much to the cuisine—hot peppers, vibrant spices, and tricks they had learned from Mayans, Aztecs, and Incas in their colonies to the south.

From the Spanish, New Orleans got a great visual change in its architecture. Two disastrous fires in 1788 and 1794 destroyed the whole city. The French city of cottages and wooden houses disappeared, to be replaced by a Spanish city of heavily walled brick houses, two and three stories high, with tiled roofs, wide arches, fanlights, and—so dear to the Spanish heart—patios and courtyards, those outdoor living rooms where a family can relax in peace and privacy, free of the vexations of the outside world. One French element retained was the galleries across the front of the buildings, stretching out over the banquettes, or sidewalks. And the Spanish added to these the wrought-iron and cast-iron railings and columns that give the French Quarter its most striking visual aspect. A stranger could think he was walking down the streets of Seville, Havana, or Merida. These covered sidewalks afford protection from both the hot sun and the rain. When it rains, a person can walk for blocks in the French Quarter without getting wet.

The Spanish regime saw many developments that were to shape the character of the colony, such as the coming of the Acadians (described below) and in the 1790s the coming of the Dominican refugees. When Toussaint L'Ouverture led the uprising of the slaves in Santo Domingo (Haiti) in 1791, they massacred all the whites they could lay their hands on. However, several thousand of them escaped and made their way to New Orleans. Many brought along their slave cooks and loyal family retainers. "Les Refugies" were true Creoles themselves, and after ten years of immigration there were as many of them in New Orleans as there were original French settlers. Quickly blending into the original population, they gave it an infusion of creativity. They established the first newspaper and the first theater in the colony. They possessed the Gallic *joie de vivre*—a love of good living, good wine, and good food. Their cooks contributed new ideas to Creole cookery, especially in the field of seafood preparation.

The Haitian rebels also proscribed the mulattoes, many of whom made their way to New Orleans, bringing with them the practice of voodooism, the black magic that was to have a profound influence on both black and white populations of the city. Food, sometimes raw and sacrificial, played a large part in the voodoo rituals.

During the French Revolution many aristocrats and royalists escaped the guillotine by moving to Louisiana. They settled in New Orleans, and they also established a colony at St. Martinsville on Bayou Teche. For a time that community was known as Petit Paris. Accustomed to a life of wealth and idleness, these aristocratic settlers had a hard time adjusting to the rough life of the colony, but near-starvation forced them to roll up their sleeves and go to work. And they were absorbed into the existing population.

Many of the great chefs of France, having lost their royal employers to the guillotine, also emi-

Café des Exiles. A gathering place for the Santo Domingo refugees in the 1790s, it is said to have become a front for the Lafitte brothers' smuggling operations somewhat later. It is now a bohemian night club called Lafitte's Blacksmith Shop. (Etching by the author)

grated to New Orleans, where they opened restaurants or took employment with wealthy families. Their influence on Creole cuisine was considerable.

All these diverse elements in the rich melting pot of New Orleans had coalesced into a single homogeneous society by the time of the Louisiana Purchase in 1803. Although the Creoles hated to become *Américains*, the period from 1800 to 1860 saw the full flowering of Creole society. And it was during that time that many of them came into the really big money. They owned cotton, sugar, and rice plantations, with whole armies of slaves to work them. In the city they owned banks, brokerage firms, commission houses, and export and import establishments. They refused to stoop to such lowbrow professions as merchandising, the buying and selling of goods. Creoles would not work at jobs requiring that they take off their coats, sit behind desks, or stand behind counters. They conducted most of their business in a casual manner in the coffeehouses, or Exchanges, as the barrooms were euphemistically called.

Outwardly the Creole men appeared to be of docile and placid disposition, but actually they were hot-tempered, overbearingly proud, and so touchy that they would fight a duel over the slightest insult, real or imagined. A common epitaph was "Mort sur le champ d'honneur."

A Creole belle, around 1873. (Courtesy of the Special Collections Division, Tulane University Library)

Many American men from above Canal Street were actually afraid to come down to the French Quarter and associate with the Creole men. As one American put it, "A few nips, a little spat, and before you even knew what happened you've got a sword through your gizzard." The Creoles loved to gamble, especially at crap shooting and stud poker. This pastime often led to squabbling and bloody encounters.

The focal center of Creole existence was *la famille*. All of life rotated around the family—the children, in-laws, *tantes, oncles,* and the *cousins* and *cousines* by the dozen. Almost all the top families were interrelated by marriage, so Creole society could very properly be called a *familistère*, a coterie of kinfolks. Creole women were closely sheltered. An outsider or stranger was never admitted to the inner circle of *la famille*, and the mothers and daughters wore veils on the street, so it was pretty much a mystery whether Creole women were really beautiful or other-

View of the riverfront in the 1870s. (Courtesy of Louisiana State Museum)

wise. A New Englander wrote that "they were angels from Paradise." An English traveler wrote that they were "rather on the plump side." It's hardly surprising if they really were plump. To the Creoles, good food and good wine were the perfect expression of the happiness of being alive. Almost any event was the signal for a grand dinner: weddings, christenings, anniversaries, birthdays, Saints' days. They'd never admit it, but they behaved as though their patron saint was Lucullus. Yet they were deeply religious, and the Catholic Church had a great deal of influence on their eating habits. The many fast days and the long Lenten season all helped promote the consumption of seafood among the

Where "soul food" began. A typical old plantation kitchen. Note the portable fireplace oven in the foreground. (Courtesy of the Special Collections Division, Tulane University Library)

Creoles and they became the world's greatest masters of seafood preparation—the *raison d'être* of this book.

Creole society had a stratified caste system as rigid as that of India. The family tree meant everything. Money did help, though it was not always of prime importance. The gradations were as follows: Creoles, Chacks, Chacas, Catchoupines, Chacalatas, Bambaras, Bitacaux, and Cachumas. Chacalatas were country cousins, or bumpkins. The name Bambara hints of "dirty hands"; they and the Bitacaux had to work at hard, dirty jobs to make a living. At the bottom rung of the ladder were the Cachumas, those who had black ancestors in their family tree. More details about that group will follow.

In 1790 New Orleans had a population of 8,000 including Creoles, free people of color, and slaves. By 1806 the population had increased to 31,000, composed of 13,500 Creoles, 3,355 free colored people, 3,500 Americans, 5,714 Europeans, and several thousand slaves. It was undeniably a slave-based economy, with blacks doing all the hard, dirty work that made the white folks rich. They cleared the plantations and worked them. They made the bricks, mixed the mortar, and built the mansions in the French Quarter, on the Esplanade, and in the Garden District. They even forged and cast the wrought-iron and cast-iron balconies. All these aspects of opulence came from the sweat of the black man's brow. And black women did some heavy sweating, too: They were the cooks, the standard bearers who brought Creole cookery to its apotheosis as an art. They cooked in private homes, in restaurants, on the plantations, and in their own houses. To the French herbs and spices in the pot they added a big dash of Love, or what is today known as "soul." It wouldn't be far from wrong to say that Creole cookery as we know it today is simply glorified "soul food" with a French accent. Go into the kitchen of any great New Orleans restaurant, and you will see these beautiful black ladies bending over their stoves: Some have been at it for as much as forty years. A white chef in a *gros bonnet,* trained in Paris, may be walking around, supervising things, but he's mostly just an ornament. In some of the old Creole families, the black cook was considered a member of *la famille.* She had lifetime tenure, and when she died, she was buried in the family tomb in St. Louis Cemetery.

The Civil War marked the beginning of the end for the Creole way of life. The great plantations lay in ruins, and the banks, brokerage firms, and other businesses were bankrupt. The Americans, now in the majority, were much more aggressive than the easygoing Creoles, and they assumed the leadership in politics, business, and finance. The Creoles kept their control over social life, however, organizing the Mardi Gras with its aristocratic secret Knewes acting out fantasies to replace the vanished realities. Creole children went to the public schools and spoke English instead of French. The soft-cadenced Creole patois, which had been their universal language, almost vanished, spoken by only a few of the elderly. Faced by the bleakest poverty, the Creoles had to sell their plantations, their French Quarter mansions, their furniture, jewels, and bric-a-brac. In 1885 their historian

A Creole kitchen in the French Quarter. The cook was often considered a member of the family. (Courtesy of the Special Collections Division, Tulane University Library)

and chief defender, Charles Gayarre, wrote that there were still 250,000 white Creoles left in Louisiana. In the years since then, even these have largely disappeared, intermarrying with the Americans and with the immigrant Germans, Irish, and Italians. They fell into the melting pot that is New Orleans. But they left their mark: They gave the city its unique Gallic character, its joie de vivre, its gracious little social customs (such as "lagniappe") going all the way back to the Marquis de Vaudreuil, and its love of parades, festivals, and spectacles with plenty of music. They gave us the Mardi Gras. But their greatest gift of all was Creole cuisine. Not only surviving but flourishing, it is one of the world's great cooking schools today.

The white Creoles jealously and vehemently tried to reserve the Creole label for themselves alone, but another group also called themselves Creole, and with much justification. They were the people of mixed blood. From the very earliest days of the colony there were many "free people of color" in the city, mostly mulattoes and quadroons, and their numbers grew as time passed. Too much emphasis and romantic attention has been given to the quadroon balls and the rich Creoles with their quadroon mistresses. They were a minority. Rather, it was a steady process of amalgamation of two races living in close proximity. In the early days there were gradations of mixed blood, each with its own label—such as quadroon, octoroon—suggesting the proportions of the blood mixture.

As the mixing continued, no one could keep up with the fractions, and these terms fell into disuse. People of all gradations called themselves simply Creole, and the name has stuck. There are tens of thousands of them in New

French Quarter Creole, 1890. (Courtesy of the Special Collections Division, Tulane University Library)

Orleans today, ranging in color from dark brown to nearly white. Many live in tight little enclaves scattered around the city, refusing to associate too much with either whites or blacks. As skilled artisans practicing masonry, carpentry, house painting, and decoration, they have long controlled a large part of the building and construction industry of the city. They are strong believers in higher education, and they put their children through college whenever possible. Their latest generation has produced prominent doctors, dentists, artists, writers, musicians, lawyers, judges, and a mayor of New Orleans. As the barriers of prejudice and segregation fall away, these latterday Creoles, well educated and ambitious, may someday surpass in accomplishment the old-time plantation-owning Creoles.

And now that I've filled you in on the Creoles, let's take a look at the Cajuns, God bless 'em.

THE COMING OF THE ACADIANS

The peninsula off the eastern coast of Canada now know as Nova Scotia was called Acadia by the French who originally settled it. It is a ruggedly beautiful country, ideal for the simple pastoral life. For this reason it may have been named after the Greek region of Arcady, which in ancient times had an almost mythic reputation as a paradise of rural peace and quiet. The peaceful French peasants and fishermen who settled Acadia give credence to this viewpoint on the origin of the name. According to another school of thought, the name is derived from Akkad, an Algonquin Indian word, the name of a small river on the peninsula. Take your choice.

To populate their colony, the French brought 400 families over from Brittany, Normandy, Santonge, Poitou, and La Rochelle. Those from La Rochelle, who were Biscayan fishermen, worked to develop the extensive fishing grounds off the coast of Acadia. Nearly all the Acadians in America today are descended from those original 400 families. They throve and multiplied, and by 1760 there were more than 25,000 of them. They were hardworking, industrious, and frugal, and they made the barren countryside of Acadia bloom like the rose. Then disaster befell them.

In the middle 1700s the English wrested Acadia away from the French and renamed it Nova Scotia. They promptly set about anglicizing the place, bringing in many new settlers from Scotland and the Midlands. At first the attitude of the English overlords toward the Acadians was an attempt at even-handed justice, but the Acadians were so strongly French, Catholic, proud, and intractable that they would not accept the overlordship of their Anglo-Saxon conquerors. They refused to take the oath of allegiance to the English crown or to exchange their Catholicism for the Anglican faith. And this stubbornness was their undoing. At a meeting in Halifax Lieutenant-Governor Lawrence and his Council decided that they could not tolerate such recalcitrance and possibly even sedition in their midst, and they resolved to expel all the Acadians.

Without knowing their destiny, the Acadians throughout the colony responded to a summons to meet in their chapels on September 5, 1755. When assembled, they were arrested and put on board ships. On this first roundup 7,000 were collected, 1,923 of them from Grand Pré alone. The British really botched this job, which has come down in history as one of the greatest infamies of all time. Whole families were broken up haphazardly, their members shipped off in different directions, never to see one another again. Naturally there was much weeping, wailing, and gnashing of teeth. Most of the Acadians were shipped to British colonies to the south—Maine, Massachusetts, Pennsylvania, the Carolinas, and Georgia. Three years later 3,000 more were deported to France. In 1763, when the Treaty of Paris gave all of French Canada to England, the Acadians were really finished, and in the end more than 25,000 of them were expelled.

January of 1765 saw the arrival of the first group of twenty Acadian exiles in New Orleans, and by May 650 more had arrived. The city fathers had no facilities for taking care of them, so they shipped them off to the Attakapas country to establish settlements. (The Attakapas Indians, before they were wiped out, were a fierce bunch, the only Indian tribe in America to practice cannibalism. They were all gone by the time the Acadians arrived, however.)

Continuing to come in groups, the exiles settled Opelousas, the "Acadian Coast" along the Mississippi in St. James Parish, and the swampy marshland parishes of St. Mary, Vermilion, and Acadia in the southernmost part of the state. They settled in the Bayou Country along Bayou Lafourche and Bayou Teche. A census taken in 1787 gave their number in Louisiana as 1,587.

Many of the Acadians who had returned to France found it difficult to readjust in the mother country, and the Spanish, who were then in control of Louisiana, sent ships to bring 1,500 of them to Louisiana. Those who had gone to Santo Domingo found the climate too hot for their liking, and they emigrated to Louisiana also. Eventually some 5,000 came to the state.

After a period of twenty years, when the English had become firmly established in Canada, they softened their attitude toward the Acadian exiles and allowed about 15,000 of them to return and resettle in the Maritime Provinces. But those who had reached Louisiana were happy in their new surroundings, and none of them went back. In 1955 the year of the bicentennial celebrations of the expulsions, an estimate of the Acadian population showed that there were approximately 200,000 in New Brunswick, 250,000 in Quebec, 150,000 in New England, 75,000 in Nova Scotia, and—the largest group of all—600,000 in Louisiana. And those figures are a generation old. It is an amazing statistic of proliferation that more than a million descendants of the original 5,000 Acadians are living in Louisiana and other southern states today.

Alexander Mouton, the Cajun governor of Louisiana at the outbreak of the Civil War, is said to have more than 10,000 living descendants today. A very good friend of the author's is a great-great grandson, Roy "Red" Mouton, soldier-of-fortune and a member of the Abraham Lincoln Brigade in the Spanish Civil War. Red says, "At one time I had over a hundred living first cousins. Met almost all of them once at a big family reunion. And I had thousands of second, third, and fourth cousins. If I could have organized all my male cousins into a well-armed battalion, who knows, we might have whupped the hell out of Franco."

To the early Acadians southern Louisiana must have seemed like an earthly Paradise after the rocky soil and frigid climate of Nova Scotia, since it's one of the best spots in America to get good vittles for the dinner table. There are fresh and saltwater fish of many varieties, plus

A Cajun cottage. The stairs led to the *garçonnière,*
where the boys slept. They could come in late at night
without disturbing the rest of the family. (Courtesy of
the Special Collections Division, Tulane University
Library)

shrimps, crabs, crawfish, oysters, turtles, frogs,
rabbits, deer, raccoons, opossums, snipes,
grouse, wild turkey, and in the winter, wild
ducks and geese. The rich alluvial soil was ideal
for growing fruits, vegetables, and grains. The
highly adaptable Cajuns quickly learned to use
all these products in their rambunctious style of
cookery. Since its roots are French, Cajun cookery is similar to Creole cookery in many ways,
but with more spices, more herbs, more hot pepper, and more gusto. As I've already said, the
best way to distinguish them is to describe Creole

as sophisticated city cooking and Cajun as country cooking—less inhibited and more daring,
slapdash, and inventive.

The early Acadians in Louisiana were small
farmers, just as they had been in Nova Scotia,
and on the side they were hunters, trappers, and
fishermen. They lived from day to day, never
trying especially to get rich. In antebellum days
Creoles, Americans, and Englishmen built up
large sugar plantations and lived in fine mansions in the bayou country, especially along the
Teche, but the Cajuns were always too proud

Cajuns carving pirogues out of cypress logs, around 1895. (Courtesy of Louisiana Wildlife and Fisheries Commission)

chopped, adzed, and whittled out of a single cypress log and that is still very much in use today. A well-made pirogue is a true work of art, of perfect symmetry and balance, with the walls cut very thin to make it light. Some say that a pirogue could navigate on a heavy dew. It's also very speedy, and pirogue races are still a popular sport among the Cajuns. The pirogue has no keel, and you need perfect balance and muscular control to keep one upright. The outsider who boldly sits down in a pirogue will always tip it over and hit the water fast. A Cajun says, "To balance de pirogue you must always part de hair down de middle." Bayou LaFourche has been called "the longest Main Street in America." There are settlements all along its banks, and the Cajuns in their pirogues are constantly paddling up and down, going to visit their "*cousines down de bayou.*" The Cajuns call everybody cousin.

Cajuns would usually get married when the boys were eighteen and the girls fifteen. They produced large families, with as many as twenty children not at all uncommon. They loved their children, and their marriages endured remarkably well. Husbands were proud of their virility, and wives were proud of their dark-eyed beauty and the strong grip they had on their husbands (He won' go 'way 'cause there's no *fille* on the Bayou can love him better'n me!) But if the families were large, they were evidently not too large. There was always plenty to eat, and nobody ever went hungry.

The Cajuns are jolly, good-natured, and gregarious; they love to go a-visiting. When a housewife hears that a group of cousins are coming down the bayou to visit, she dashes into the kitchen and whips up a big pot of jambalaya or gumbo, enough to feed thirty people. If forty

and independent to work for the owners. They stuck to their own simple pursuits and continued to live in their small houses. When the great plantations were ruined by the Civil War, the Cajuns escaped unharmed since they had virtually nothing to lose.

Before good roads were built in the present century, it was very difficult to reach the Cajun country. This isolation helped the Cajuns to preserve their customs and language. They spoke a type of French that was the same as that spoken at the French court in the early 1600s, very different from the patois and "gombo" spoken by the Creoles in New Orleans.

In the old days the Cajuns traveled mainly by pirogue, a sort of light, shallow canoe that they

An Acadian girl. (Courtesy of the Special Collections Division, Tulane University Library)

show up, she'll throw some more rice and shrimp in the pot, and everybody will feast well. Creative improvisation is the keynote of Cajun cookery. The Cajun housewife can whip up a good dinner out of almost anything that's edible—including even an alligator, as some of the recipes in the back of this book will show.

One of the typical Cajun festivities is the all-night dance called a *fais-do-do*. Whole families attend, down to the youngest children and infants. A separate room called the *parc aux petits* (park for the young uns) is set aside for them to sleep in. The old *tante* who watches over them pacifies them with a lullaby:

Fais-do-do, Minette,
Fais-do-do mo pite bébé,
Quan quinze ans aura passé
Minette va se marier.

Go to sleep, Minette,
Go to sleep my pretty baby,
When fifteen years have passed,
Minette is going to get married.

This song is said to be the source of the name "fais-do-do." Rather tame today, these dances were formerly very exclusive affairs, attended by only close relatives and friends, and any outsider who attempted to "crash" risked getting a knife stuck in his ribs.

The Cajun musicians who provide the music for these dances have built up a school of music in their own distinctive idiom. It bounces, jumps, swings and sways, laughs and cries. The Cajun bands are always among the most popular features at the Jazz and Heritage Festivals held in New Orleans each year. They have a melodic, hard-driving beat that makes conventional jazz bands seem slow.

A Cajun kitchen. Despite its bare simplicity, some of the world's greatest cookery originated in the Cajun kitchen. (Courtesy of the Special Collections Division, Tulane University Library)

Butchers and fishmongers at the French Market, around 1890. (Courtesy of Louisiana State Museum)

Many Cajuns have moved to New Orleans. Some of them work in the great restaurants, where they put their own ideas to work. Some of the greatest dishes on the menus today are of Cajun origin: jambalaya, filé gumbo, crawfish bisque, crawfish étouffé, frog legs piquante, turtle soup, turtle stew, soft-shell crabs, redfish courtbouillon, and dozens of rice dishes.

OTHER INFLUENCES
ON THE CUISINE

There have been other influences grafted onto the Creole-Cajun cuisine. The many Italians who came to New Orleans in the last half of the nineteenth century have had considerable influence on the city's cookery. Today there are more people of Italian descent in New Orleans than of any other group. They even outnumber the Frenchmen.

One unusual group of citizens in New Orleans came from Sicily but were originally of Albanian extraction. When the Turkish overlords of Albania in the early nineteenth century expelled thousands of Christians who refused to accept Islam, many moved to the town of Contessa Entellina in Sicily, and subsequently emigrated to New Orleans. Most of the Italians in New Orleans are Sicilians, and a large proportion of them are Albanian-Italians from Contessa Entellina. They are good citizens and good cooks. One of them, Vic Schiro, once served as mayor of the city.

Another interesting ethnic group are the Yugoslavians, from the province of Dalmatia on the Adriatic coast. (Before World War I they were Austrians.) Since ancient Roman days, the Dalmatians have been great cultivators of shellfish. Many emigrated to southern Louisiana and settled in the bayous and marshes east of the Mississippi River, where some of the best oyster-growing waters in the world are located. Today the Yugoslavians control virtually the whole of the oyster-growing and distribution industries in Louisiana. They're excellent seafood cooks, too, and New Orleans has several good Yugoslavian restaurants.

Our seafood cuisine even has a bit of Chinese influence. In the 1860s Lee Yuen of Canton, China, moved to southern Louisiana to engage in rice farming, but when he saw how plentiful the small "sea-bob" shrimp were, he decided to go into the shrimp-drying business. Around 1873 he built a shrimp-drying platform in the

Chinese waltz, Manila Village, 1890. After the shrimp had dried in the sun, the Chinese fishermen and their wives danced on them barefoot to remove the shells. (Courtesy of the Special Collections Division, Tulane University Library)

THE ROOTS OF JAZZ

"Jazz is like Creole gumbo, there's a little of everything in it. It draws from African work chants, European and American folk music, grand opera, French quadrilles, Spanish dance forms, Negro spirituals—almost any kind of music played or sung in New Orleans during the nineteenth century when the city was one of the nation's chief musical centers."

Richard Binion Allen,
Curator, William Ransom Hogan
Jazz Archives,
Tulane University Library

"One of my pleasantest memories as a kid growing up in New Orleans was how a bunch of us kids playing would suddenly hear sounds. It was like a phenomenon, like the Aurora Borealis maybe. The sounds of men playing would be so clear, but we wouldn't be sure where they were coming from. So we'd start trotting, start running, 'It's this way!' 'It's that way!'—and sometimes after running for a while you'd find you'd be nowhere near that music, but that music could come on you anytime like that. The city was full of the sounds of music ...New Orleans was the city of pleasure. For the least significant occasion there would be music. There would be music for christenings, baptisms, weddings, deaths—for any occasion. There were countless places of enjoyment that employed musicians, not including private affairs, balls, soirees, banquets, marriages, funerals, Catholic communions and confirmations, picnics at the lakefront, country hayrides and advertisements of business concerns."

Danny Barker
Musician and jazz historian,
formerly assistant curator of the
New Orleans Jazz Museum,
from his unpublished autobiography

Yes, Yes, the roots of jazz in New Orleans go very deep—back to the African jungle, to the Caribbean islands, to France, Spain, and England. From 1800 to about 1850, the Negro slaves were given Sundays off for rest and recreation. They assembled in "Congo Square," a large open field adjoining the French Quarter on Rampart Street. There they sang, chanted, and danced the dances they had brought with them from Africa. The dances were variously called Congo, Calinda, and Bamboula. Sometimes they were slow and graceful, and at others they were wild and frenetic. Some of these dances were certainly the ancestors of some of the later jazz dances, the shuffle, shag, stomp, clog, and buck and wing. And elements of the songs and chants worked their way into blues, gospel songs, spirituals, work chants, and "field hollers." The only instruments available to the Congo Square dancers were crude drums (cowhide stretched over hollow logs or barrels), bells, cymbals, and small homemade percussion instruments.

Jazz could have happened only in New Orleans, with its complex set of sociological circumstances and its robust and pervasive musical culture. As in Latin America, it was a Catholic society, and Sunday was a day of fiesta, much different from the abstemious sabbaths of the Protestants. After the Civil War, when real musical instruments became available to the Negroes, they transformed everything they heard around them into instrumental music, from French minuets and quadrilles to Dahomey chants. Unable to read music and unfamiliar with the classical uses of their instruments, they started from scratch and wrested fresh new sounds from

Only in New Orleans

"The city was full of the sounds of music."
Photo by Johnny Donnels

ON THE ORIGIN OF THE WORD "JAZZ"

The new music that came out of New Orleans had to struggle along for about 20 years until it found a name. They just called it "dirty rags" or "blues." "Jass" was an Elizabethan slang term meaning vaguely "to do things with gusto and enthusiasm," but in the red-light district in Chicago, the word took on different connotations. When Tom Brown's white Dixieland Band went to Chicago in 1915, their detractors spread the rumor that they were "playing that dirty New Orleans jass music." They promptly called themselves "Brown's Dixieland Jass Band," and then the word caught on and spread like wildfire. The next white band to go north called itself the Original Dixieland Jazz Band. They became immensely famous in Chicago and New York and even went overseas to spread the gospel in London.

The term "Dixieland" originally was applied to white New Orleans jazz, which depended more on syncopation and drive for its effect than the Negro music, which was "bluesy" and improvisational. Dixieland is now used loosely to refer to all kinds of jazz with the New Orleans spirit in it.

their instruments. After the Civil War every social club, burial society, and fraternal order had its brass marching band for funerals, parades, and festivals. Most of the bands doubled as dance bands, playing at night for balls and dances. Their music was generally collective, spontaneous improvisation—something that formally trained "straight" musicians could never have accomplished.

Around 1895 Buddy Bolden came along and drew all the loose ends together. Jazz had put down its tap root, and it was here to stay.

shallow waters off the shoreline of Barataria Bay. A whole village of stilts grew up around the original platform as more Chinese immigrants moved in. Groups of Filipinos also joined in the enterprise. The community was called Manila Village, or more commonly Chinamen's Platform. Other platforms were established at Bassa Bassa and Bayou Brouillaeau. A Chinese named Ting Ting organized the shrimp-drying business on a mass-production basis and shipped them out by the barrel, all over the world.

The industry flourished in those days of no refrigeration because fresh shrimp were highly perishable, and dried shrimp would keep indefinitely. Much of the product was shipped to China, where there was a huge demand for it. Chinese restaurants all over the United States also ordered and paid high prices for the shrimp. When the Creole-Cajun cooks discovered that these salty little devils make one of the world's best gumbos, the local markets took over from the China trade, and thousands of barrels of dried shrimp were sold at the French Market in New Orleans. First refrigeration and then freezing led to the decline of the industry, and hurricanes eventually destroyed most of the platforms. You can still buy small dried shrimp today—they're sold as a snack in bars and cocktail lounges—but they're very expensive. No more dried-shrimp Chinese-Creole gumbo, alas!

SHORT BIOGRAPHY OF A CREOLE BUILDING

Down in the heart of the French Quarter (where nobody speaks French and nobody has a quarter, as they used to say) at the corner of Royal and St. Peter Streets there's a historic old building called the "Skyscraper." It was built in 1810 by Dr. Yves Le Monnier, a wealthy physician, for use as an office and residence, and it had a triple-decker slave quarter on the patio to house the servants. You can still see the doctor's monogram, YLM, entwined in the beautiful wrought-iron work of the balconies, which are said to have been imported from Seville, Spain. When first constructed, the building was only three stories high, but even then it was so tall that the neighbors feared it might topple over on their small houses. When a fourth story was added in 1876 and it really became the tallest building in the French Quarter, it was dubbed "Skyscraper." The "oval room" on the front corner of the third floor, which was Dr. Le Monnier's drawing room, has an oval-shaped domed ceiling, and it is considered by many architects to be the most beautiful room in the city. Nobody knows how the dome was constructed or what holds it up. It seems to float in the air.

By the 1880s the building had changed hands several times, and it was badly rundown. The upper stories served as a tenement residence for vagrants and newly arrived immigrants, and a Chinese restaurant and an Italian grocery store occupied the ground floor. Then George Washington Cable came along and made the building world famous. One of the best stories in his book *Old Creole Days* is about "Sieur George," as everybody called him, a dried-up little old man who lived in a small room on the top floor of the Skyscraper and jealously guarded a mysterious little black trunk under his bed. The nosy neighbors thought he was a retired pirate or something and that the trunk contained a million dollars. When Sieur George died, everybody rushed in to open the trunk. What they found were wads

Monogram of Dr. Le Monnier in
the wrought-iron balconies of the
Skyscraper.

The Skyscraper.

of used and useless lottery tickets. For many years afterward the Skyscraper was called "Sieur George's House."

Since the rents were low and the rooms large and airy, the Skyscraper became a natural habitat for writers and artists. For a while in the 1920s, Sherwood Anderson, flushed with success and notoriety from his recently published *Winesburg, Ohio,* occupied the "Oval Room" apartment, and here he lorded it over the local literary scene for a while. And for a short time he had a guest who would someday outshine him. He took in a homeless fledgling writer from Mississippi named William Faulkner and let him sleep on the valuable antique rosewood sofa. Since this feller was a heavy drinker, Anderson

lived in mortal fear that he would some night kick the arm off that rosewood sofa. The tensions got so bad that Faulkner finally moved over to Pirate's Alley to a pad of his own, where he could kick the gong around as much as he pleased.

Pat O'Brien's, the most famous bar in America (with the possible exception of McSorley's Wonderful Saloon) got its start in a cubbyhole on the ground floor of the Skyscraper. Pat kept bar and his partner, Charlie Cantrell, ran a blackjack table in a dark corner. Every time Cantrell got two dollars ahead he gave it to Pat, who would run out and buy a quart of "Green River" to keep the bar going. George Oeschner was the office boy, floor sweeper, and bouncer. Today

Pat O'Brien's is an enormous bar and cabaret a half block down St. Peter Street, and more booze is sold there each year than in any other bar in America. The owners are semiretired millionaires who raise race horses and daffodils as a hobby.

Johnny Donnels and Maggi Hartnett, next door neighbors, have had their art galleries on the ground floor and their studios on the second floor of the Skyscraper for many years. We've had some memorable parties and seafood dinners in those places. Donnels has switched from painting to photography in recent years and has gained an international reputation. Many of his photos are included in this book.

Some of the best jam sessions in the history of New Orleans jazz have been held in the Skyscraper. Such greats as George Lewis, Kid Thomas, Percy Humphries, Jim Robinson, Louis Nelson, Raymond Burke, and Paul Crawford have gathered there for Chimney Sweeper's Shrimp Boils, and afterward they jammed, blowing their horns until the plaster cracked.

The author of this volume, a resident of the Skyscraper off and on for twenty-five years, is writing these lines in the third floor front studio on the right side of the illustration. I'm sitting here scribbling and drinking beer and praying that the ancient plaster ceiling won't fall on my head. It's the heavy antique type of plaster ceiling meant to last a hundred years, and this one has lasted almost two hundred. The ceilings in these old Creole houses have a domino effect.

When the one on the top floor falls, so does the one on the floor below, and so on down to the ground. (There are no basements in these buildings. When they were built, the water table was only two feet below the level of the ground.) Although the walls are typically eighteen inches thick, their bricks were handmade and carelessly dried in the sun instead of kiln-baked, and they were glued together with river mud instead of mortar. If you punched a hole in the plaster of a wall, the whole wall might come running out like the sand in an hourglass.

The once mighty oaken beams in these old Creole houses measure $12'' \times 12''$ and $8'' \times 8''$, but they're so riddled with the holes eaten out by hundreds of generations of termites that they're as brittle and light as cork—a heavy cough could cause disaster. Johnny Donnels says the beams in the Skyscraper are held together by the termites inside holding hands, and if they ever let go we're done for.

My reason for dragging the Skyscraper into this chronicle is to give the reader a glimpse of the post-Creole Bohemian way of life of the French Quarter. In my third floor "cooking laboratory" I have kitchen-tested hundreds of Creole-Cajun recipes and fed the results to hundreds of friends. This experience later enabled me to open my own seafood restaurant. And cumulatively these experiments—on my friends and on the public—have led to the creation of this cookbook. Thank God that all the guinea pigs survived!

Chapter 2

The Appurtenances of the Art

THE INDISPENSABLE VEGETABLES

A few vegetables are indispensable for Creole-Cajun cookery, and a short discussion of them is in order.

CREOLE TOMATOES

The large vine-ripened Creole tomato is one of the glories of Louisiana cookery. Creole tomatoes have a pronounced acid flavor and are used to make delicious sauces, stews, gumbos, and so on. In fact, the very term "à la Creole" usually denotes a tomato sauce of some sort, and when it's made with fresh Creole tomatoes, its flavor will be distinctive. To peel a Creole tomato, stick a fork in the "eye" and dip it in hot water for a few seconds. The skin will come right off. Or hold one over a gas flame until its skin splits. There's no need to "seed" fresh tomatoes used in most Creole or Cajun dishes.

The large "beefsteak" vine-ripened tomatoes available in most parts of the country in the summertime are a good substitute for Creole tomatoes. "Hot-house tomatoes," those pale tasteless things found year-round in the grocery stores, are not very suitable for cooking purposes. They're picked green and stored in gas-filled warehouses to ripen. By the time they reach the consumer, they're almost devoid of flavor.

When fresh vine-ripened tomatoes are not available, use canned tomatoes for cooking. The plum-type tomatoes, *pomodori pelati*, favored by Italian and Spanish cooks are especially good.

SCALLIONS (SHALLOTS), GREEN ONIONS, AND CHIVES

For some strange reason, scallions are called shallots in southern Louisiana. This is a confusing error of nomenclature, because the true shallot is a small bulb that's widely used in France but hardly ever found in Creole recipes. Therefore, to avoid confusion we will use the term "scallion" throughout this book. Tender green onions are even more widely available than scallions and hence more frequently used. The scallions and green onions are used mostly for their green tops, which impart a delicious flavor and texture to roux, gumbos, soups and stews, and they're also an excellent garnish. Scallions and green onions are interchangeable in this book.

Fresh green chives are so scarce that they are used principally for garnish. However, they are excellent when used as a substitute for scallion or green onion tops in cooking.

ONIONS

Chopped onions are an indispensable ingredient of many Creole and Cajun dishes. Either the large yellow onions or the white ones may be used. The latter are usually stronger and have a more pungent flavor.

GARLIC

The bulb of contentment and love (the ancients regarded it as an aphrodisiac), garlic is extensively used in Creole and Cajun cooking. The Cajun truck farmers grow "horse garlic," a large bulb that is much milder than imported garlic and can be used more generously. Contrary to widespread opinion (and sometimes prejudice), when cooked for a good long while, garlic does not have a pronounced odor or taste. It blends almost imperceptibly with other ingredients and gives savour to the final dish. I double the amount of garlic called for in most recipes if it's going to have a long, slow cook because I find that most recipe makers are too timid in its use. Spanish and Greek cooks make a famous garlic soup that's neither odoriferous nor overflavored. It's not only delicious but, as we said, an excellent aphrodisiac—maybe! Powdered, granulated, and dehydrated garlic do not have the delicious flavor of the fresh product, and they should be used only in emergencies.

GREEN PEPPERS

Throughout the whole South, green sweet peppers are called "bell peppers," but since this book will—I certainly hope—have circulation outside the South, I'll stick to the term "green peppers." Along with tomatoes, scallions, and onions, chopped green peppers are an indispensable ingredient of many Creole-Cajun dishes. Stuffed green peppers are also a favorite dish.

As for hot peppers, they're so important that I'm giving them special treatment at the end of this chapter.

OKRA

The delicious mucilaginous vegetable that Creoles and Cajuns use to thicken and flavor their gumbos, soups, and stews is okra. Widely used all over the South, okra has never gained much popularity in the rest of the country, probably because of its slick and sliding texture. A taste for it is something that has to "grow" on you.

Okra is a very ancient vegetable. The Sumerians were probably the first to domesticate and cultivate it. The ancient Egyptians used it as a food, and in addition they pounded the dried seed pods to make a high-grade papyrus. From Egypt it spread all over Africa, becoming one of the staple foods of the jungle tribes, who cooked their meals in a big communal stew pot. According to one theory, it was via these Africans that the seeds reached America. Okra was originally called gombo (spelled with an "o"), which is a pure Tshi tribal word from the Gold Coast of Africa. It is said that Africans brought as slaves to America hid the seeds in their ears. Since they were stripped naked on shipboard, that was about the only place available for concealing their small belongings.

Another version of the okra story is that the seeds were brought to Louisiana by the French colonists who settled New Orleans in the early 1700s. According to this version, the word gumbo is a Portuguese corruption, "quingumbo," of an African word, "quillobo," used by the natives of Angola and the Congo.

No matter what its origins, when okra was combined with the shrimps, crabs, and oysters of Louisiana, it reached the peak of its glory, and the world got that beautiful dish Creole Gumbo. With its lilting acidic flavor, okra does magic things to any kind of stew. Fresh young okra pods are the best, but frozen okra is very good. Freezing has the advantage, of course, of making the product available year-round. Freezing also makes it transportable, so that it can be purchased in supermarkets anywhere in the country. Canned okra may be used when neither fresh nor frozen okra is available.

If looks are important, okra should not be cooked in iron, tin, or copper utensils. Its high acidity causes these metals to turn it black, but neither flavor nor food value is affected. Black is beautiful when it comes to gumbo. The Cajuns down on the bayous have been cooking black gumbo in black iron wash pots as long as anyone can remember. It's the only utensil big enough to provide for a "fais-do-do," or a family reunion with fifty cousins.

If you want to preserve okra's pretty green color, use stainless steel or porcelain enamel pots, or ovenproof glass or earthenware casseroles. If you'd like to make gumbo without okra, I'll tell you how when I get to the story of filé later in this chapter.

THE SPECIAL INGREDIENTS

MUSHROOMS

Good fresh mushrooms add flavor to many Creole-Cajun dishes. I don't recommend the use of canned mushrooms, which have the flavor and texture of library paste and are not worth the exorbitant price charged for them. Wild mushrooms can be extremely dangerous, so don't try gathering them yourself—unless, of course, you're an expert mycologist. An amateur can end up in the morgue. Anyway, wild mushrooms don't have as good flavor as the tame commercial mushrooms do. In the spring of the year the Cajuns down in the swamps gather willow mushrooms, a type of fungus growing on the trunks of willow trees. When properly prepared, willow mushrooms are said to rival in flavor the truffles of France and Italy. When cooked wrong, however, they taste like sawdust or hickory chips. Dried Chinese or Italian mushrooms are excellent in many Creole-Cajun dishes but not very authentic.

ARTICHOKES

These delicious vegetables thrive in the warm, humid climate of southern Louisiana, and they're a great favorite with Creole and Cajun cooks. Oyster and artichoke soup is one of the greatest triumphs of the whole Creole repertoire of soups. Shrimp-stuffed artichokes (see index) are among the best of the Italian contributions to New Orleans cuisine.

MIRLITONS

In the same family with the squash and cucumber, the mirliton is also known as vegetable pear,

custard marrow, and chayote, its Mayan name. It was brought to Louisiana by the Spaniards from their colonies to the south, and it has been popular ever since. The mirliton has a bland, mild flavor, which makes it a perfect foil for delicately flavored seafood, such as shrimp and crabmeat. Shrimp-stuffed mirliton (see index) is a favorite Cajun dish.

Other vegetables popular with Creole cooks are celery, asparagus, and eggplant. For salad greens they like watercress, chicory, romaine, escarole, and garden lettuce. A Creole cook will not touch a head of iceberg lettuce if anything else is available.

Lemons, of course, are widely used in flavoring seafood sauces, and grated lemon peel is used to flavor many soups and stews. Slices of lemon are used to garnish many soups, and the lemon wedge is the most popular of all garnishes for fish dishes. Lime juice, lime slices, and wedges, which are used the same as lemon, may be even better for some dishes than lemon.

ALMONDS

The distinctive ingredient used in the great Creole seafood amandine dishes is the almond. Sliced almonds are preferred, either natural or blanched. Slivered almonds are too coarse. Almonds are a great addition to some seafood soups and stews. Before using almonds, you should gently cook them in butter, stirring constantly until they are a golden deep yellow. Never brown almonds or their flavor will be too strong.

PECANS

Another Louisiana staple that has not been well enough used in the cuisine is the pecan. Sliced thin and prepared like almonds, they are used in the same ways. A trout meunière pecandine is as good as trout amandine, or better.

RICE

The great Louisiana food staple is rice. The state raises more rice than all the rest of the country put together, and the average Louisianian eats almost as much rice per annum as a Chinese. A big bowl of hot rice is to be found very frequently on Creole or Cajun dinner tables. But it's not the sticky, gummy mess that many Northerners call rice. When the Creoles cook it, every grain is separate, dry, and thoroughly cooked.

In the old days, rice was washed and boiled in order to clean it and remove the starchy flour that was mixed in with the rice. Modern machinery is now able to clean the rice thoroughly before it's packed, so washing and boiling for the purpose of cleaning are no longer necessary. Follow instructions on the package for cooking, which usually reads: Proportions, 1 cup rice, 2 cups water, 1 tsp salt. Place all in a pot and bring to the boil, cover the pot tightly, and cut the heat very low. Steam for fifteen minutes until the rice has absorbed all the water. Cooking tip: Add a tablespoon of vegetable oil, olive oil, or lard to the pot when the water begins to boil, and stir well. This will keep the rice grains from sticking together.

However, many Creole purists and restaurant chefs prefer the old-fashioned method of cooking rice by boiling it. Here's how it's done:

CREOLE BOILED RICE

You'll need two cups of rice, six cups of water, and two teaspoons of salt. Bring the water to a boil, add the salt, add the rice slowly, and boil until the rice is soft. Pour it into a colander or wire strainer to drain. Place the colander in a preheated oven, and let the rice swell up and dry out for ten to fifteen minutes.

No self-respecting Creole or Cajun cook would ever use precooked "instant" rice. It's a tasteless, inferior product, and it's not even instant. It takes almost as long to prepare as regular rice.

The black Creoles of New Orleans invented a delicious rice cake, or fritter, called a *calas*, and the calas vendors, in gingham dresses with

Calas vendors selling their wares at the railroad station. (Fortier Collection)

starched white aprons, each one carrying a basket on her arm, were a familiar sight on the streets of the French Quarter. They had a familiar vending song that went:

Belles calas!
Madam mo gaignin calas,
Mo guaranti vous ve bons,
Belles calas, belles calas!

Beautiful rice fritters!
Madam, I have rice fritters,
I guarantee they are good
Beautiful rice fritters,
beautiful rice fritters!

CALAS

Boil a cup of raw rice with a teaspoon of salt in a quart of water until the rice is soft and mushy. Drain and smash the rice into a paste. Dissolve a yeast cake in water, and add it to the paste. Let it rise overnight. Next day add to the paste four beaten eggs, a cup of flour, a half cup of granulated sugar, a half teaspoon each of powdered nutmeg, ground allspice, and powdered cinnamon, and mix well to make a thick batter. Drop heaping tablespoons of the mixture into deep hot fat (350°), and fry until golden brown. Drain the calas on absorbent paper, and keep them warm by covering them with a towel until all of them have been cooked. Before serving, sprinkle generously with powdered confectioner's sugar. Calas in the early morning with a cup of café au lait was a standard Creole breakfast in the good old days.

CORN PRODUCTS

Ever since Louisianians learned from the Indians how to use them, corn products have ranked high on the list of Creole and Cajun staples: corn bread, hoe cakes, hush puppies, hominy, and hominy grits. Corn flour is the best of all coatings for frying fish and oysters (cornmeal is still very popular for this purpose, but it doesn't give as good results as the flour). For many years the standard Cajun breakfast was *"couche-couche,"* a delicious cornmeal mush served with sugar and milk, or cream, or clabber (curds and whey).

In the old days enormous quantities of hominy were eaten in Louisiana. The slaves on the plantations ate it along with their fatback and turnip greens. Rich or poor, black or white, everyone liked it. Oyster-hominy soup is a delicacy that would satisfy any epicurean palate. Hominy also makes a good gumbo. Canned hominy, now available in the stores, saves a lot of work, but for those hardy souls who like to do things right and in the old-fashioned way, here are the instructions for making lye hominy.

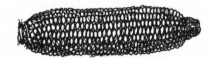

HOMINY

Soak two gallons of dried shelled corn in water for 48 hours. Add a bit of bicarbonate of soda to inhibit fermentation. Place the corn in a large pot with plenty of water. Tie a half gallon of hardwood ashes in a cloth bag, and place it in the pot. Boil for five to six hours, or until the corn grains separate easily from their outer shells. Be sure to use plenty of water, so that the corn does not stick to the bottom of the pot and scorch. When it's done, run cold water over the corn to cool it, and then separate the grains from the husks by working them in the palms of the hands. Rinse the cleaned grains three or four (or

more) times in fresh water to remove all trace and taste of the ashes. Keep the moist hominy refrigerated until ready to use, or dry it thoroughly and store it in cloth bags.

To make grits, grind dried hominy grains coarsely. Homemade hominy has a much better flavor than the canned commercial variety, but gad, it shore is a lot of work! None of the good things in life come easily.

Grits are the darling dish of Dixieland. As a side dish, they go beautifully with fried fish. Fried grits are also delicious. The boiled grits are allowed to cool and harden. Then they are cut in thin slices and fried brown in butter or bacon drippings. It comes as a surprise to many that grits are a popular dish throughout Italy, where they're called *polenta*. Among Northerners a liking for grits seems to be an acquired taste, but it's something worth learning because they're wholesome and economical.

To cook grits, boil a cup of dry grits and a teaspoon of salt in five cups of water for 30 minutes. Serve with butter or redeye gravy (ham gravy).

Never use instant grits. They have as little character as instant rice or instant coffee or instant what-have-you. The trend toward instant everything is one of the worst food developments of the twentieth century.

HERBS AND SPICES

One of the chief characteristics of Creole and Cajun cookery is a skillful use of herbs and spices—never too much and never too little, but they're always there. Handling herbs and spices requires practice. The amateur and the beginner have a tendency to overdo it, so take it easy until you learn how.

The spices most frequently used are allspice, cloves, nutmeg, mace, cinnamon, ginger, saffron, turmeric, cumin, mustard seed, black and white pepper, anise, caraway, and cardamon. Spices are always dried and may be used whole or ground. Prepared Creole mustard made from the whole ground seeds is a great New Orleans favorite for making pungent seafood sauces, such as Remoulade. When black pepper is called for in a recipe, you'll get much better flavor if you use fresh ground pepper. No good cook can do without pestle and mortar or a pepper mill.

The dried herbs most frequently used are thyme, basil, bay leaf, and filé (see "The Story of Filé" below). Others are oregano, chervil, marjoram, savory, and tarragon. The fresh herbs most frequently used are parsley, chives, basil, and thyme. Basil in particular was a revered plant among old-time blacks. If you grew in your front yard a male basil plant with narrow leaves next to a female plant with broad leaves, they would keep away the evil eye, and no one could cast a voodoo spell on your house.

Mixed shrimp and crab boil spices are a thing unto themselves, and their use is described in the chapters on shrimp and crabs.

The flavor of spices and herbs deteriorates rapidly once their containers have been opened and they are exposed to the air. Discard your stock every few months and purchase a new supply if you want to be a good cook.

BUDDY BOLDEN

Buddy Bolden (1878–1931) is now generally recognized as the "father of jazz." He was the first man to play the stuff as we know it, and his band was the first jazz band. They started playing in 1895. Of course, jazz didn't spring full-grown out of Bolden's noodle as Athena sprang from the brow of Zeus. Ragtime was already there, and so were the blues, spirituals, and other sources. Bolden and his band were the catalysts who welded all these diverse elements together in a new idiom. Since they were not exactly Sunday school types and did not come from a high-class or "dicty" environment, they rebelled against the clean "legitimate" music prevalent in their times and searched for a new voice. Their music was deliberately barrelhouse, low-down, dirty raggedy, gully-low, gut-bucket, raunchy, and full of connotations of sex. They could neither read nor write music; they played by ear, "faked" it.

Bolden has become a legend, a myth. It's a shame that there was no recording equipment in those days, because all we know about his playing is hearsay—and very little of that. They say he was the greatest cornet player who ever lived. He had such volume that when he played for a picnic over in Algiers, you could hear him all the way across the river in the French Quarter. Yet he had such control that he could play the blues low enough for you to hear the dancer's feet shuffling across the floor. His following was enormous, and when he played for a picnic, party, parade, or dance his "Chillun," as he called them, would come from miles around.

Bolden and his band were strictly "uptown," from the black neighborhood around Perdido and South Rampart Streets, a few blocks above Canal. There is no question but that jazz was a black invention.

Bolden's personal life was as wild as his music. He was crazy about booze and women—the epitome of dissipation. But the human frame can take only so much abuse. During a Labor Day parade in 1907 his mind exploded, and he went beserk and started slinging his horn around. They locked him up in the East Louisiana Hospital at Jackson, and he spent the last 24 years of his life there, forgotten by the world to whom he had given a new kind of music and joy. An old musician friend who visited him at the hospital in the late twenties said, "He didn't know who I was, he didn't know who he was, and he didn't care about nothin' at all."

The Father of Jazz

BUDDY BOLDEN'S BLUES

Thought I heard Buddy Bolden say
You're nasty, you're dirty, take it away,
You're terrible, you're awful, take it away,
I thought I heard him say.

I thought I heard Buddy Bolden shout:
"Open up that window and let that bad air
out,
Open up that window and let that bad air
out."

I thought I heard Judge Fogarty say
"Thirty days in the market, take him away.
Get him a good broom to sweep with, take
him away"
I thought I heard him say.

I thought I heard Frankie Dusen shout,
Gal, gimme that money, I'm gonna beat it
out,
Cause I thought I heard Frankie Dusen shout.

This is one of the few songs that can be ascribed to Buddy Bolden. It was his theme song, and it was originally called *Funky Butt Blues*. There were many verses and versions of the song. This one was recorded by Jelly Roll Morton, who was a walking reservoir of the early jazz material. The Frankie Dusen referred to in the song was Bolden's trombone player. When Bolden persisted in the evil habit of running off and drinking up the band's payroll money, they threw him out of his own band, and Frankie Dusen assumed the leadership.

Bolden's bands always had 5 to 7 members. In 1895 the band consisted of Brock Mumford, guitar; Frank Lewis, clarinet; Willy Warner, clarinet; Willy Cornish, valve trombone; Bolden, cornet; and Jimmie Johnson, bass viol.

But the herb of all herbs among both Creoles and Cajuns is filé, and let's pause here while I tell you all about it.

THE STORY OF FILÉ

For hundreds of years the Choctaw Indians have had a settlement at Bayou Lacombe on the North Shore of Lake Pontchartrain. And they had a way of making gumbo long before the white man and the black man arrived. They invented filé (pronounced feelay). The tender green leaves of the sassafras tree are gathered, dried, and ground to a powder. Only a few tablespoons of the powder will thicken a whole pot of gumbo and give it a flavor that's spicy and pleasant. The filé must always be added after the pot is removed from the fire. If allowed to boil, it becomes stringy and unpalatable. Okra and filé should never be used together in a gumbo or it will be as thick as mud. The Creoles in New Orleans used filé only in the wintertime, when fresh okra was not available, but many Cajuns prefer filé gumbo year-round. They pass a big bowl of filé around at the table, so that all the guests may take as much as they want.

The Indians also supplied dried bay leaves (laurel), an essential flavoring element in most Creole soups and stews. At the old French Market there were always several Choctaws sitting in the shade of the arcade, peddling their small caches of filé and dried bundles of bay leaves.

On several visits to Bayou Lacombe a few years ago I was fortunate enough to meet one of the last of those Indian filé makers. His name was Nick Ducré, and he was over eighty-five, very proud, wise and independent. He owned a

One of the last of the Choctaw Indian filé makers of Bayou Lacombe on the North Shore.

few acres of very valuable land on the banks of the bayou. Rich folks had built up bayou estates all around him, but he clung to his land and kept it in a primitive state with plenty of game—coons, possums, squirrels, rabbits, and even a few deer. A great story teller, he told us much about the good old days in the early part of the century. Once a month he would take a schooner across the lake to New Orleans and sell his filé and bay leaves at the market at the New Basin Canal. He would sell out in one day, buy himself a pint of whiskey, and sail for home that night, a happy Indian.

Like many Cajuns even today, Nick was a strong believer in the "fifolay" (*feu follet*), known to others as swamp fire, jack-o'-lantern, will-o'-the wisp. He thought it was a type of ghost, the spirit of some departed person. Nick warned us solemnly that if we were ever walking down the

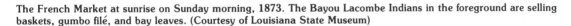

The French Market at sunrise on Sunday morning, 1873. The Bayou Lacombe Indians in the foreground are selling baskets, gumbo filé, and bay leaves. (Courtesy of Louisiana State Museum)

road late at night and saw a fifolay coming toward us, we would have to get out of the road and hide in the bushes until it passed. You don't go fooling around with a fifolay, or all sorts of bad things can happen. The cows will go dry, the horses will get the colic, or you'll fall down and break a leg or something. Nick had me so spooked I was afraid to go out and look at Bayou Lacombe in the moonlight.

At our last parting Nick gave me a sample jar of his homemade filé, and I made a pot of gumbo with part of it. Because I didn't realize just how strong it was, I overdid it. That gumbo got so thick, the stirring spoon stood upright in it. I have saved the rest of that filé as a memento of one of the best Indians I ever knew.

So whenever you eat gumbo filé, give a thought to the almost vanished Choctaws of Lacombe. Filé of a commercial grade can be purchased at any grocery store in New Orleans and in the Cajun country, but the homemade kind is stronger and tastier. If you can't find an Indian source, you can make it yourself by pounding dried sassafras leaves with pestle and mortar. And while you're at it, pound up a few bay leaves for a terrific flavoring element.

If you live outside this area, you can order filé from the dealers listed at the end of this book.

But the single most important flavoring element in both Creole and Cajun cooking is neither a spice nor an herb, but the roux—and this calls for a bit of explanation.

DISSERTATION ON ROUX

The roux is the soul essence of most Creole-Cajun cooking. It's a subject that mystifies the uninitiated, but it's really very simple. To a Louisiana cook making a roux comes as natural as breathing. "Roux" comes from the French term "roux beurre," which means reddish-brown butter, and that's exactly what it is—flour or cornstarch browned with butter or other fat, shortening, or vegetable oil. The roux was used for centuries in French cookery for thickening sauces, soups, and gravies, but it was regarded as peasant stuff by the masters of haute cuisine, who preferred the classic brown (espagnole) sauce.

It wasn't until the roux reached the New World that it became the backbone of a whole new cuisine. When the Creole-Cajun and black cooks of New Orleans took hold of the delicate French roux, they whammed it and whacked it until it became something alive, strong and vibrant, a perfect backdrop for cooking the seafood, game, and vegetables that were available in the region.

The chief function of a roux is to contribute a deep, resonant, browned flavor to any dish it's used in, and it thickens the dish and gives it body. Some of the things it does are almost metaphysical. It makes food slide gently down the tongue, and it tickles the taste buds as it passes by. For some mysterious reason, a good roux inhibits spoiling or souring of a soup or stew.

There are still two schools of thought on roux making. Many aristocratic Creoles think a light golden-colored roux is best. But most Cajun and black cooks prefer a roux that's dark brown, as rich a hue as you can get it without scorching or burning it. The latter type has a very pronounced and recognizable flavor.

The great Escoffier thought the dark brown peasant style of roux, made with flour, was indigestible, and he went to great lengths to explain why a cook should use cornstarch instead of flour. If he had come down to Thibodaux talking like that, they would have ridden him out of town on a rail. When a good cook uses them, either method is satisfactory.

HOW TO MAKE A ROUX

Only a serenely patient cook should try to make a roux. A jumpy, nervous person will scorch or burn it every time. Our instructions here call for butter, but you can use clarified bacon drippings, lard, shortening, vegetable oil, or even olive oil.

To make an average-size roux, melt a half stick (four tablespoons) of butter in a heavy skillet over low heat, add four tablespoons of flour, and stir it in until the mixture is creamy and free of lumps. Turn the heat very low and continue to stir, scraping the bottom of the skillet, for at least twenty-five minutes. When a roux reaches its climax and is done, it begins to brown very rapidly, and you must be on your toes to keep it under control and not let it scorch or burn. If it does, you must throw it out, clean the skillet perfectly, and start all over again—a very tedious business. Some perfectionist aficionados of the art, using very very low heat and lots of patience, can carry a roux for an hour or more before it reaches maturity, and they swear that this is the best roux of all.

When you've brought your roux to the shade of brown you want, you can set it aside until you're ready to use it, or you can add onions, scallions, green peppers—whatever vegetables and seasonings the particular recipe calls for—to the roux in the skillet and keep on cooking until the vegetables are soft and transparent but not browned.

Many cooks make roux in large amounts and freeze it in small individual packets, so that they won't have to go through this complex rigamarole every time they cook.

ESSAY ON H-H-H-HOT PEPPERS!

Acadiana, the country down around Lafayette and New Iberia, might well be called the hot underbelly of America because most of the hot peppers and pepper sauces consumed in the country come from that area. It's the home of McIlhenny's Tabasco, Trappey's Mexi-Pep, and countless other brands of fiery hot sauces, as well as bottled pickled peppers of all kinds, dried pepper pods, the powdered red pepper universally known as Cayenne, and crushed red pepper flakes and seeds so hot they make your hair stand on end. Along the highway the pepper fields spread in all directions, with the plants growing in long rows, flourishing and green. The hot sun, humid atmosphere, and rich alluvial soil of the region are ideal for pepper culture, and the natives make the most of it. Even the smallest farms have a few acres of peppers, and

PEPPERS

they sell their crop to the pepper sauce factories and the canneries. They raise many different kinds of peppers: Anaheim chilis, Louisiana sports, red and green tabascos, serranos, cayennes, torridos, jalapenos, Bahamian reds, and bird's eyes. The last, as the name suggests, are small as a bird's eye, but so hot they can make you gag, choke, and holler for ice water.

Hot pepper adds zest to foods of all kinds, especially seafoods, and the Creoles and Cajuns, well aware of this fact, use cayenne and the liquid pepper sauces generously. Many of the recipes in this volume call for a smidgin of hot pepper, generally specified as cayenne or Tabasco. However, any of the well-known liquid pepper sauces, such as Trappey's, Zatarain's, or Crystal, may be substituted for Tabasco. And powdered cayenne may be substituted for any of the liquid sauces.

Eating hot peppers, raw or pickled, is a popular indoor barroom sport among Louisianians, and those who can stand the heat will sit at the bar eating the peppers and downing them with beer. It's hard to say whether it's masochism or machismo. The pepper eaters say that once you get used to them they're not very hot, that it's all a state of mind. Hot peppers are said to cure stomach ulcers and hemorrhoids, but the believers haven't produced any clinical proof. One thing is certain: they produce Mexican heartburn. Like the common cold, this ailment has no known cure. Take two aspirins and go to bed and wait.

Because some people do eat hot peppers just for the fun of it, Mr. Bernard Trappey, of Trappey's Food Products in New Iberia, holds a "World's Championship Hot Pepper Eating Contest" every two years, and I'm proud to say that I helped with the contest held in 1974. When I was traveling around in the wilds of Yucatan, a Mayan Indian gave me some peppers that were the hottest I had ever tasted. I

Bernard Trappey, pepper pickler and sponsor of the "World's Championship Hot Pepper Eating Contest."

recognized immediately that I had found a "breakfast of champions" and sent some seeds to Mr. Trappey. The seeds germinated, and the plants grew and produced abundantly. Mr. Trappey labeled the new pepper the "secret weapon" and entered it in the final heat of the contest, where it crowned the champion. The Yucatecos call the pepper Habanero.

Trappey's Food Products in New Iberia is one of the state's largest producers of Creole-style food products. The company turns out some delicious pickled hot peppers and two different pepper sauces—Mexi-Pep, which is comparatively mild, and Trappey's Hot Sauce, which is very hot. Mr. Bernard Trappey is a distinguished gastronome himself, one of the founders and a charter member of the Original Ancient Order of Creole Gourmets. He gave me the organization's recipe for Redfish Courtbouillon included in this book.

As you drive south on the highway from New Iberia you come to Avery Island, which is not really an island but just happens to be separated from the mainland by bayous. It's one of the unique places of the world, with salt domes rising into the air like miniature mountains and enormous salt mines flourishing under the ground. Down under the salt there are great pools of oil that the wells on the surface pump forth night and day. On 2500 acres of land are grown 750,000 hot pepper plants, which in turn provide the principal ingredient of one of the world's most famous sauces, Tabasco. Some fifty million bottles of Tabasco a year are sold in 100 different countries all over the world. There isn't a bar in the land without a bottle of Tabasco on the shelf for making Bloody Marys.

Edmund McIlhenny created the sauce more than a hundred years ago. A friend returning from the Mexican War had given him some

"Mr. Tabasco," Walter S. McIlhenny, inspects the fermenting mash from which his sauce is made.

seeds, and he planted them in his garden, where they thrived for a good many years. During the lean years after the Civil War, McIlhenny struck on the idea of making a sauce out of the peppers, and he called it Tabasco. The fat was in the fire, and it has been flaming mightily ever since. Tabasco is strictly a copyrighted proprietary trademark, but it has become such a common household name that it's listed in the dictionary. The company has fought and won many trademark-infringement lawsuits against competitors who have tried to label their sauces "tabasco"— much as the manufacturer of Coca-Cola has been able to protect that name.

The distinguishing characteristic of Tabasco is that it's hot as hell, much hotter than any of its competitors. Incidentally, it also has aroma and savour. These qualities are obtained by aging the ground-up peppers in vinegar in oaken casks, in much the same way that Jack Daniels whiskey is aged. However, the effect is reversed: aging makes the whiskey milder, but it makes the peppers hotter. It's the long, slow process of aging that gives Tabasco its distinctive tang and heat. Most sauce manufacturers are just in too big a hurry.

Walter Stauffer McIlhenny has been president of the Tabasco Company since the 1950s. A grandson of Edmund McIlhenny, he rules for the benefit of the fifty-five to sixty other heirs of the founder who are stockholders. He is a sort of benevolent despot, but since he took charge of the operation, the sales of Tabasco have increased fifteen times over, so nobody's complaining.

A bon vivant, gourmet, and authority on Creole cuisine, Walter Stauffer McIlhenny has contributed several of his recipes to this book.

Chapter 3

Gumbo, Jambalaya, and Other Classic Soups and Stews

CREOLE GUMBO, LA SOUPE DIVINE

Creole Gumbo has deep and diverse roots and many ancestors. It's descended from the French peasant's pot-au-feu and the fisherman's bouillabaisse, from the communal pot of okra stew simmering on the tribal fire in an African village and from the boiling pot of crabs and shrimp tended by Choctaw Indians on the north shore of Lake Pontchartrain. Gumbo is a mystique. Like jazz and the blues, it has overtones of voodoo, mumbo-jumbo, and the Shaman's secret ritual. But best of all, it just tastes good. It's a one-dish meal, nourishing and filling, and it sticks to your ribs. Oh, it's just impossible to describe it. You'll have to come on down to New Orleans and try it. But

as I stated before, the purpose of this book is to evangelize the subject of Creole cookery so that any gourmet in Iowa or Idaho can do with the vittles just what they do in the Crescent City. The basic products are available in any good supermarket in almost any city or town in the land.

There are as many ways to make gumbo as there are cooks. No two cooks make it just alike, and for that matter, no cook makes it exactly the same way twice. It's an improvisational thing, like early jazz. You just take off with whatever tune is handy, and then you travel. You throw in a lot of blue notes, flatted fifths, discords, and glissandos to spice it up, and the end result is almost always satisfying. A Creole cook can take a handful of chicken wings or a turkey carcass or a piece of sausage or a few shrimp and crabs and whip up a gumbo. There are seafood gumbos, chicken gumbos, wild duck and squirrel gumbos, meat and sausage gumbos, okra and filé gumbos, and even a Lenten gumbo called gumbo z'herbes, in which seven different types of greens are used.

All gumbos have two things in common: They all start off with a roux, and they all use either okra or filé as a thickening and flavoring agent. Bloody arguments and duels have been fought over whether okra or filé makes the best gumbo. The adherents of each school simply refuse to listen to those of the other. They're as irreconcilably split as Ghibelline and Guelph. I will try to present both sides, so that you can judge for yourself.

The small neighborhood restaurants in New Orleans are where you will usually find the best gumbo. For many years we had a colorful little restaurant and bar at the corner of Bourbon and St. Peter Streets called The Bourbon House. The food was good and cheap, especially the Creole Gumbo, and the drinks were generous and low-priced, so it was only natural that The Bourbon House became the nucleus of the whole French Quarter. Adam Beeler was the bartender-cook and general factotum, and Robert Silliman was the black waiter and maître d', as well as Father Confessor and Lord Protector of about half the lost souls in the French Quarter. You could learn a lot about making Creole Gumbo just by watching Adam Beeler cook. At work in his kitchen, he was a no-nonsense cook. He put just about everything he had in the refrigerator into his gumbo pot, and it usually turned out very good—but sometimes it misfired and was just awful! There's an apochryphal story about Adam and his gumbo and Ro-

bert, said to have come from some of the restaurant's regulars. It seems that a few years ago the city passed a new law requiring that garbage cans be on the sidewalk for collection by 5 p.m. One day Robert yelled into the kitchen, "Hey, Adam, the garbage truck is coming." And Adam yelled back, "Tell him to leave three cans today."

It takes a bit of moola and plenty of elbow grease to make a really deluxe Creole gumbo. At the Skyscraper a dozen friends would pitch in and share the expense and the endless peeling and chopping. These gumbo parties were happy affairs, and nobody ever went home hungry or in a blue funk. We often had a backdrop of good jazz or blues and rhythm or somebody plunking banjos and guitars.

Here's our recipe for the type of gumbo we made at those parties. Remember that making gumbo is a very flexible thing, and you can omit or make substitutions for any of the ingredients given here. Freewheel it!

CREOLE GUMBO
(Serves 12 or more)

  5 **lb fresh heads-on shrimp (or 4 lb frozen shrimp tails)**
12 **live crabs (or 1 lb frozen crabmeat)**
  4 **dozen oysters and their liquor**
  1 **chicken, about 2 lb**
  1 **lb stewing beef, diced small**
  1 **meaty hambone**

½ lb country ham, diced
4 strips bacon
3 large onions, chopped
2 green peppers, chopped
6 scallions with their green leaves,
   chopped
4 cloves garlic, minced
1 cup chopped celery
¼ cup chopped parsley
3 lb fresh (or 4 pkg frozen) okra, sliced
4 large Creole tomatoes, peeled and diced
   (or a 32-oz can)
2 bay leaves
1 tsp thyme
2 tbsp Worcestershire sauce
½ tsp cayenne
1 tsp freshly ground black pepper
4 tbsp salt (or more)
6 quarts stock or water (or more)
4 tbsp butter and 4 tbsp flour (for the roux)
   steamed rice

The operation requires several utensils, a big skillet, a big stew pot, and several smaller pots for steaming.

First the roux: Melt the butter in the skillet, add the flour, and stir until dark brown, keeping the fire very low. To the roux in the skillet add the chopped onions, green peppers, scallions, garlic, and celery and stir them in well. Adding more butter if necessary, cook the vegetables until they're limp and transparent, but don't brown them. Add the okra and keep cooking until the okra loses its gummy consistency. Put this mixture into the large stew pot. Clean the skillet, and fry the strips of bacon and the diced country ham slowly until browned. Add the ham to the pot, and drain the bacon on a paper towel. Crumble it and

add to the pot. Shake the diced stewing beef in a paper bag with seasoned flour, coating it well, and add it to the bacon grease in the skillet. Sear the beef until it's browned on all sides, and add it to the pot.

While you were doing all the above, your assistant cooks should have been performing the following operations: Cut the chicken into pieces, place them in a pot, and cover with water, adding a teaspoon of salt. Boil for 30 to 40 minutes, or until tender. Remove the chicken and add its cooking stock to the big pot. Remove the skin from the chicken, cut the skin into very small pieces, and add it to the pot. Remove the chicken meat from the bones, dice it, and add it to the pot.

Wash the shrimp and cover them with water in a pot, adding a little salt. Bring to the boil and cook for five minutes, or until they're pink and easy to peel. Take them out and cool them in the sink. Save the shrimp stock in the pot. Peel the shrimp and set them aside. Take the heads and the shells off the shrimp, place them in some sort of flat-bottomed container, and crush them thoroughly with a pestle or an empty bottle. Pour this mixture into the shrimp water in the pot, and boil it vigorously for 15 minutes. Strain the liquid through triple cheesecloth into the big stew pot. The stuff inside the shrimp's head is like the tomalley of a lobster—a nectar of the gods—and this stock will really give kick to the gumbo. So will the crab stock (see below).

Wash the live crabs thoroughly, put them in a pot, cover with boiling water, and boil for 20 minutes. Remove the crabs and pour the stock into the large stew pot. Clean the crabs. Remove the top shells and scrape the spongy gills off. Break off the mouth parts, and re-

STORYVILLE

Storyville—"Down the line" on Basin Street. Tom Anderson's Saloon and Dance Hall was located on the corner. Tom Anderson was the unofficial "Mayor" of Storyville. The parlor house next door belonged to Gertrude Dix, who later married Tom Anderson. The mansion with the onion-shaped Byzantine cupola was Arling-ton Hall, run by Josie Arlington. The house with the triangular cupola was Lulu White's Mahogany Hall, the most famous house of them all. All these mansions were elaborately furnished with fine furniture, carpets, velvet draperies, tapestries, chandeliers, and expensive statuary and paintings.

In the early 1890s houses of prostitution were spreading out all over New Orleans, even into respectable neighborhoods, and the whole real estate market was endangered. To remedy the situation the city fathers passed an ordinance, introduced with good intentions by Alderman Sidney Story, establishing a legalized red light district of about a dozen square blocks behind the French Quarter. To the alderman's chagrin, the public immediately pinned the name "Storyville" on the area, conferring on him a dubious immortality. Most New Orleanians simply called it "The District." From 1898 to 1917, Storyville was the most famous, glamorous, and notorious cesspool of iniquity on the face of the earth, encompassing all forms of vice for all tastes. It was in 1917 at the height of World War I that Secretary of the Navy Josephus Daniels made the city close The District down to protect our clean-cut Navy boys from sin and disease.

Many people have the mistaken idea that jazz was born in Storyville whorehouses. In fact, jazz was born in the black neighborhood above Canal Street. The parlor houses sometimes hired "professors" to play the piano and perhaps a string trio or a blues

Basin Street Blues

singer now and then, but the jazz bands were too noisy and raucous for the "genteel" atmosphere the houses were trying to put across. It was in the numerous cabarets and dance halls in The District that the bands found steady employment. These places nurtured jazz through its childhood and puberty until it became a full-grown art form, rough and ready and rowdy. Among the most famous dance halls were Pete Lala's Place, 101 and 102 Ranch, Tuxedo, Rice's, Abadie's (Aberdeen's), Fewclothes, Big 25, Frenchman's, Tom Anderson's, and Frank Early's.

Among the musicians who played in these dance halls were Freddie Keppard, Joe Oliver, "Big Eye Louis" Nelson Delisle, Emanuel Perez, George and Achille Baquet, Sidney Bechet, "Pops" Foster, Kid Ory, Lorenzo Tio, Zue Robertson, Henry Tio, Johnny and "Baby" Dodds, Buddy Petit, Jimmy Noone, Papa Celestin, Alphonse Picou, A. J. Piron, Jelly Roll Morton, Louis Armstrong, Mutt Carey, Clarence Williams, and Bunk Johnson. Some of these musicians went on to become internationally famous. All of them were Negroes or Creoles of mixed blood. No white musicians played in Storyville. But the young white musicians who were later to create "Dixieland Jazz" were sitting around listening and learning.

Storyville was undeniably the hothouse where jazz reached full bloom.

BASIN STREET BLUES

Won'tcha come along with me
To the Mississippi?
We'll take the boat to the land of dreams
Steam down the river down to New Orleans;
The band's there to meet us,
Old friends to greet us,
Where all the light and the dark folks meet,
This is Basin Street:

Chorus
Basin Street is the street,
Where the elite always meet, in New
  Orleans,
Land of dreams. You'll never know how nice
  it seems,
or just how much it really means.
Glad to be, Yes, siree, where welcome's free,
Dear to me, Where I can lose
My BASIN STREET BLUES.

Spencer Williams, (1889–1965) was a nephew and ward of Lulu White, the famous madam of Mahogany Hall. An entertainer at a very early age, he later wrote some of the greatest all-time jazz standards: *Basin Street Blues, Mahogany Hall Stomp, I Ain't Got Nobody, I Ain't Gonna Give Nobody None O' My Jelly Roll, Everybody Loves My Baby, I've Found a New Baby, Royal Garden Blues,* and *Shim-Me-Sha-Wobble.* He left New Orleans in 1907 to work in Chicago and New York, where he gained fame. He went to Paris in 1925 to write material for Josephine Baker's hit revues. He returned to America, but in 1932 he and Fats Waller went back to Paris and took the place by storm. Williams married an English girl and lived for many years in London, Stockholm, and Paris. He died at Flushing, New York, in 1965.

move the "apron" on the bottom of the crab. Twist off the fins, legs, and claws. Crack the claws and put them in the main pot. Break the body into two halves and drop them in. Be sure you've scraped out all the crabfat from the corners of the top shells and from the body cavity and added it to the pot, because a gumbo wouldn't be fit to eat without this delicious stuff (see "The Fabulous Story of Crabfat" in Chapter 5). Crush the crab shells, legs, and fins in the bottom of a pot as you did the shrimp shells. Cover them with water and boil vigorously for 15 minutes. Strain the liquid and add it to the main cooking pot.

Add the oyster liquor to the pot. Get as much of this stuff from your oyster dealer as you can, a quart or two if possible, but if you can't get that much, the chicken, shrimp, and crab stock (plus water if needed) will do.

You are now ready to light the fire under the big stew pot. Add the tomatoes, parsley, hambone, and all the flavoring elements except the salt. The liquid should cover everything in the pot by about two inches, so add more liquid if necessary. You can use fish stock, oyster liquor, chicken bouillon, a combination of all these, or just plain water. Bring the pot to a boil, then lower the heat, place an asbestos pad under the pot to prevent scorching, and boil gently for 1½ to 2 hours. You can't overcook it; the longer it cooks, the better. Stir it occasionally and scrape the bottom with a metal kitchen spoon. If there's a black residue on the tip of your spoon, it means you're scorching it, and you'd better slow down. If it really begins to burn and has an acrid, scorched smell, you must cut off the heat, remove the gumbo from the pot, clean all the burned material off the bottom of the pot, rinse it out, replace the gumbo, and start cooking again. Thus chastened, you'll use moderation and sense. A stew containing roux will always scorch if you don't keep a close watch on it and cook slowly.

About 30 minutes before the gumbo is done, start cooking your rice. Bring 12 cups of water to a boil, and add a tablespoon of vegetable oil (keeps the grains separated), 4 teaspoons of salt, and 6 cups of rice. Stir the mixture vigorously, and when it returns to the boil, turn the heat very low, cover the pot tightly, and cook for 15 minutes or until all the water is absorbed. Let it set for a few minutes, and then taste for doneness. Never stir steaming rice until it's done.

Ten minutes before serving the gumbo, add the shrimp and the oysters to the pot, and stir them in.

Now comes the last and critically important act: adjusting the salt. A good gumbo must have plenty of salt in it if it's to be as savoury as it should be. Keep adding salt to the pot and stirring it in until it achieves this deep, rich savour. Don't be timid! A bland gumbo is a disaster.

Serve the gumbo in large preheated soup bowls. Place a half cup of rice in the bottom of each bowl and ladle the gumbo over it, making sure that each bowl gets a generous share of all the elements—shrimp, crab, and oysters. (Option: Many hosts prefer to pass around a bowl of hot rice and let the guests add exactly the amount they want.)

I like a good full-bodied imported red Burgundy with my gumbo, but many prefer the lighter white wines.

Antoine's Restaurant, as seen from Royal Street. (Sketch by Roscoe Misselhorn)

Antoine's is America's most famous restaurant, and deservedly so. Its grand cuisine, fine wines, and the sheer ambience of "Dinner at Antoine's" make for an unforgettable experience. It's not just a tourist attraction, either. Many New Orleanians consider it their favorite restaurant, and they dine there as often as their pocketbooks will allow. Many of the classic dishes of Creole cuisine were invented by Antoine's—Oysters Rockefeller, Pompano en Papillote, and Crawfish Cardinale, for instance.

Antoine Alciatore came to New Orleans from Marseilles in 1840. He opened a boardinghouse on St. Peter Street, offering bed and board to all and sundry. The board was better than the bed, though, and his dining room became so crowded he couldn't accommodate the crowds who wanted in. This led him to give up room renting and open a restaurant on St. Louis Street. He had two sons, Jules and Fernand. Jules succeeded to the ownership of Antoine's, and Fernand opened his own restaurant, La Louisiane, which became almost as famous as Antoine's. Jules was an inventive genius and developed most of the specialties for which Antoine's is now famous. He was succeeded by his son Roy, who in turn was succeeded by Roy Guste, a fifth-generation member of the royal family of Alciatore.

OYSTER GUMBO A LA ANTOINE

(Serves 6 or more)

This is a bit of haute cuisine. Antoine's would never give anyone their recipe for Oysters Rockefeller, but sixteen years ago the late, great Mr. Roy Alciatore gave me his recipe for Oyster Gumbo. Like all great cooking it's very simple and easy to prepare.

- 3 tbsp flour
- 5 tbsp butter
- 6 raw hard-shell crabs, cut in pieces
- 2 bay leaves
- 1 tsp thyme
- 1 lb raw okra, sliced
- 6 raw tomatoes with skins removed and chopped fine
- 1 quart oyster liquor
  salt and pepper to taste
- 1 lb peeled raw shrimp
- 5 dozen raw oysters

Make a good roux with the flour and butter by allowing it to brown (but not burn) while stirring constantly over a low flame. To the brown roux add the raw hard-shell crabs cut into several pieces. Stir and cook a little, and then add the bay leaves and the thyme. Add the raw sliced okra and allow to cook awhile. Then add the tomatoes and allow to cook some more. Next add a quart each of oyster liquor and water at the same time. Season with salt and pepper to taste. Allow the gumbo to simmer for an hour and a half. Ten minutes before serving, add the shrimp and the raw oysters. Serve with boiled Louisiana rice.

CRAB GUMBO

(Serves 8 to 10)

- 3 dozen large fat live crabs (or 3 lb frozen crabmeat)
- 3 lb fresh or frozen shrimp
- 2 lb sliced fresh okra (or 3 pkg frozen)
- 2 large onions, chopped
- 1 green pepper, chopped
- ¼ cup chopped parsley
- 3 cloves garlic, minced
- 5 Creole tomatoes, peeled and chopped (or a 32-oz can)
- 2 bay leaves
- ½ tsp thyme
- ¼ tsp cayenne
- ½ tsp freshly ground black pepper
- 3 tbsp butter
- 3 tbsp flour
  salt to taste

Peel the shrimp and set aside. There's no need to devein them. Save the heads and shells.

Wash the live crabs thoroughly in the sink. They'll protest vigorously, but ignore them. Place them in a large pot, cover with boiling water, and add a little salt. After the water returns to the boil, cook the crabs for 20 minutes. Take them out of the pot and place them in the sink to cool. Save the stock in the pot. Crush the shrimp shells and heads with pestle and mortar, or use a bottle and a flat-bottomed pan. Add this mixture to the stock in the pot. Remove the crab claws and set aside. Remove the top shells of the crabs, scrape all the crabfat out of the corners of the shells, and save it. Twist off the legs and fins. Crush the top shells and the legs and fins with pestle and mortar, and add them to the stock pot. Boil all these shells vigorously for 30 minutes, and then strain off the liquid through a triple layer of cheesecloth. This makes a beautiful stock for your gumbo.

In a large heavy skillet melt the butter, add the flour, and make a roux. To the roux add the onions, green pepper, and garlic, and cook until the vegetables are soft and transparent. Add more butter if necessary. Add the okra to the skillet, and cook it until it loses its gummy consistency and is smooth. Add the crabfat, parsley, bay leaves, thyme, cayenne, and black pepper to the skillet and stir them in, cooking a little longer.

Put the skilletful of vegetables in a large stew pot and add the tomatoes. Crack the crab claws and put them in. Clean off the crabs' bodies by removing and discarding the gills (or "dead man's fingers"), the mouth part, the small bag next to it at the front, and the sex parts (or "apron") on the bottom. Clean out the body cavity and save all the fat, the yellow liver (tomalley), and any red coral (eggs) that may be present. Add all this—the "caviar" of the crab—to the pot. Discard the intestine, the white stringy thing in the body cavity. Break the crab bodies into halves, cut each half into two or three pieces, and add to the stew pot. Next add the shrimp. Add enough of the strained stock to the stew pot to cover all contents by one inch. If more liquid is necessary, add fish stock or bouillon. Simmer for an hour, add the shrimp, cook for a half hour more, and at the end add salt carefully. The gumbo should be salty and savoury. Preheat soup bowls, place a little steamed rice in the bottom

of each, and ladle the gumbo over the rice. Serve piping hot, with hot crunchy French bread. A white Chassagne-Montrachet or Pouilly Fuissé will go beautifully with this gumbo.

CRAB-HOMINY GUMBO
(Serves 6 to 8)

2 dozen large fat live crabs (or 2 lb frozen crabmeat)
2 lb fresh okra, in ½″ slices
2 large onions, chopped
1 16-oz can tomatoes, drained and chopped
1 16-oz can hominy
3 cloves garlic, minced
4 tbsp chopped parsley
¼ tsp cayenne
½ tsp freshly ground black pepper
3 tbsp lard (or shortening)
2 tbsp flour
salt to taste

Wash the live crabs thoroughly in the sink. Place them in a large pot and cover with boiling water. After the water comes to the boil, cook the crabs for 20 minutes. Remove and cool them. Save the water. Twist off the crab claws, legs, and flippers, and set them aside. Remove the top shells of the crabs, and scrape off the spongy gills. Clean out all the crabfat in the corners of the shells and save it. Also save all the crabfat and yellow liver from the crab's body cavity. Break off the mouth part and remove the apron from the body. Crack the body into two halves and pick out all the meat.

(See instructions for crab picking in Chapter 5 under "How to Eat Boiled Crabs.") Crack the crab claws and pick out their meats. This picking is a tedious chore, but it's worth the bother. You should get about two pounds of the meat and the crabfat.

Place the crab shells, legs, and flippers in a flat-bottomed pot, and smash them up with a pestle or a heavy bottle. Cover with part of the water the crabs were boiled in. Boil vigorously for 30 minutes to extract the essences. Strain the liquid, set it aside, and discard the shells.

In a large pot or Dutch oven (aluminum or stainless steel preferred to iron, which turns okra black) heat the lard and add the flour to make a roux. Add the onions and garlic and cook until transparent. Add the okra and cook until it loses its gummy consistency. Add the hominy, tomatoes with their juice, parsley, cayenne, black pepper, and about a tablespoon of salt. Cover the materials in the pot by about an inch with the crab water, the juice from the shells, and the crabfat. Simmer for an hour. Add the crab meat, and then simmer for a half hour more. At the end adjust the salt. The gumbo should be salty and savoury, hot and peppery, and thick. Serve it in preheated soup bowls over mounds of steamed rice.

SEAFOOD-SAUSAGE-CHICKEN GUMBO FILÉ
(Serves 8)

2 lb heads-on shrimp (or 2 lb frozen tails)
3 dozen oysters and their liquor

1 3-lb chicken, cut up
1 lb Andouille sausage or Creole smoked sausage, chopped fine
2 large onions, chopped
½ cup celery leaves, chopped fine
4 scallions with their green leaves, chopped fine
½ tsp thyme
1 bay leaf
½ cup butter
½ cup flour
¼ tsp cayenne
salt and freshly ground black pepper to taste
filé powder
steamed rice

Place the cut-up chicken pieces in a pot, add the chopped sausage, cover with water, and add a teaspoon of salt. Boil for 45 minutes. Remove the chicken and sausage and save the broth. Remove the chicken meat from the bones, dice it, and set it aside. Wash the shrimp, cover with water in a pot, add a little salt, and boil for five minutes. Remove the shrimp from the pot, peel (do not devein), and set aside. Return the heads and shells to the shrimp broth in the pot, and boil vigorously for 15 minutes. Strain this broth into the chicken broth.

Make a roux of the butter and flour. When the roux is browned, add the onion, celery leaves, and scallions. Cook slowly until the vegetables are soft and transparent. Stir in the thyme, bay leaf, cayenne, and black pepper. Place the roux-vegetable mix, sausage, and chicken in a stew pot and cover by one inch with the chicken-shrimp broth, adding water or chicken bouillon if necessary. Simmer for one hour. Add the shrimp, oysters, and oyster liquor, and cook for 10 minutes longer. Adjust the salt. Turn off the heat and let the gumbo sit for five minutes. Then you can either add two tablespoons of filé powder and stir it in well or place the filé bottle on the table and let the guests add their own. About a half teaspoon per bowl is average.

Serve in preheated gumbo bowls with a little rice in the bottom of each bowl. French bread on the side and a dry red wine are called for.

SHRIMP-TASSO GUMBO
(Serves 8)

The Cajuns have a type of dried beef called tasso that's a cousin to the pemmican of the Indians and the jerky beef of Western frontiersmen. Rubbed with salt and spices before being dried, it has a pungent flavor and makes a delicious gumbo when combined with shrimp and okra. It is sold in neighborhood groceries throughout the Acadian country. In other areas jerky dried beef or corned beef can be used as a substitute.

2 lb tasso
3 lb fresh heads-on shrimp (or 2 lb frozen tails)
3 lb fresh okra (or 4 pkg frozen), sliced
2 large onions, chopped
1 green pepper, chopped
4 cloves garlic, minced
1 32-oz can tomatoes
3 tbsp lard or bacon drippings

3 tbsp flour
¼ tsp cayenne (or more)
salt and freshly ground black pepper to taste

Cover the tasso chunks with water and soak them overnight. Drain. Cover the tasso with fresh water and boil gently for two hours, or until it is soft and tender. Take it out, dice it, and set it aside. Cover the shrimp with the water the tasso was boiled in, and boil for five minutes. Remove the shrimp, peel, and set aside. The stock in the pot may be too strong and salty for use as gumbo stock, so taste it and dilute with fresh water until it's palatable.

Melt the lard in a large skillet, add the flour, and make a brown roux. Add the onions, green pepper, and garlic to the roux, and cook until the vegetables are wilted. Add the sliced okra to the skillet and continue cooking until the okra loses its gummy consistency. Chop the tomatoes and add them to the skillet. Cook a little longer, add the cayenne and black pepper, and stir well. Place this mixture in a stew pot, and add the tasso and shrimp and enough tasso-shrimp stock to cover by one inch. If necessary, add water. Cook at a slow boil for 45 minutes more. Add salt if necessary. Ladle over rice in preheated soup bowls.

JAMBALAYA

After gumbo the most famous Creole-Cajun stew is jambalaya. The word is probably derived from "jambon," which means ham in both Spanish and French. The "a la ya" is

JAMBALAYA (On the Bayou)

Goodbye Joe me gotta go, me oh my oh,
Me gotta go, pole the pirogue down the
   bayou,
My Yvonne, the sweetest one, me oh my oh,
Son of a gun, we'll have big fun on the
   bayou!

Chorus
JAM-BA-LA-YA and a crawfish pie, and filé
   gumbo,
Cause tonight I'm gonna see my ma cher-a-
   mio.
Pick guitar, fill fruit jar and be gay-o,
Son of a gun, we'll have big fun on the
   bayou,
Thibo bayou.

Thiboudaux, Font-tain-eaux, the place is
   buzzin,
Kinfolk come to see Yvonne by the dozen
Dress in style and go hog wild, me oh my oh,
Son of a gun, we'll have big fun on the
   bayou!

Settle down far from town, get me a pirogue
And I'll catch all the fish in the bayou.
Swap my mon to buy Yvonne what she need-
o,
Son of a gun, we'll have big fun on the
   bayou!

French Quarter restaurant at the turn of the century.
(Etching by William Woodward)

This isn't strictly a jazz song—it's country music, by the greatest country musician of them all. Hank Williams was no Cajun, but he caught their spirit perfectly. When the song first came out in the early fifties, it was at the top of the Hit Parade for weeks. It made jambalaya almost as famous as Creole gumbo. The jazz bands picked the song up, and it's still frequently played in New Orleans.

probably an African expletive which can be interpreted as either acclaim or derision. Jambalaya was a well-known dish even before Hank Williams's Hit Parade song came along and made it nationally famous. Millions have sung the song without knowing anything about what the dish was like. The recipes herewith will give you a chance to really get on the bandwagon. Jambalaya started out as a poor man's catch-all, utilizing any leftover meats, sausages, shrimp, or fish that might be lying around, and stretching them a long long way with plenty of rice. If a poor Cajun family had five or six kids, it's a safe bet they ate jambalaya several times a week. Like red beans and rice, it kept people from starving during depressions and recessions.

But the consummate artistry of Creole and Cajun cooks has lifted jambalaya above its humble beginnings to a higher plateau, and it is now served with pride and joy in the mansions of the wealthy and in high-toned restaurants. This dish is a close cousin of the Spanish paella, and it probably originated down around New Iberia, which, as its name suggests, was originally a Spanish settlement. However, there's another town with a Spanish name, Gonzales, up near Baton Rouge, that calls itself the Jambalaya Capital of the World. Its citizens hold a jambalaya festival every year. They cook big black iron wash pots full of the stuff, and people come from all over to sample the rich and redolent fare. A real Gonzales jambalaya is so peppery hot, spicy, and rich that the uninitiated can barely cope with it, but an aficionado of the art can consume a half gallon of it and ask for more. The version of Creole Jambalaya here is lighter fare than the Gonzales product.

CREOLE JAMBALAYA
(Serves 8 to 10)

2 lb raw shrimp, peeled
2 cups raw rice
1 lb Andouille sausage or Creole smoked sausage
½ lb cooked chicken, diced
½ lb country ham (or boiled ham), diced
½ stick butter
4 tbsp flour
2 16-oz cans beef broth (or 3 cups bouillon)
4 cloves garlic, minced
3 medium white onions, chopped fine
6 scallions with their green leaves, chopped
4 Creole tomatoes, peeled and chopped (or a 16-oz can tomatoes, drained and chopped)
1 small green pepper, chopped
1 bay leaf
½ tsp thyme leaves
⅛ tsp ground cumin
⅛ tsp ground cloves
⅛ tsp ground allspice
¼ tsp cayenne (or more)
salt and freshly ground black pepper to taste

Melt the butter in a thick-bottomed pot or Dutch oven, cook the sausage and ham until lightly browned, and stir in the flour. Add the onions, scallions, green pepper, and garlic, and cook until the vegetables are soft and transparent. Stir in the chopped tomatoes and their juice. Stir in the bay leaf, thyme, cumin, cloves, allspice, cayenne, and black pepper. Add the beef broth and mix well. Add the raw shrimp and the chicken. Stir in the raw rice. Season with salt, approximately a tablespoon to start. The liquid in the pot should just cover the contents. Add more broth or bouillon if necessary. Bring it to the boil, and then cut the heat very low, cover the pot, and cook until the rice is done. (The rice will absorb most of the moisture. A jambalaya should be damp but not soupy.) Adjust the salt and serve at once to 8 or 10 hungry people. Anybody who doesn't have a really good appetite should not be allowed to eat jambalaya.

Wash it down with a good full-bodied red wine.

SHRIMP JAMBALAYA
(Serves 6)

Among connoisseurs of jambalaya, the plain Shrimp Jambalaya is considered unsurpassable, and they think it's a waste of time to make it any other way.

- **4 lb raw shrimp, peeled**
- **2 cups raw rice**
- **½ stick butter**
- **4 tbsp flour**
- **2 medium white onions, chopped**
- **3 scallions with their green leaves, chopped**
- **2 cloves garlic, minced**
- **1 small green pepper, chopped**

- **2 tbsp parsley, chopped**
- **1 16-oz can tomatoes, drained and chopped**
- **2 16-oz cans beef broth (or 3 cups bouillon)**
- **⅛ tsp ground cloves**
- **⅛ tsp ground allspice**
- **½ tsp thyme leaves**
- **¼ tsp cayenne (or more)**
  salt and freshly ground pepper to taste

Melt the butter in a thick-bottomed pot or Dutch oven, add the flour, and cook over low heat to make a light golden roux. Add the onions, scallions, green pepper, garlic, and parsley, and cook until the vegetables are soft and transparent. Add the tomatoes and their juice and the beef broth, and mix well. Add the cloves, allspice, thyme, cayenne, and black pepper. Season with salt, about a tablespoon to start. Add the shrimp and cook for five minutes. Stir the rice in well. The mixture in the pot should be just covered with broth, so if necessary, add more broth or bouillon. Bring to the boil, and then cut the heat very low, cover the pot, and cook until the rice is tender. Adjust the salt. Serve a good red or white wine; let your taste buds make the choice.

SHRIMP-OYSTER JAMBALAYA
(Serves 8)

To the recipe for Shrimp Jambalaya (above) add two dozen oysters and their liquor. If the oysters are large, cut them in half. In a small

saucepan, poach the oysters in their liquor until they're firm and plump and their edges curl. When the Shrimp Jambalaya is done, fold in the oysters and the liquid, stirring gently so as not to tear the oysters apart.

SHRIMP AND BEEF JAMBALAYA

(Serves 6)

- 2 lb raw shrimp, peeled
- 1 lb round steak or stewing beef, diced
- ½ stick butter
- 3 tbsp flour
- 2 medium onions, chopped
- 1 small green pepper, chopped
- 1 rib celery, chopped
- 4 scallions with their green leaves, sliced fine
- 2 tbsp chopped parsley
- ¼ lb fresh mushrooms, sliced
- 1 16-oz can tomatoes, drained and chopped
- 2 16-oz cans beef broth (or 3 cups bouillon)
- 2 cups raw rice
- ¼ tsp cayenne
- ½ tsp thyme
- 1 bay leaf
  salt and freshly ground black pepper

In a heavy, thick-bottomed pot or Dutch oven melt the butter and sear the diced beef until it's browned on all sides. Add the flour and mix well. Add the onions, green pepper, celery, and scallions, and cook until the vegetables are soft and transparent. Add the tomatoes, mushrooms, parsley, thyme, bay leaf, and shrimp.

Add the beef broth, cayenne, and black pepper. Add a tablespoon of salt as a starter. Stir in the raw rice. The liquid should just cover the contents of the pot, so add more broth or bouillon if necessary. Bring to the boil, and then lower the heat to a gentle simmer, cover, and cook until the rice is tender. Adjust the salt and serve at once.

Beer is good with this, and so is imported Burgundy. If you prefer white wine, try a Chablis or a Liebfraumilch.

COURTBOUILLON MEANS LOVE AND AFFECTION

The third great stew in the hierarchy of Creole-Cajun cookery is the renowned Redfish Courtbouillon.

As I told you in Chapter 1, we used to lead the high life at the old Skyscraper at the corner of Royal and St. Peter Streets in the French Quarter. There was a party almost every night and almost always a pot of something good simmering on the stove. I've mellowed a little and put aside the high life with other childish things, but I still like to get stewed and whip up a seafood stew for a pretty girl and sing in my best Donald Duck voice: "A loaf of bread, a pot of stew, and you. . . ." The dolls really hate my singing, but they usually swear by my stew. Don't ever forget that from way back in time seafood has been known as the best of aphrodisiacs—and a brain food to boot. A dozen oysters on the half-shell or a good seafood stew will get you further with a nice girl than a quart of booze. I'm not sure what it will do for your I.Q., though.

Courtbouillon (pronounced coobyong) is definitely a Cajun dish. It's redolent with the odors of bayou and swamp, but it has worked itself into the highest echelons of Creole-Cajun cookery and is served with pride by many famous restaurants in New Orleans and in the homes of rich and poor alike.

In classic French cookery a courtbouillon is just a watery stock, but as they did with most of the other effete French ideas, the Creoles and Cajuns took hold of it and whammed it around until it became a great big stew—pungent, rich, and satisfying. Cajun folksingers have about a half dozen songs about redfish courtbouillon, most of them based on the theme "I want some coobyong, Mama, and your love and affection"—typical Gallic forthrightness and warmth.

The following recipe was given to me several years ago by Mr. Bernard Trappey of New Iberia, one of the founders of the Original Ancient Order of Creole Gourmets, so it must be authentic. At least I've tried it many times, and it always turns out good.

About the fish, as the name indicates, this dish is best when made with the redfish, also called channel bass (*Sciaenops ocellatus*), but you can substitute any firm white-fleshed fish, such as red snapper, gaspergou, catfish, sheepshead, cobia, or striped bass and get good results.

REDFISH COURTBOUILLON I

(Serves 12 to 16)

10 lb redfish, cut in 2″ cross sections
¾ cup olive oil or fat
¾ cup flour
1 16-oz can tomatoes
1 6-oz can tomato paste
fish stock or water
1 cup claret or Burgundy
2 lemons, sliced
4 cloves garlic, minced
1 rib celery, finely chopped
3 bay leaves
½ tsp thyme
½ tsp ground allspice
1 small green pepper, chopped
½ lb fresh whole button mushrooms (or larger mushrooms, sliced)
½ cup chopped parsley
salt, freshly ground black pepper, and cayenne to taste
steamed rice

Use a large, thick-bottomed iron pot (or a stew pot with an asbestos pad under it). Heat the olive oil or fat and add the flour. Lower the heat and, stirring constantly, make a dark brown roux. Drain the tomatoes, chop finely, and add with their juice to the pot. Add the tomato paste. Cook and stir occasionally until oil rises to the surface and the mixture is a smooth pulp. Stir in 2½ quarts of fish stock or water and a cup of claret or Burgundy, and mix well. Add the lemon slices, garlic, celery, bay leaves, thyme, allspice, green pepper, mushrooms, and parsley. Season with salt, black pepper, and cayenne.

Let this mixture simmer for 30 to 45 minutes, stirring occasionally and scraping the bottom of the pot to make sure it's not sticking. Rub the fish pieces with salt, freshly ground black pepper, and cayenne. Add the fish pieces to the pot and raise the heat. When it returns to the boil, lower the heat and cook at a slow boil for 20 minutes, or until the fish is tender and flakes when tested with a fork, and the liquid is the consistency of medium gravy. Serve the fish and sauce on steamed rice, and garnish with chopped parsley. The one that gets the greasiest chin is the biggest Creole gourmet. Wash it down with a good dry claret or Burgundy, and top off the whole dinner with Benedictine or Chartreuse served along with a rich black chicory coffee with a small twist of lemon peel in it.

REDFISH COURTBOUILLON II
(Serves 8 to 10)

If possible, have the fish dealer save the heads, backbones, tails, and trimmings for you so that you can make a fish stock according to the following instructions. (You should always keep a supply of this wonderful stuff in the freezer, in several small containers. It has many many uses, as you will find throughout this book. If you do not have fish stock on hand, you can substitute beef or chicken stock or bouillon, but the end result will not be as good.)

FISH STOCK
   4 **lb fish heads, bones, tails, trimmings**
   4 **quarts water**
   4 **cloves garlic, crushed**
   3 **onions, coarsely chopped**
   4 **tomatoes, chopped (or a 16-oz can)**
   1 **cup parsley, coarsely chopped**
   2 **ribs celery with leaves, chopped**
   2 **bay leaves**

½ **tsp each basil, thyme, and freshly ground black pepper**
¼ **tsp cayenne**
4 **tsp salt (or more to taste)**
¼ **tsp saffron (optional)**

Place all the ingredients in a stew pot, and boil vigorously for 30 minutes. Adjust the salt. It should be strong and savoury. Strain the liquid through a double layer of cheesecloth and set aside until needed. Discard the vegetables and bones.

THE COURTBOUILLON
   4 **lb redfish fillets, cut in 3″ pieces**
   ½ **cup bacon drippings or shortening**
   ½ **cup flour**
   2 **large onions, chopped**
   2 **ribs celery, chopped (1 cup)**
   4 **scallions with their green leaves, thinly sliced**
   1 **green pepper, chopped**
   2 **cloves garlic, minced**
   1 **cup dry red wine**
   1 **16-oz can tomatoes, drained and chopped**
   1 **6-oz can tomato paste**
   2 **quarts fish stock**
      salt and freshly ground black pepper to taste
      steamed rice

In a heavy iron pot or Dutch oven, heat the bacon drippings, add the flour, and stir over a low fire to make a dark brown roux. Add the onions, celery, green pepper, scallions, and garlic, and cook slowly until the vegetables are well done and beginning to fall apart, adding more shortening or broth if necessary. Add the tomatoes, tomato paste, wine, and fish stock, mix well, and simmer for one hour, stirring occasionally and scraping the bottom of the pot to keep it from sticking. Rub the fish pieces with salt, black pepper, and cayenne, and place them in the pot. Raise the heat to the boil, then cut it low, and simmer for 20 minutes or until the fish is tender and flakes with a fork. Serve the fish and the sauce over mounds of steamed rice in preheated soup bowls, with plenty of hot crunchy French bread and a good full-bodied wine, red or white.

SWAMP CATFISH COURTBOUILLON

(Serves 8 to 10)

The Cajuns down in the swamps catch catfish day and night, and they dote on Catfish Courtbouillon, with plenty of roux to make it thick and plenty of spices to jazz it up.

4 lb catfish fillets, cut in 3″ pieces
1 cup vegetable oil
1 cup flour
2 onions, chopped
6 scallions with their green leaves, sliced
½ cup chopped parsley
1 cup chopped celery
1 16-oz can tomatoes, drained and chopped
1 6-oz can tomato paste
3 cloves garlic, minced
1 lemon, sliced
2 bay leaves
½ tsp thyme
¼ tsp ground allspice
¼ tsp mace
¼ tsp ground cloves

2½ quarts fish stock or water
½ cup dry red wine
¼ tsp cayenne
salt and freshly ground black pepper
steamed rice

Heat the oil in a large iron pot or Dutch oven. Add the flour and stir to make a dark brown roux. Add the onions, scallions, parsley, garlic, and celery, and cook until the vegetables are soft and transparent. Add the tomatoes with their juice and the tomato paste. Add the bay leaves, thyme, allspice, mace, cloves, lemon slices, red wine, cayenne, and black pepper, and mix well. Add the fish stock or water and simmer for one hour, stirring occasionally and scraping the bottom to keep from sticking. Add the salt and adjust carefully. It should be salty and savoury.

Rub the fish pieces with salt, freshly ground black pepper, and cayenne, and place them in the pot. Raise the heat to a boil, then lower the heat, and simmer for 20 minutes or until the fish is tender and flakes with a fork. Serve the fish and sauce over mounds of steamed rice in preheated soup bowls.

The Cajuns have another freshwater fish, called a gaspergou, which makes an excellent substitute for catfish in this recipe. Some Cajun courtbouillon fanciers think the gaspergou stew is even better.

Gaspergou, or freshwater drum. (Drawing by Duane Raver, Jr., courtesy of Louisiana Wildlife and Fisheries Commission)

BOUILLABAISSE—A SEAFOOD SYMPHONY

Bouillabaisse has become the world's most famous seafood stew. It originated on the south coast of France in the vicinity of Marseilles, a city that has gained eternal fame by tacking its name onto the dish. Legend has it that the dish got its name when one Marseilles fisherman was teaching another how to make it. He gave only two commands, "Bouilli!" (boil) and, fifteen minutes later, "Baisse!" (stop). It started out as a humble fisherman's potpourri, a method of using "trash fish"—obscure or unattractive species that came up in the net but were usually thrown back into the sea because there was no ready market for them. (About half the fish that come up in a modern fishing dragger's trawl are "trash fish" and get thrown back. This is a tragic waste because most of these fish are edible.) Chief among the French trash fish—and, the purists say, indispensable for a real bouillabaisse—is the *rascasse*, an ugly-looking thing with a big mouth, goggle eyes, and fins like the sails of a hang glider. Three American species closely related to the rascasse and having the same flavor are the sea robin, the sculpin (nicknamed by fishermen "the Presbyterian minister"), and the scorpion fish of California. I have proved many times over that these monstrosities are not an absolute necessity for a good bouillabaisse. But a number of different kinds of fish and shellfish are helpful

Rascasse.

to the flavor, and a few fat-fleshed fish, such as Spanish mackerel, should be included, if possible, for "sweetnin'."

I went out on a fishing dragger once and brought back sixteen different species of "trash fish," about fifty pounds in all. When I got home to my cooking "laboratory" in the Skyscraper, I filleted the fish and made a big batch of fish stock out of the heads, bones, and trimmings. I put the fish fillets in a big ten-gallon pot, added shrimp, oysters, and crabmeat, and covered it with the fish stock. Then I invited about twenty-five hungry friends in, and they happily stashed away the whole potful. Nobody was squeamish about the term "trash fish."

I can't expect my readers to find such a wide variety of fishes, so I will give a recipe with products obtainable at any fish market. Have the market save you the heads, bones, and tails of the fish, about four pounds, so that you can make the fish stock.

SAFFRON IS A MUST

BOUILLABAISSE

(Serves 10 or more)

FISH AND SHELLFISH
- 1 lb speckled trout fillets
- 1 lb redfish fillets
- 1 lb red snapper fillets
- 1 lb flounder fillets (or any other kind of fish available in the market, such as sheepshead, white trout, Spanish mackerel, mullet)
- 1 lb peeled raw shrimp
- 2 dozen oysters (about a pint)
- 1 lb crawfish tails (optional)
- 1 lb crabmeat (optional)

VEGETABLES AND OTHER INGREDIENTS
- 1 cup olive oil
- 12 cloves garlic, minced
- 2 large onions, chopped
- 3 large tomatoes, peeled and chopped (or a 16-oz can)
- ½ tsp powdered saffron
- 4 scallions with their green leaves, thinly sliced
- 3 tbsp chopped parsley
  salt and freshly ground black pepper to taste

BOUILLABAISSE STOCK
- 4 lb fish heads, bones, tails, trimmings
- 4 quarts water
- 2 large onions, coarsely chopped
- 3 large tomatoes, coarsely chopped (or a 16-oz can)
- 2 ribs celery with leaves, coarsely chopped
- 1 cup parsley sprigs
- 2 bay leaves
- ½ lemon, sliced
- ½ tsp each basil, thyme, and freshly ground black pepper
- ¼ tsp cayenne
- 4 tsp salt (or more to taste)

Place all the ingredients listed under "Bouillabaisse stock" in a pot and boil vigorously for 30 minutes. Strain through triple cheesecloth, squeezing the bag to extract all the essences. Discard the gunk in the bag and set the stock aside.

Heat the olive oil in a skillet, and cook the onions, garlic, scallions, parsley, and tomatoes just until wilted. Stir in the saffron. Season with salt and freshly ground black pepper. Place all of this mixture in the bottom of a large pot—or a large earthenware casserole if you want to be completely authentic. Now add the fish fillets and the shellfish. Add enough fish stock to cover the things in the pot by two inches. If you don't have quite enough stock, use some water. After the mixture comes to the boil, cook it for exactly 15 minutes, and cut off the heat. While it is boiling, lift the fillets in the pot gently with a kitchen spoon and move them around a little to keep them from being too tightly packed together. Taste the broth and adjust the salt. It should be salty and savoury, not too much and not too little. Cover the bottoms of extra large soup bowls with thin slices of garlic bread (see Madame Bégué's Creole Bouillabaisse), and fill the bowls with fish, shellfish, and broth. Sprinkle

A group of Creole gentlemen, trenchermen all, enjoying a breakfast at Madame Bégué's. (Courtesy of the Special Collections Division, Tulane University Library)

In the 1870s Monsieur Hippolyte Bégué, a butcher in the French Market, opened a breakfast restaurant for his butcher friends. Those hard-working fellows began work several hours before dawn, and by 11 a.m. they were always ravenously hungry and thirsty. M'sieur Hippolyte assuaged their thirst downstairs at his bar, and Madame Bégué served them enormous breakfasts upstairs. Though of German extraction, Madame became one of the finest Creole cooks in New Orleans, and the fame of her breakfasts spread. During the Cotton Centennial of 1884-1885, the tourists discovered the restaurant. They displaced the butchers, and from then on until 1910, no visitor to New Orleans could call his visit complete without a breakfast at Bégué's. Unfortunately, the Bégués left no descendants to carry on their establishment. Today the super-swank Royal Sonesta Hotel has memorialized Madame by calling its restaurant "Madame Bégué's, but they'll have to do some hustling to equal her skill with a skillet.

fresh chopped parsley, or chopped green onion leaves on top. Do not leave the fish in the pot too long or they'll get soft and overcooked. At some establishments the fish and shellfish are served in one bowl and the broth in another, but the peasants like them mixed together, and so do I.

The three hallmarks of a good bouillabaisse are: (1) It should be garlicky as hell. (2) It should be a golden yellow color and have a slight flavor of iodine from the saffron. (3) The fish should not be overcooked, and the dish should have a fresh tang of the salt sea in it. When you have mastered the art of making bouillabaisse, you can call yourself a master chef.

NOTE: New Englanders should add littleneck quahaugs in their shells, mussels in their shells, and the tails and claws of small lobsters to their bouillabaisse.

MADAME BEGUE'S CREOLE BOUILLABAISSE
(Serves 6)

New Orleans, in spring-time—just when the orchards were flushing over with peach-blossoms, and the sweet herbs came to flavor the juleps—seemed to me the city of the world where you can eat and drink the most and suffer the least. At Bordeaux itself, claret is not

better to drink than at New Orleans. . . .
Claret is, somehow, good in that gifted place
at dinner, at supper, and at breakfast in the
morning. . . . At that comfortable tavern on
Pontchartrain we had a bouillabaisse than
which a better was never eaten at Marseilles:
and not the least headache in the morning, I
give you my word; on the contrary, you only
wake with a sweet refreshing thirst for claret
and water.

William Makepeace Thackeray, *The Roundabout Papers (1856)*

Mr. Thackeray had eaten a Creole bouillabaisse the night before at Boudro's Restaurant on the lakefront. Whether it was or was
not better than the Marseilles version we don't
know, but one thing is certain: It was entirely
different. The Creoles use only two species of
fish, the red snapper and the redfish. The
skinned fillets of the fish are rubbed with herbs
and spices in a manner that was probably
never practiced in France. The liquid in the
Creole bouillabaisse is more of a sauce (with
roux in it) than the French version, which is a
clear broth, made yellow by the saffron. And
in the Creole version the fish are precooked
before they reach the final cooking in the
sauce. It's a delicious dish, but we'll never
know whether it's the same article that
Thackeray ate. Boudro's and Madame Bégué's
may have made it differently because, as I've
said before, no two Creole cooks ever do anything just alike.

THE DRY MARINADE
- 1 tbsp dried parsley flakes
- ¼ tsp powdered thyme
- ¼ tsp basil
- ¼ tsp powdered bay leaf
- ½ tsp ground allspice
- ¼ tsp cayenne
- 1 tsp powdered garlic (or 2 tsp finely minced fresh garlic)
- ½ tsp freshly ground black pepper
- 1 tsp salt

THE BOUILLABAISSE
- 6 4-oz fillets (or slices) of red snapper, skinless
- 6 4-oz fillets (or slices) of redfish, skinless
- 2 tbsp flour
- 2 cups fish stock
- 1 large onion, finely chopped
- 2 cloves garlic, minced
- 1 cup dry white wine
- 1 16-oz can tomatoes, chopped
- ½ tsp powdered saffron
  olive oil
  salt and freshly ground black pepper
  garlic bread

If you don't have a skillet large enough to hold
the 12 pieces of fish, you'll have to cook them
in shifts. Make a simple stock by placing the
heads, tails, and bones of the snapper and
redfish in a saucepan with a quart or more of
water. Boil for 30 minutes and strain through
triple cheesecloth. You need only two cups.

Rub the dry marinade thoroughly into each side of the fish fillets. Set them aside.

Make garlic bread in advance as follows: Put six cloves of garlic through a garlic press, and mix the pulp with two tablespoons of olive oil. Cut 12 thin slices of French bread, and brush on one side with the garlic-oil mixture. Fry the bread on both sides in olive oil until golden brown. Set aside and keep warm.

Now to cook the fish, place a quarter cup of olive oil in the large skillet and heat it. Turn the heat low. Sprinkle the finely chopped onion in the pan. Place the fish fillets in the skillet on top of the onion, and cook gently for five minutes. Turn them over with a spatula and cook five minutes more. Remove the fish pieces, place on a platter, and keep warm. Add the flour to the skillet and blend well with the olive oil and onion, making sure it's free of all lumps. Stir in the minced garlic. Add the dry white wine, the fish stock, and the tomatoes. Cook for 15 minutes until the mixture thickens a little. Stir in the saffron, and season to taste with salt and freshly ground black pepper. Return the fish fillets to the sauce, and *bouilli!* (boil) for five minutes, then *baisse!* (stop).

Put two slices of fried bread on the bottom of each of six preheated soup bowls. Place one slice of red snapper on one slice of bread and a slice of redfish on the other. Ladle the sauce over the fish, sprinkle with chopped parsley, and serve at once.

When you see what a hard job it is to make this brew, you'll understand why Antoine's makes you order it 24 hours in advance.

SHRIMP BOATS A-COMIN'

SHRIMP BOATS A-COMIN'

They go to sea with the evening tide
and their womenfolk wave their good-bye,
Ils s'en vont. There they go!
While the Louisiana moon floats on high,
And they wait for the day they can cry:

Chorus
SHRIMP BOATS is a-comin', their sails are in
*   sight*
SHRIMP BOATS is a-comin', there's dancin'
*   tonight*
Why don't-cha hurry, hurry, hurry home,
Why don't-cha hurry, hurry, hurry home?
(look, here the) SHRIMP BOATS is a-comin',
There's dancin' tonight.

Happy the days while they're mending the
*   nets,*
'Til once more they ride high out to sea.
Ils s'en vont. There they go!
Then how lonely the long nights will be
Til that wonderful day when they see

Chorus
SHRIMP BOATS is a-comin', their sails are in
*   sight*
SHRIMP BOATS is a-comin', there's dancin'
*   tonight*
Why don't-cha hurry, hurry, hurry home,
Why don't-cha hurry, hurry, hurry home?
(look, here the) SHRIMP BOATS is a-comin',
There's dancin' tonight.

This isn't traditional New Orleans jazz, but we must include it here because it's so appropriate to our subject. It was a nation-wide hit when it first came out, and it's still frequently played today by the jazz bands of New Orleans.

Chapter 4

The Succulent Shrimp

Shrimp are the glory of New Orleans. We eat them for breakfast, lunch, dinner, and 'tween-meal snacks. We're close to the source of supply. Down near the Gulf, towns like Golden Meadow, Houma, Morgan City, and Delcambre have some of the largest shrimp fleets in the world, and they supply over half the shrimp the nation consumes. Shrimp have become the most universally popular seafood item in America today. Freezing, fast transportation, and distribution are the secret of the shrimp's meteoric rise to fame. A homemaker in Dubuque, Iowa, or Boise, Idaho, can get all the good frozen shrimp she needs at her supermarket. Shrimp are one of the few seafood products that can be frozen without

damage to their flavor or quality. They will keep for months in the freezer.

The Creole and Cajun methods of cooking shrimp are the best and most refined in the world, and with an abundant supply of fresh heads-on shrimp available at almost all times, it's no surprise that New Orleans rules the field of shrimp cookery.

Shrimp are amazingly versatile. They can be boiled, broiled, sautéed, fried, stewed, grilled—in short, they can be cooked in almost any manner. And there are hundreds of sauces that go well with shrimp. I've been collecting shrimp recipes for twenty-five years, and at present I have more than 500, all different.

A handful of jumbos.
(Courtesy of Louisiana Wildlife
and Fisheries Commission)

THE DIFFERENT TYPES OF SHRIMP

Several different types of shrimp are available in New Orleans: lake shrimp, river shrimp, Gulf shrimp, and Campeche shrimp from the Gulf of Campeche in Mexico. (The Gulf of Campeche was the most lucrative fishing ground for the Louisiana shrimp fleet until Mexico passed a law setting the 200-mile limit. The local shrimp industry has suffered greatly.) There is variety in color and species: white shrimp, brown shrimp, and red and pink shrimp.

Shrimp dealers grade shrimp by "count"—for instance, "20-count" means twenty shrimp per pound. A classification table would be approximately as follows:

Grade name	Count per pound
Giant	10-12
Jumbo	15-20
Large	20-25
Medium	25-35
Small	35-45
Titi (very small)	75-100

SHRIMP FACTS

When you're buying raw shrimp in the shell, the most important thing is to make sure they're fresh. They should be firm and glistening and have a fragrant saltwater odor. If they look dried up in their shells or are mushy and have a definitely bad smell, pass them by because they may be headed over the hill. (Oddly enough, though, this is not an iron-bound rule. Some shrimp connoisseurs, especially among Latin Americans and Orientals, insist that the shrimp should have a rich, high smell).

Remember when buying that it takes 1½ to 2 pounds of heads-on shrimp in the shell to produce a pound of peeled shrimp. Twelve peeled 20-count shrimp make a good individual helping when shrimp are served in casseroles or pastry shells with sauces. For Shrimp Boil parties, allow two pounds of 20-count heads-on shrimp for each person. A true aficionado can stand around for hours peeling and eating boiled shrimp and swilling beer. For a Barbecued Shrimp party allow a pound and a half per person. Barbecued shrimp are rich and buttery, so the average person eats fewer of them. For a shrimp cocktail serve six large or eight medium shrimp. For baked stuffed shrimp, four of the giant 10-count shrimp will make a big meal.

The heads and shells of shrimp can be used to impart a delicious flavor, as will be demonstrated in some of the recipes that follow.

There's no hygienic reason in the world for deveining a shrimp, even though in the extra large jumbos and giants the vein is large and unattractive. Would you sit down and try to devein an oyster? Oysters and shrimp feed on the same clean microscopic sea organisms. New Orleanians smile when they see a Yankee tourist sitting in a restaurant eating boiled shrimp. He peels each shrimp carefully and then laboriously deveins it. No native would ever do that. On extremely rare occasions, at certain times of the year, shrimp may acquire more of an iodine flavor than they usually have. If you have any doubts about a batch of shrimp you've bought, boil a couple for five minutes and eat them. If the iodine taste is

excessively strong, then you can go to the trouble of deveining the rest of the batch, either before or after cooking.

One of the best ideas that have come out of having lots of shrimp available is the small three-ounce packet of spices prepared especially for boiling shrimp and crabs. Such packets, called simply "Shrimp Boil" or "Crab Boil," are on sale in groceries all over Louisiana at a very reasonable price. Each one contains about 20 different spices, some of them very rare. You could never duplicate the mixture yourself. The closest you could come would be to use a whole package of mixed pickling spices. Shrimp boil spices go under a variety of brand names: Yogi, Rex, and Zatarain's, to name a few. If they're not on sale in your neighborhood, you can order them from the suppliers listed in the appendix of this volume. They give such good flavor to boiled shrimp and boiled crabs that it's worth going to a bit of trouble to obtain them.

There is now a liquid shrimp boil "spice" on the market, but it's a sad synthetic thing made of chemicals and is not as good as real spices.

If you eat plenty of shrimp you'll never have a goiter, because they supply the iodine the thyroid gland needs. The various other vitamins they contain are said to be needed by certain other glands. Many people believe shrimp are a good aphrodisiac. Certainly they contain a good amount of protein, as well as some of the calcium, phosphorous, copper, zinc, sulphur, magnesium, and other rare elements essential to good metabolism. Let no one deny it, shrimp are one of the greatest of health foods.

And they taste so damn good!

THE SHRIMP BOIL—A SOCIAL INSTITUTION

The best of all ways to eat shrimp is to boil them, peel them yourself, plop them down your gullet, and wash them down with plenty of good cold beer. As a jubilant festive occasion, the Shrimp Boil and Beer Bust is the Southern equivalent of the New England clambake, so easy to do and such good clean fun for young and old.

About twenty years ago a group of us French Quarter Bohemians organized a boiled shrimp and beer club called The Guild of Chimney Sweepers (in honor of the annual dinner Charles Lamb threw for the young chimney sweeps of London). Each year a little before or after Mardi Gras (Fat Tuesday), we throw a big shrimp boil for our friends. At our last big party we boiled 400 pounds of shrimp and 400 fat crabs for 200 guests, and we drank eight thirty-gallon kegs of beer. For music we had Kid Thomas and his Algiers Stompers, the famous old gut-bucket jazz group from Preservation Hall, and the Olympia Funeral Marching Band. We struck a doubloon (bronze medallion) as a souvenir of this joyous

shindig. It all just goes to show you what a helluva mystique can be built up around the beautiful shrimp. It's sacred everywhere to gourmets and Bacchanalians.

HOW THE CHIMNEY SWEEPERS BOIL LARGE QUANTITIES OF SHRIMP

NOTE: The Chimney Sweepers have found that a new thirty-gallon galvanized garbage can makes an ideal utensil for boiling large amounts of shrimp (or crabs or crawfish), but if you have any doubts about this, use a thirty-gallon stainless steel stock pot or even an old black cast-iron wash pot. When you buy the garbage can, put some water in it to test it (products are getting shoddy these days). Before using the can for cooking, place a half gallon of warm water and a pound of bicarbonate of soda in it, and scrub the inside thoroughly with a plastic scrubber. This will neutralize the acids used in the galvanizing process.

When boiling shrimp by the hundreds of pounds, you should divide them into 25-pound batches and boil one batch at a time. Trying to cook more at one time is foolhardy, because those in the center of the pile will come out raw. Fill your 30-gallon pot one third full of water, and add six large onions, coarsely chopped; a whole bunch of celery with leaves, coarsely chopped; two whole heads of garlic, coarsely chopped; three lemons, sliced; a pound of salt; a half pound of cayenne; five three-ounce packages of "Shrimp Boil" spices; a half bottle of Worcestershire sauce; and a quart of white wine. Boil all this stuff for an hour to make a good strong liquor. Put 25 pounds of shrimp in a pillowcase, and lower them into the pot of boiling liquor. Make sure they're loosely packed so that the hot water can circulate all around them. By trial and error we found that the ideal cooking time for 25 pounds is approximately 25 minutes. Of course, the time is much less for smaller batches. Use the same cooking liquor over and over for each new batch; it gets richer and richer all the time. Allow two pounds of shrimp for each guest, although a really hungry Chimney Sweeper can eat six pounds of boiled shrimp any old day. A recipe for a sauce to dip the shrimp in is given after the basic recipe below.

A SMALL CHIMNEY SWEEPER'S BOILED SHRIMP DINNER
(Serves 5)

10 lb raw heads-on shrimp (20-count)
 1 cup salt
 1 lemon, sliced
 ½ bunch celery with leaves, coarsely
  chopped
 2 large onions, coarsely chopped
 ½ head of garlic, chopped

 4 tbsp Worcestershire sauce
 2 pkg "Shrimp Boil" spices or 1 pkg mixed
  pickling spices
 1 tsp cayenne (more if you like it hot)

Put all but the shrimp in a large pot and add enough water (about a gallon) to cover.

Let the mixture boil rapidly for 30 minutes to make a strong liquor. Put the shrimp in, and when the liquor comes back to the boil, cook for 10 to 15 minutes, or until the shrimp are firm and peel easily. Sample one. If it's undercooked it will taste like library paste. If it's overcooked, the shells will shrivel and be hard to peel, so cook them fast! When the shrimp are done, remove them from the pot to the sink, and run cold water over them to stop the cooking process. It's like cooking al dente spaghetti, and the time is about the same.

SAUCE FOR 10 POUNDS OF BOILED SHRIMP
 2 bottles chili sauce (no ketchup, please!)
 ½ bottle horseradish
 1 medium onion, grated
 ½ cup finely chopped fresh parsley
 1 small rib celery, grated
  juice of ½ lemon
 ½ tsp celery seeds
 ½ tsp toasted poppy seeds
  salt and freshly ground black pepper
 ½ tsp Tabasco

Mix all the ingredients well and chill. Peel the shrimp, dip 'em in this sauce, and wolf 'em down. Drink plenty of beer to help the process along.

This is an ideal sauce for shrimp, lump crabmeat, oyster, lobster, and clam cocktails. It tastes so good, I'm thinking of someday bottling it to make myself some moola.

SHRIMP BOILED IN BEER

If you substitute beer for water in the recipe above, you'll get a pleasant surprise. The taste is wonderful, and it just might make hair grow on your chest. To my way of thinking, there's a terrific affinity between shrimp and beer—but perhaps you've already guessed that by now!

SHRIMP BOILED IN LOUISIANA ORANGE WINE

Oranges are grown extensively in the extreme southern part of Louisiana around Buras. Since South Louisianians would rather drink than eat, much of the crop goes into making orange wine—a palatable potable that's also good for boiling shrimp. Mix a half gallon of orange wine with a half gallon of water and use it instead of water in the basic recipe above. If you can't find orange wine but still want to try wine-boiled shrimp, use a California dry white wine or a Burgundy, either red or white.

The important thing about this process is the stirring, which must be done frequently. Since the shrimp at the bottom cook first, stir them upward until they reach the top. However, keep the pot tightly covered when you're not stirring. When the shrimp are done, they should be bright red and firm, but they shouldn't taste fishy—or like library paste! The right flavor of "doneness" takes a little practice to learn. Sample them now and then.

STEAMED SHRIMP

Up in Maryland and the Chesapeake Bay country, they like to steam their shrimp and crabs instead of boiling them, and up in New England, steaming lobsters instead of boiling them is the accepted method. Steaming keeps the tomalley intact so that it doesn't become a gooey mess. Because of the amount of stirring involved, it's not good practice to try to steam more than five pounds of shrimp at a time. The heads drop off when you try to cook too many at a time.

- **5 lb raw heads-on shrimp in their shells (20-count)**
- **½ cup salt**
- **2 lemons, sliced**
- **2 ribs celery, coarsely chopped**
- **1 large onion, coarsely chopped**
- **6 cloves garlic, chopped**
- **1 pkg "Shrimp Boil" spices or ½ pkg mixed pickling spices**
- **½ tsp cayenne or Tabasco**

To start the process, place a half cup of water in the bottom of a pot. Later the shrimp will produce their own liquid. Place half the shrimp in the pot, tear the bag containing the spices open, and sprinkle the spices on the shrimp. Place the other seasonings and vegetables on top of the shrimp, and then add the other half of the shrimp. Fire up, cover the pot, and wait for it to start steaming. They will be done in about ten minutes. Serve them with the cock-tail sauce above.

ALL YOU'VE ALWAYS WANTED TO KNOW ABOUT BARBECUED SHRIMP

One of the most delicious seafood dishes to come out of New Orleans is barbecued shrimp, and once you've eaten it, you'll never forget it. When Johnny Donnels and I want to impress distinguished out-of-town visitors, we throw a shrimp barbecue at his studio on the second floor of the Skyscraper. We bought a big, deep stainless steel pan that will hold twenty pounds of shrimp (enough for fifteen guests), and after the shrimp are cooked, we place the pan on a table in the center of the room. The guests gather 'round and pluck the shrimp out, peel them and devour them, and they dip chunks of hot French bread in the sauce in the pan and and. . . .

Barbecued shrimp have been around for a long, long time, and they've been served at many restaurants, but they've been brought to a peak of perfection by Pascal's Manale, up-town on Napoleon Avenue. People come from miles around to eat their barbecued shrimp, and on weekend nights the place is so crowded, you have to wait two or three hours to get a table.

It is said that Manale's secret recipe for this dish is buried in the center of a two-ton con-crete block under the office safe. A friend of mine, Mrs. Ivy Whitty, solved the riddle by hir-ing a cook who used to work at Manale's. The cook could neither read nor write, but she had all the treasured secrets in her head. Working together, that cook and Mrs. Whitty perfected a barbecued shrimp recipe that may not be Manale's, but it is sublime.

It's amazing that such a good dish could be so simple, but there's nothing in it except shrimp, butter, and black pepper. If you try to add anything else—herbs, spices, Worcester-shire, whatever—you'll spoil it for certain. It's important to use fresh shrimp with their heads and shells on if you can find them. The tomalley inside the shrimp's head, which is like the tomalley of a lobster, adds a real punch to the sauce in the pan. (However, if you can't find fresh shrimp, frozen unpeeled shrimp tails will make a dish that's almost as delicious and better than almost any shrimp dish you could find in the average seafood restaurant.)

At first glance it seems that the recipe calls for too much black pepper, but you'll discover later that it's just right. The heat cooks out of it—well, sort of. Always open a fresh can of black pepper when making this dish so that it will be fully aromatic and pungent. The general rule for butter is one stick per pound of shrimp plus a couple of sticks for the pan.

BARBECUED SHRIMP I
(Serves 4)

5 lb fresh shrimp with heads on, if possible (or 5 lb frozen unpeeled shrimp tails)
7 sticks of butter
 black pepper, as instructed

Wash the shrimp. Spread them out on a thick layer of newspapers on a table, and leave them there for a full hour or more, so that they'll drain thoroughly. They must drain com-pletely and be as dry as possible because water hurts the flavor of the sauce. Spread the shrimp in a big flat baking pan (even a turkey roasting pan will do). Place the sticks of butter on top of the shrimp, and sprinkle on the black pepper in a thick layer, $\frac{1}{16}$ inch to $\frac{1}{8}$ inch deep, covering the whole top surface. Place in a preheated 350° oven and cook for 45 minutes, stirring gently and turning the shrimp over every 15 minutes to make sure they're all saturated with the sauce. The shrimp are still firm when done. But watch them, because if they begin to shrink up and the shells get crinkly, they're being overcooked.

Bring the shrimp to the table in the pan they were cooked in, and let the guests gather around the table and pick their shrimp out of the pan, peel them, dip them in the butter-pepper sauce in the pan, and eat 'em happily. Provide plenty of hot French bread, so the guests can dip chunks of it in the sauce. Everything should be washed down with voluminous quantities of cold beer. And give thanks to Mrs. W. and her cook, who taught us this beautiful rigamarole.

NOTE: Many people like to eat barbecued shrimp, shell and all, without peeling them, but this is a dangerous practice, because their sharp, pointed beaks can easily punch holes in your innards.

BARBECUED SHRIMP II
(Serves 1)

18 shrimp tails in the shell
1 stick butter, melted
black pepper

This is a good way to prepare barbecued shrimp in some far off inland town where fresh heads-on shrimp aren't available but frozen shrimp are.

Arrange the shrimp on a metal sizzle platter of the type used for broiling steaks (or use a small flat baking pan). Pour the melted butter over them. Sprinkle with a generous layer of black pepper. Place under the broiler flame for four or five minutes, then turn each shrimp over, sprinkle on more black pepper, and broil for four minutes more. Take the shrimp directly to the table on the sizzle platter. After they've cooled sufficiently, peel them with your bare hands and eat them. It's a messy business, and you'll need plenty of napkins, but they're so delicious it's well worth the muss and fuss. Cold beer is the best accompaniment, but a robust imported red Burgundy also goes beautifully with this dish.

SHRIMP A LA CREOLE (SAUCE PIQUANTE)
(Serves 8 or more)

The most famous stew to come out of New Orleans, Shrimp à la Creole has spread all over the United States. But in some places, far from home, it has become a godawful mess. It's so easy and profitable to cheat with it—a few tomatoes and a few lonely shrimp, poured on a pile of gummy rice, and the cheapest, lowliest cafeteria or restaurant can tag it "à la Creole." In the hands of a Creole or Cajun chef the dish can become a thing of transcendant beauty—spicy, hot, and full of flavor. In fact, in New Orleans they don't even call the sauce "Creole"; they call it "Sauce Piquante," which means piquant and hot.

6 lb heads-on 20-count shrimp
1 stick butter
½ cup flour
1 heart of celery, chopped fine
  (about 1 cup)
1 large green pepper, chopped
4 cloves garlic, minced
6 scallions with their green leaves, sliced
  thin
2 medium onions, chopped
3 large fresh Creole tomatoes, peeled and
  diced (or a 16-oz can of tomatoes,
  drained and chopped, with their juice)
3 tbsp chopped fresh parsley
1 6-oz can tomato paste
½ tsp cayenne or Tabasco
  juice of 1 lemon
½ tsp thyme
½ tsp basil
¼ tsp ground cumin
¼ tsp oregano
¼ tsp mace
¼ tsp ground cloves
¼ tsp ground allspice
2 bay leaves
1 cup imported Burgundy
2 cups (or more) shrimp or fish stock, or
  bouillon
  salt and freshly ground black pepper to
  taste
  steamed rice (about 6 cups)

It takes about six pounds of heads-on raw shrimp in their shells to make four pounds of peeled shrimp. If you can't find fresh heads-on shrimp, five pounds of frozen shrimp tails in their shells will do, and their shells can still be used to make stock. If you can't make shrimp stock, use bouillon or plain water although the flavor will of course not be as good.

Peel the six pounds of heads-on shrimp and set them aside. There's no need to devein them. Place the heads and shells in a flat-bottomed pot, and pound them with a pestle or a thick bottle. Pour six cups of water over the shells, and boil for a half hour. Strain the liquid through double cheesecloth. This is your shrimp broth, tasty and useful for making your sauce.

Melt the butter in a thick-bottomed pot or Dutch oven, add the flour, and make a brown roux. Add the celery, onions, scallions, green pepper, and garlic, and cook until the vegetables are soft and transparent but not brown. Add more butter or shrimp broth, if necessary. Add the tomatoes, tomato paste, parsley, cayenne, lemon juice, Burgundy, all the herbs and spices, and the bay leaves. Add two or more cups of the shrimp stock. It should be very juicy and semifluid at this stage. Season with salt and freshly ground black pepper. Mix well, bring to the boil, and then cut the heat low and simmer very gently for an hour or more. If it gets too thick, add more shrimp stock or bouillon. Stir now and then with a large kitchen spoon, scraping the bottom of the pot. If the spoon comes up with black residue on the tip, you're scorching it, so lower the heat and take it easy.

After the sauce is well cooked, add the peeled shrimp, raise the heat a little, and cook for three to five minutes more. Cut off the heat and let it cool down. Like most seafood stews, it has a better flavor if allowed to age overnight. Here are three good tips to avoid spoilage of your beautiful stew. Never leave the lid on a pot of stew while it's cooling, or it may sour. Never refrigerate a pot of stew until it has cooled down to room temperature, or it may sour. If the pot is sitting on a shelf or table, place a spoon under it so the air can circulate underneath. At the beginning of my chef's career I spoiled hundreds of dollars worth of gumbos, chowders, soups, and stews before a wise old chef came along and whispered these secrets into my stupid wooden ear.

To serve your shrimp à la Creole, heat the sauce and shrimp the next day, but don't boil it. Ladle shrimp and sauce over a layer of freshly steamed rice in the bottom of preheated soup bowls or individual casseroles. You need about six cups of cooked rice for eight people. Serve a chilled Chablis or Clos Vougeot along with it, and your guests should be enraptured.

REMOULADE—A ZINGY SAUCE

Remoulade sauce is one of the glories of Creole cuisine, and Shrimp Remoulade (it's pronounced ruma-lahd) is the most popular appetizer in New Orleans restaurants. Also served frequently in the home, it's a familiar standby for buffets and cocktail parties.

There are two types of remoulade sauce, the zippy and sometimes very hot type, red or brown, that uses Creole or Dijon mustard as a base, and the white type that uses fresh homemade mayonnaise and is milder in character but has such a delicious flavor that it's preferred by many connoisseurs.

SHRIMP REMOULADE (WHITE)

    3 lb shrimp, boiled and peeled
    1 pint homemade mayonnaise
    1 pint sour cream
    2 cloves garlic, finely minced
    2 tbsp chopped onion
    2 tbsp chopped sour pickle
    2 tbsp capers
    3 hard-cooked eggs, chopped
    1 tsp anchovy paste (or 2 chopped fillets)
    2 tbsp fresh parsley, chopped
    1 tsp paprika
       salt and white pepper to taste

Boil the shrimp in lightly salted water for five minutes (after the water returns to the boil). Let them cool and then peel them and set them aside.

Mix all the sauce ingredients together well, and if the mixture isn't zingy enough, add more salt and more lemon juice or vinegar to make it sharp as a razor. Place the shrimp in a flat glass bowl and pour the sauce over them. Marinate in the refrigerator for several hours or overnight. As an appetizer for a dinner, they can be served six to a plate on a bed of shredded lettuce. For a cocktail party snack, leave them in the bowl and spear each shrimp with a toothpick so the guests can pick them up.

This sauce is also a beautiful accompaniment to crabmeat, crawfish, steamed lobsters, and steamed mussels.

Mr. Jean Galatoire came to the United States from France at the turn of the century, with him his three nephews. They chose New Orleans to settle in because of its French atmosphere. They formed a partnership with Victor Bero in 1902. "Victor's" had been a leading New Orleans restaurant since 1840. In 1905 they bought Victor out, and Galatoire's was on its way. It is probably the best seafood restaurant in America today. Their trout meunière amandine, trout marguery, and broiled pompano are unsurpassed anywhere, and their shrimp dishes are all superb fare. After Mr. Justin Galatoire died, the management was taken over by David Gooch, a fourth-generation member of the family. Galatoire's has one tradition that has never been breached, even for governors, senators, or anyone else. They do not accept reservations. If you go during the rush hour you'll have to wait in line on the sidewalk. New Orleanians get around this by going to Galatoire's during the off hours when it's easier to get a table and the dining is more leisurely.

HOMEMADE MAYONNAISE FOR REMOULADE

- 2 egg yolks
- 1 pint olive oil (or vegetable oil)
- ¼ tsp Tabasco
- ½ tbsp powdered mustard
- ¼ cup lemon juice (or vinegar)
- ½ tsp salt
  white pepper

If you try to cheat by using one of those awful commercial mayonnaises, your sauce will be a bust. There's no substitute for a good homemade mayonnaise. Place the egg yolks in a mixing bowl, add the flavoring elements, and beat them together. Add the oil one drop at a time at first and then in a slow, steady stream as you continue the beating. Keep beating until all the oil is absorbed. If it curdles or is too thick, you've added the oil too fast. Start over again, using a new egg yolk in the bowl, and add the curdled mixture to it slowly. The final mixture should be velvety, creamy, and smooth, and it should have a full-bodied zest.

SHRIMP REMOULADE GALATOIRE (RED)

The late, great Mr. Justin Galatoire of the far-famed Galatoire's Restaurant gave me his recipe for Shrimp Remoulade twenty years ago, and it's as alive and vibrant now as it was then, possibly even better since it has aged and acquired a patina.

- 3 lb shrimp, boiled and peeled
- 1 cup olive oil
- 4 scallions with their green leaves
- 2 ribs celery
- 3 small cloves garlic
- 1 tbsp chopped fresh parsley
- 6 tbsp Creole mustard
- 3 tbsp paprika
- ½ cup vinegar
  salt and freshly ground black pepper

Put all the vegetables through the small blade of the grinder, chopping them very fine. (You can use a blender or food chopper for this chore.) Place the vegetables in a mixing bowl and add the mustard, paprika, salt, pepper, and vinegar. Add the olive oil slowly and mix well. Place the boiled peeled shrimp in the sauce and let them marinate for three or four hours. As an appetizer, they can be served on a bed of shredded lettuce, or as Mr. Galatoire suggested, in addition to being served as an appetizer, they can be used as a garnish for other seafood dishes. A very wise man was Mr. Justin Galatoire.

CAJUN SHRIMP REMOULADE (RED)
(Serves 4)

Down in Acadiana they like their remoulade sauce very hot—"piquante" they euphemistically call it to fool the unwary. To get the heat they use fresh horseradish and fresh or pickled hot peppers (serranos, tabascos, cayennes, jalapenos, or birds' eyes). Many Cajuns grow a few horseradishes in their gardens just for flavoring their seafood sauces. Grated fresh horseradish is so hot and pungent that it electrifies your nostrils and brings tears to your eyes when you just smell the stuff.

2 lb boiled and peeled shrimp
4 tbsp olive oil
2 tbsp Creole mustard
2 tbsp vinegar
1 tsp fresh horseradish
1 tbsp finely minced hot peppers, fresh or pickled
2 tsp paprika

2 tbsp finely minced celery
2 scallions with their green leaves, finely chopped
1 tbsp parsley, finely minced
salt and freshly ground black pepper to taste

Combine the vinegar with the mustard, horseradish, paprika, and salt and pepper. Gradually add the olive oil and blend well. Add the chopped peppers, scallions, celery, and parsley, and mix well. Place the shrimp in a flat glass bowl and pour the sauce over them. Stir the shrimp around to coat them thoroughly. Place them in the refrigerator to marinate for at least three hours, but overnight is even better. Serve them on shredded lettuce, and provide plenty of cold beer or chilled wine to lower the heat.

TUJAGUE'S SHRIMP REMOULADE
(Serves about 100)

If you're giving a little party for about 100 guests, you may very well consider using the Tujague's Restaurant bulk formula for Shrimp Remoulade, which the owner, Mr. Philip Guichet, has given me. This should be a group effort, because it's a hell of a job to peel thirty pounds of raw shrimp and chop all those vegetables very fine.

STEP 1
30 lb shrimp, peeled while raw
½ lb powdered red pepper or cayenne
½ lb salt
1½ gallons water

Two famous restaurants in the same building, 1890. (Courtesy of the Special Collections Division, Tulane University Library)

Madame Bégué's was upstairs and Tujague's downstairs at the corner of Decatur and Madison Streets opposite the French Market. Today Tujague's is still there after 125 years. Mr. Otis Guichet, the present co-owner says, "In the 1890s our six-course table d'hote dinner cost 50¢, and that included a bottle of wine and a glass of Cognac with your coffee."

Place the water in a very large pot on the stove, add the red pepper and salt, and bring to the boil. Add the 30 pounds of shrimp to the pot, and when it returns to the boil, cook for 12 to 15 minutes, stirring frequently so that the shrimp will cook uniformly. When the shrimp are done, pour off the cooking water. Do not rinse or wash the shrimp. Spread them out on a flat surface to allow them to cool.

STEP 2
 3 **heads lettuce**
 2 **whole bunches celery**
 4 **whole bunches scallions with their green leaves**
 4 **large yellow or white onions**
 1 **gallon Creole mustard**
 1 **quart yellow mustard**
 1 **lb paprika**
 1 **gallon Wesson oil**

Chop all the vegetables up very fine and place them in a very large mixing pan. Add the Creole mustard, the yellow mustard, and the paprika. Mix well; then add the oil slowly, blending it in thoroughly. Add the 30 pounds of cooled shrimp to the sauce and mix well. Chill in the refrigerator—if it's big enough! Serve on beds of shredded lettuce on small plates. Your 100 guests should love you after all the work you've put into this enterprise!

AVOCADO

SHRIMP-STUFFED AVOCADOS
(Serves 8 as appetizers, 4 as a full meal)

There's a small Italian bar and restaurant called Ruggiero's on Decatur Street opposite the French Market. Although it's located in the midst of touristy boutiques, it has nevertheless kept its character as a neighborhood restaurant frequented by New Orleanians and French Quarterites. At Ruggiero's they feature good seafoods. They have an old-fashioned oyster bar with a marble top on it, and the oysters are usually good and salty. Over the years they've featured some far-out dishes that less venturesome restaurants wouldn't touch but that I myself devour with gusto: stuff like fried octopus and squids and, best of all, shrimp-stuffed avocado. Their formula is a trade secret—and you can't blame 'em, it's so good. However, I've puttered around with this dish for years in my Skyscraper cooking laboratory, and here's a good way to do it.

"JELLY ROLL" MORTON

Drawing by Emily Davis

WININ' BOY BLUES

I'm the winin' boy. Don't deny my name,
I'm the winin' boy. Don't deny my name, my
* name,*
Winin' boy, Don't deny my name,
Pick it up and shake it like sweet Stavin'
* Chain,*
I'm the winin' boy, Don't deny my name.

Mama, Mama, Mama, look at Sis:
Mama, Mama, won't you look at Sis, look at
* Sis.*
Mama, Mama, look at Sis,
She's out on the levee doin' the double twist.
I'm the winin' boy. Don't deny my name.

See that spider climbin' up the wall!
See that spider climbin' up the wall, the wall,
Well, you see that spider climbin' up the
* wall,*
Goin' up there to get her ashes hauled.
I'm the winin' boy, Don't deny my name.

Jelly Roll's most famous song was heard most recently in the movie "Pretty Baby." Winin' has nothing to do with wine. It's a contraction of "winding," a sexual technique. Jelly Roll himself was the original winin' boy, a great favorite of the Storyville ladies in their off hours. Tony Jackson, who was also a great Storyville "professor," wrote a song called *I've Got Elgin Movements in my Hips with Twenty Years Guarantee.* The hot pianos of Jelly Roll and Jackson had a great deal of influence on early jazz musicians.

Greatest of the jazz pianists

Jelly Roll Morton (real name: Ferdinand Joseph Le Menthe) was one of the giants of the Golden Age of Jazz, the greatest of all jazz pianists. He was born in Gulfport, Mississippi, in 1885 and moved to New Orleans at an early age with his family. Against his family's wishes he learned to play hot piano, and he was still very young when he became a "professor" in the plush sporting houses on Basin Street. As with everyone else in those times, his style was basically ragtime in the beginning, but he developed a unique style of his own that was very advanced in harmonic conception, and full of the barrelhouse gusto of the new jazz that he was helping to develop. He could wrest sounds out of a piano of a type that had never been heard before. He was creative and could take an old blues or ragtime theme and make a completely new tune of it. As a composer he was prolific, and many of his compositions became jazz classics. Among them were *King Porter Stomp*, *Grandpa's Spells*, *Milenberg Joys*, *Wildman Blues*, *Winin' Boy Blues*, *Wolverine Blues*, *Shoe Shiner's Drag*, *The Crave*, *Perfect Rag*, *Frog-I-More Rag*, *The Pearl*, *Kansas City Stomp*, and *Mamie Desdoume's Blues*.

He was a flashy showman and loved fancy clothes and diamonds. He had a diamond embedded in a front tooth to add sparkle to his smile. Needless to say, the girls were crazy about him, and he reciprocated in kind. He was an expert pool shooter, and when the music business was slow, he could walk into a poolroom and win several hundred dollars in a night's play.

He left New Orleans in 1915 and went on to fame and riches in Chicago, California, and New York. He organized several small hot bands that toured the country extensively, spreading the gospel of jazz far and wide. They made more than 35 records, many of which were solid hits. In 1928 his orchestra played at the Roseland in New York. He retired to Washington, D.C., but in 1938 Alan Lomax brought him out of seclusion long enough to record 12 long-play records on the history of jazz for the Library of Congress. His autobiography, *Mr. Jelly Roll*, recorded and transcribed by Alan Lomax, is a landmark of jazz literature. He died in California in 1941. At the funeral someone who was curious about that diamond-studded tooth opened his lips. The diamond has disappeared. *Sic transit gloria.*

4 avocados
1 cup shrimp tails, boiled, peeled, and
   diced (or use whole tiny "titi" shrimp)
1 cup crabmeat
1 tbsp chopped parsley
1 medium onion, chopped
2 cloves garlic, minced
¼ tsp crushed red pepper seeds
¼ cup Marsala wine
   Parmesan cheese, grated
2 tbsp olive oil
   salt and freshly ground black pepper

Cut the avocados in half and remove the seeds. Heat the olive oil in a skillet, and cook the onion and garlic until soft but not brown. Add the parsley, shrimp, crabmeat, condiments, and wine, and continue cooking and stirring until they're well mixed and the flavors are blended. Fill the avocado halves with this mixture, piling it up in a mound. Sprinkle with Parmesan. Place oiled aluminum foil on the bottom of a baking pan and lay the avocados on it. Bake in a medium hot oven until the tops are browned. They can be served either hot or cold, but they're at their very best when refrigerated overnight and served chilled the next day. And along with them try a nice bottle of Valpolicella.

OPEN SESAME!

Gone but of blessed memory is Victor's Cafe and Bar, which was located at the corner of Chartres and St. Louis Streets in the French Quarter. It was the habitat for many years of the Bohemian set of artists and writers, and the hard-drinking and eating TV and radio people from the WDSU studios across the street. After he'd known you for a couple of years, the generous manager, Vernon Dusaulles, would give you an almost unlimited tab if you just paid up now and then. Vernon built us a small swimming pool in the backyard patio, and it was great fun on a hot summer day to float around in the pool while drinking mint juleps out of paper cups.

But the great feature at Victor's was Estrellita (which of course means "star"), a beautifully wizened little black lady, about seventy-five years old, who ran the kitchen with an iron hand and an iron skillet. She made the best roux in New Orleans, and its flavor was perceptible in nearly all her dishes, dark brown and oniony. She didn't give a damn about the printed menu out front. She'd whip up whatever she felt like cooking, often some ancient Creole thing from the back of her mind, and the management out front would have to go along with it and feature it as "Tonight's Special." Estrellita's "Specials" eventually became famous, and the management was glad to go along with them. For her regular customers who were there almost every night she would often cook up something special. One night she said to me, "Sugar Britches, I'm gonna cook you somethin' special tonight, has you ever et bennes?" "No, Ma'am," I replied, "what are they?" "Well, my ancestors they brought two things over here from Africa with them, okra and bennes, and they're both mighty good." And then it dawned on me, "bennes" is the African word for sesame seed. They've been eaten for thousands of years all over the Middle East, and Moslem traders introduced them to all parts of Africa, where they were highly valued both as a flavoring agent and as a source of cooking oil.

FRIED SHRIMP WITH SESAME SEEDS

Peeled raw shrimp
beer batter (see below)
sesame seed
deep hot fat

Dry the shrimp as thoroughly as possible with paper towels so the batter will cling to them. Use a deep fry pot with a wire basket, and heat the fat to 375°. (A Cajun trick is to throw a wooden match into the fat, and if it lights, your fat is ready.) Dip the shrimp in the batter, and then dip them in sesame seeds, picking up as many seeds as will cling to them. Place the shrimp in the wire basket and fry very quickly until they're golden but not brown. Be careful not to overcook. Serve them piping hot. Their flavor is unique.

BEER BATTER
  1 cup flour
  1 cup beer
  ½ tsp baking powder
  1 tsp salt
  ⅛ tsp black pepper

Place the beer in a mixing bowl and sift the flour, salt, baking powder, and black pepper into it. Mix it well (but not too much), adding a little more beer if necessary. You can use it immediately, but it will work better if you let it "set" for a couple of hours. It will keep for several days in the refrigerator, and a little fermentation improves its flavor.

FRIED SHRIMP AND ANCHOVY

This is a great snack to serve at cocktail parties, or you can serve it to impress a particular lady friend in the cool of evening.

  1 lb peeled raw shrimp
  1 can rolled anchovies
  beer batter (see above)

Cut the anchovy rolls into halves (a whole roll is too strong in flavor). Shape a shrimp into a circle. Embed half an anchovy roll in the center of the circle, spearing all the way through with a toothpick, as shown in the drawing. This holds the anchovy in place and makes the shrimp keep its shape. After you've fixed all the shrimp this way, dip them in beer batter, place them in a frying basket, and fry in deep hot fat (375°) until golden. Do not overcook. Serve with homemade tartar sauce (see below).

TARTAR SAUCE
Most of the commercial tartar sauces on the market today are a disgrace to the art of good eating. They're loaded with preservatives and lack the tang of fresh homemade mayonnaise. Here's a fresh tartar sauce that's loaded with flavor.

  1 cup homemade mayonnaise
  2 tbsp finely chopped onion
  2 tbsp chopped sweet pickle

1 tbsp finely chopped parsley
juice of 1 lemon
salt to taste

Mix all the ingredients well and chill before using.

BUTTERFLY FRIED SHRIMP
(Serves 4)

Some of the chefs in the small Chinese restaurants scattered around New Orleans are past masters at the art of butterfly fried shrimp. The butterfly cut makes the shrimp turn out crispier and crunchier than plain whole fried shrimp.

2 lb raw shrimp in their shells
beer batter (see above)

Peel the raw shrimp but leave the last segment of shell and the tail on. Holding each shrimp on its back, split it down the inside with a small knife, cutting from the tail toward the front. Don't cut all the way through until the final inch or half inch. Spread the shrimp out in the classic butterfly shape. Dry them well with paper towels. Holding each shrimp by the tail, dip it in the batter. Place the shrimp in the bottom of a frying basket, and fry in deep hot fat (375°). The cooking time is very brief, just until they're golden but not browned. Drain on paper towels and serve piping hot with tartar sauce, soy sauce, or Chinese sweet and sour sauce (see below).

CHINESE SWEET AND SOUR SAUCE
If you can get it, use the tart plum sauce found in Chinese grocery stores. If not, finely chopped pineapple with an equal amount of pineapple juice will do.

This sauce goes beautifully not only with butterfly fried shrimp, but with a wide variety of fish and shellfish dishes, fried, broiled, or sautéed. You should always keep a supply of it in the fridge or freezer. It's a great substitute for that ungodly concoction called ketchup.

1 cup Chinese plum sauce (or ½ cup minced pineapple and ½ cup pineapple juice)
1 clove garlic, put through a garlic press
¼ cup lemon juice (or diluted vinegar)
¼ cup sherry
¼ cup soy sauce
¼ cup sugar
¼ tsp cayenne or Tabasco sauce
sprinkling of powdered ginger
salt if necessary

Mix all the ingredients together and chill in the refrigerator. Serve the sauce in small individual dishes along with each helping of butterfly fried shrimp. The shrimp should be dipped in the sauce before they're eaten.

SWEET AND SOUR SHRIMP MILBY
(Serves 4)

Like many other French Quarter artists, Frank Milby is a whiz kid in the kitchen. He likes to experiment and doodle, freewheel it, and play by ear with his taste buds as a guide, and nine times out of ten his experiments turn out beautifully. Here's one of them.

2 lb shrimp, peeled
½ stick butter
1 cup honey
juice of 2 lemons

Melt the butter in a skillet, and cook the shrimp 1½ minutes on each side. Add the lemon juice and honey, and simmer for a few minutes more. Serve with noodles or rice.

MILBY'S CREOLE MUSTARD AND HONEY SHRIMP

(Serves 4 to 6)

Another sweet-sour-pungent Frank Milby brainstorm is Creole Mustard and Honey Shrimp. Sounds weird but tastes great.

2 lb peeled shrimp
½ stick butter
1 cup honey
½ cup Creole mustard
   juice of 1 lemon
   salt to taste

Melt the butter in a skillet, and cook the shrimp 1½ minutes on each side or until they're pink and firm. Add the lemon juice, honey, Creole mustard, and salt, and simmer for a few minutes more. Serve with Chinese noodles and perhaps some Chinese plum wine or some warmed saki.

BROILED SHRIMP DELICADO

(Serves 4 or more)

Here's a shrimp recipe that was given to me by a master chef who modestly refuses to let me use his name, but his dish is a glory. Part of the secret, of course, lies in the saffron, which imparts an indescribable flavor to the marinade. It's expensive stuff, but what the hell, shrouds have no pockets, so indulge yourself now and then. Use the stringy type of saffron that cooks commonly call "pussy hair." Grind up enough of it with pestle and mortar to make one teaspoonful of powder.

2 lb large raw shrimp (20-count) in their shells

THE MARINADE
   1 tsp powdered saffron
   4 cloves garlic, finely minced
   ½ cup onions, minced
   1 tsp paprika (real Hungarian if you can get it)
   1 stick butter
   ½ cup vegetable oil
   1 tbsp A-1 steak sauce
   1 tsp Tabasco
   ¼ cup sherry
   1 tsp salt
   ¼ tsp freshly ground black pepper

Peel the raw shrimp, leaving the tail section on. Split them down the inside and butterfly them.

For the marinade, heat the butter and vegetable oil in a skillet and mix well. Stir in the saffron. Add the garlic and onions, and cook until the onions are soft and transparent. Add the other ingredients and simmer gently for a half hour. Let it cool.

Place the shrimp in a flat glass bowl or other container, and pour the marinade over them. Let them soak for a half hour, turning them over now and then so they'll be well coated and saturated. Place the shrimp in a large broiler pan or on a cookie sheet, pour the marinade over them, and broil on each side for five minutes or until lightly browned.

Serve piping hot, with hot, crispy, crunchy French bread, and of course a good vibrant wine, either white or red. Beer is also good with this dish.

CREAMED SCAMPI I
(Serves 6)

The Italians call shrimp "Scampi," and the things they can do with the succulent little scamps is nothing short of miraculous. Here's a formula I've developed that's one of the most popular items on the menu of my little seafood restaurant.

6 dozen raw shrimp (20-count), peeled
1½ sticks butter
3 tbsp flour
1 pint cream
2 cloves garlic, put through a garlic press
1 tomato, peeled and diced
½ cup dry white wine
   juice of a lemon
   salt and freshly ground black pepper

Melt a half stick of butter in a skillet, stir in the flour, and mix well. Remove from the fire and add the cream slowly, a little at a time, mixing well. Return to the fire and cook slowly, stirring constantly. Add the garlic, lemon juice, and white wine, and season with salt and pepper. Keep cooking and stirring until the mixture thickens. Taste it and adjust the seasonings. It should be sharp, salty, and garlicky. Peel and dice a tomato into fine cubes and stir it in. The tomato should just heat through and not cook. Keep the sauce warm while cooking the shrimp.

Heat the stick of butter in a skillet, and cook the shrimp approximately 1½ to 2 minutes on each side. Be careful not to overcook them. When all the shrimp are cooked, stir them into the sauce. Serve in six preheated individual casseroles or pastry cups, allowing twelve shrimp per helping. An imported Chablis or Pouilly-Fuissé goes well with this dish.

CREAMED SCAMPI II
(Serves 4 to 6)

3 lb raw heads-on shrimp (20-count) in
   their shells (about 2 lb when shelled)
½ stick butter
4 scallions with their green leaves
2 tbsp fresh chopped parsley
3 tbsp flour
2 cups shrimp stock
½ cup dry white wine
1 cup cream
3 egg yolks
¼ tsp nutmeg
   salt and freshly ground black pepper

Peel the shrimp and save their heads and shells. Place the heads and shells in a small pot, and pound them with a pestle or a thick flat-bottomed bottle. Cover with six cups of water, and boil for 30 minutes or until about half the liquid evaporates. Strain the stock through double cheesecloth, and set aside.

Melt the half stick of butter in a skillet or Dutch oven, add the flour, and stir until well blended. Add the scallions, parsley, and nutmeg, and season with salt and pepper to taste.

Cook slowly for 10 minutes, stirring to blend. Add enough of the shrimp stock to make it slightly creamy. Add the white wine. Continue to cook and stir. Add the shrimp and cook for 10 minutes. Mix the egg yolks and cream in a bowl, and add two tablespoons of the hot pan sauce, stirring rapidly to prevent curdling. Pour this mixture into the main pan, and stir rapidly to blend it in well. Serve at once in hot toasted pastry shells or on slices of trimmed toast or in individual preheated casseroles. It calls for a good white wine, perhaps one of the Alsatian wines or a Liebfraumilch.

SHRIMP VICTORIA

(Serves 8)

This dish is featured at Brennan's Restaurant, and they have given me permission to reproduce it.

Note that they use sour cream, one of the most delicious weapons in the arsenal of the seafood cook. It can often be substituted for mayonnaise or sweet cream in various sauces with spectacular results. The fresh basil in this recipe also adds a kick.

4 lb raw shrimp, peeled and deveined
   (about 7-8 lb in the shell)
1 cup butter (2 sticks)
¾ cup scallions, thinly sliced
½ cup sliced fresh mushrooms
1 bunch fresh basil
⅔ cup dry white wine
⅔ cup heavy sour cream
1¼ tsp salt

½ tsp white pepper
3 tbsp Worcestershire sauce
   about ⅓ cup white roux (1 tbsp butter,
   1 tbsp flour, ¼ cup hot milk)

Melt the butter in a large heavy sauté pan or saucepan. Add the scallions, mushrooms, and basil, then add the shrimp, and cook until they begin to appear glazed and slightly translucent. Stir in the wine and cook for about two minutes. Add cream, salt, pepper, and Worcestershire, and mix thoroughly. Then add several tablespoons of the white roux, and cook for a minute or two. If the sauce is thin, add the rest of the roux. Remove the pan from the heat, allow to stand for a few minutes uncovered, and then stir in the sour cream. Serve immediately on preheated dinner plates, taking care to divide the shrimp and the shreds of basil evenly and to arrange them attractively. Brennan's recommends a Meursault or a Johannisberger Riesling with this dish.

SHRIMP A LA NEWBURG

(Serves 6 to 8)

I've wrestled for years with various classic Newburg recipes, twisting them around to develop one that I really like. For instance, I've eliminated eggs from the formula. With good butter, cream, brandy, and sherry, the sauce is rich enough. Omitting the eggs also simplifies the cooking process, because you don't have to use a double boiler. And I've thrown in a few chopped fresh mushrooms just for the hell of it.

6 dozen shrimp (20-count), peeled
1½ stick butter
6 tbsp flour
1 pint cream
1 pint milk
1½ tsp salt
½ tsp freshly ground black pepper
½ tsp nutmeg
½ cup sherry
½ cup chopped fresh mushrooms
2 oz fine brandy

Melt a half stick of butter in a saucepan, stir in the flour, and mix it well. Remove the pan from the fire and stir in the milk, a little at a time, stirring constantly. Then add the cream and mix well. Return to the fire and cook slowly, stirring often. Add the salt, pepper, nutmeg, sherry, and mushrooms. Keep cooking and stirring until the mixture thickens. Keep the sauce warm while cooking the shrimp.

Melt a stick of butter in a large skillet, and add the shrimp. Stir around, and when the shrimp are good and hot, add the brandy and flame it. After the flame dies out, stir and cook the shrimp until they're firm, about three minutes. Don't overcook. Using a slotted spoon, add the shrimp to the Newburg sauce, mixing well. Serve in six preheated individual casseroles with toast triangles and steamed rice on the side. And of course a good dry white wine.

This dish is unbelievably rich and filling and you should always face it with a good hefty appetite and sharpened taste buds.

SHRIMP NEWBURG AU RHUM

In the early days on the sugar plantations the rich planters nearly always had a still house,

and during the cane-grinding season they'd turn out a year's supply of a rich, dark home-made rum called "tafia." There were no revenooers in those days, and you could produce as much rum as you wanted for home consumption. Some of the planters even made enough to dole out a small quota to their slaves on Christmas, New Year's, and the Fourth of July.

Since there was a plenteous supply, it was only natural that "tafia" should work its way into plantation cookery, especially in dishes where brandy or wine was called for. In the Newburg recipe above, substituting two ounces of rum for the brandy when sautéing the shrimp will give you Shrimp Newburg au Rhum.

SHRIMP-CRABMEAT ROYALE
(Serves 6 to 8)

2 lb peeled raw shrimp
6 live fat crabs (or ½ lb frozen crabmeat)
1¾ sticks butter
½ cup flour
1 cup fresh sliced mushrooms
4 scallions with their green leaves,
     finely chopped
½ cup chopped fresh parsley
1 pint milk
1 pint cream
½ cup sherry
     juice of 1 lemon
½ tsp cayenne

salt and freshly ground black pepper to taste

Boil the live crabs for 20 minutes in salted water. Pick out their meats and save all the crabfat. Melt a stick of butter in a large skillet, and cook the shrimp about three minutes on each side. Sprinkle the lemon juice over them. Add the crabmeat and crabfat to the skillet, and mix it well with the shrimp. Melt a quarter stick of butter in a small skillet, and cook the mushrooms and scallions until limp. Stir in the parsley. Add this mixture to the shrimp and crabmeat.

Melt a half stick of butter in a saucepan, add the flour, and mix well. Remove from the fire and add the milk, a little at a time, at first stirring well or beating with a small wire whisk. Add the cream and whisk some more. Add the cayenne, sherry, salt, and pepper. Return to the fire and cook gently over low heat until the mixture thickens. Put the shrimp-crab mixture and the sauce together in a large saucepan, and cook slowly for ten minutes more, or just until it's well heated through. Serve in preheated individual casseroles or in lightly toasted pastry shells.

SHRIMP CANAPE A LA IRMA

This is a featured appetizer at Arnaud's Restaurant, whose owner, Mrs. Germaine Wells Cazenave, gave me the recipe twenty years ago.

2 lb boiled and peeled shrimp
4 scallions with their green leaves, minced
1 clove garlic, minced

2 tbsp flour
  butter as needed
  fish broth as needed
¼ cup claret
¼ cup white wine
4 egg yolks
  trimmed toast
  bread crumbs
  Parmesan cheese

Cook the minced scallions and garlic in butter until lightly browned. Add the flour and stir it in to make a roux. Add fish broth to achieve the thickness desired. Slice the shrimp fine and put them in the sauce. Cook for about 20 minutes. Mix claret, white wine, and egg yolks and add to the sauce to "tighten" it. Spread on toast slices, cover with mixed bread crumbs and Parmesan cheese, and bake in a preheated 350° oven until golden brown.

NOTE: If you don't have any fish broth lying around, you can use the water that the shrimp were boiled in, but boil it down some to strengthen it.

BAKED STUFFED SHRIMP
(Serves 4)

The giant 10-count shrimp are very large. For an individual serving, four of these shrimp stuffed with a good seafood dressing and baked will make a big meal for the hungriest of gourmets.

16 giant (10-count) shrimp
1 medium onion, diced
2 tbsp green pepper, minced

1 cup crabmeat
6 large oysters, poached until firm and minced
1 cup boiled shrimp, minced
2 tbsp celery, minced
3 cloves garlic, minced
1 tbsp Creole (or Dijon) mustard
1 tbsp Worcestershire sauce
¼ tsp cayenne or Tabasco
4 eggs
¼ loaf French bread
2 tbsp butter
1 tbsp dry white wine
   salt and freshly ground black pepper to taste
   sherry

Peel the shrimp but leave the last shell segment and the tail on. Butterfly the shrimp by splitting down the inside and spreading them out. Remove the vein.

Melt the butter in a skillet, and cook the celery, onion, garlic, and green pepper until lightly browned. Moisten the bread and knead it to a paste. Beat the Worcestershire, cayenne or Tabasco, wine, and mustard into the eggs until thoroughly mixed, and pour over the bread, adding the vegetables, crabmeat, oysters, and minced shrimp. Season to taste with salt and black pepper, and mix well. Divide the stuffing into 16 portions, and press one on each of the butterflied shrimp. Place the shrimp on a buttered cookie sheet, and brush the top of each shrimp with melted butter. Bake in a 400° oven for 15 to 20 minutes until lightly browned. Before serving, brush the tops of the shrimp again with butter, and sprinkle a few drops of sherry on each. Serve rice on the side.

You can also prepare smaller shrimp, such as 20-count, in this manner, but allow six shrimp for each serving.

SHRIMP-STUFFED MIRLITONS
(Serves 6)

The mirliton, also called vegetable pear or chayote, is a pear-shaped squashlike vegetable that migrated to southern Louisiana from the Caribbean or from Yucatan, probably during the Spanish regime. "Chayote" is a Mayan Indian word, and since the Mayans perfected the squash, perhaps they also developed the chayote. When it reached Louisiana, it became a great favorite with both Cajun and Creole cooks. Probably the best way to use it is to stuff it with shrimp dressing.

3 large mirlitons
1 lb peeled raw shrimp, chopped
4 strips bacon, fried brown and crumbled
3 scallions with their green leaves, thinly sliced
1 medium onion, chopped
2 cloves garlic, minced
1 small rib celery, minced
1 green pepper, diced
2 tbsp chopped parsley
1 stick butter
2 tbsp sherry
¼ loaf French bread
¼ tsp Tabasco
   bread crumbs, buttered
   salt and freshly ground black pepper

Boil the mirlitons. It takes about 45 minutes to cook a large mirliton all the way through. Cut them in half and dig out the meats, but leave the shells intact. Mash up the meats and the seeds (they're edible) into a pulp, and set aside. Melt the butter in a skillet, and cook the onion, scallions, garlic, celery, and green pepper until they're soft and transparent but not browned. Add the mashed mirliton, chopped shrimp, crumbled bacon, chopped parsley, sherry, and Tabasco. Mix well and cook slowly for 15 minutes, stirring constantly. Add stock or bouillon if necessary. Moisten the French bread, knead it to a paste, and add it to the pan. Mix well and cook 10 minutes longer. Fill the mirliton shells with the mixture, and cover the tops with buttered bread crumbs. Bake in a preheated 350° oven for 20 minutes or until the tops are browned.

SHRIMP-STUFFED GREEN PEPPERS
(Serves 12 as appetizer, 6 as full dinner)

1½ lb cooked peeled shrimp
 1 medium onion, chopped
 2 tbsp minced celery
 2 tbsp chopped fresh parsley
 1 tsp Worcestershire sauce
 ½ cup tomato sauce
 2 cups cooked rice (or more, depending on size of peppers)
 2 tbsp butter
 ¼ cup bread crumbs
 6 medium-sized green peppers
 ¼ tsp cayenne

 2 tbsp white wine
 salt and freshly ground black pepper to taste

Cut the shrimp into ¼" pieces, reserving six whole shrimp to garnish the tops of the peppers. Cook the onions and celery in butter until tender. Add the parsley, Worcestershire, cayenne, salt, black pepper, and tomato sauce. Cook for five minutes, add the cooked rice, and mix thoroughly. Cut off the tops of the peppers to form cups, and remove the seeds and white pulp. Cover with hot water, add salt, and simmer for five minutes. Don't let them get too soft. Drain the peppers and fill with the shrimp-rice mixture. Top each with bread crumbs, and dot with butter. Place the stuffed peppers in a greased casserole and cover. Bake for 20 minutes, uncover, and bake 10 minutes more. Garnish with finely chopped parsley and the whole reserved shrimp.

SHRIMP-STUFFED CHERRY TOMATOES
(An hors d'oeuvre)

½ lb cooked peeled shrimp
 1 pint cherry tomatoes
 1 scallion with 3" of its green leaves, minced
 6 to 8 pitted black olives, chopped (Greek olives if possible)
 2 hard-boiled eggs, finely chopped
 ⅛ tsp Tabasco
 salt and freshly ground black pepper to taste

Wash and drain the cherry tomatoes, removing stems, if any. Cut a thin slice off the top of each tomato, and scoop out the pulp. Set the tomato shells aside to drain. Chop the shrimp very fine, and mix with the scallions, olives, eggs, Tabasco, salt, and black pepper. Stuff the mixture into the tomato shells. Chill in the refrigerator before serving with cocktails.

NOTE: Either flaked fresh cooked crabmeat or cooked chopped crawfish is a good substitute for shrimp in this nifty appetizer.

SHRIMP-STUFFED EGGPLANT
(Serves 6)

> 2 lb raw peeled shrimp, chopped
> ½ lb lean ham, diced
> 3 large eggplants, halved
> 12 scallions with their grean leaves, sliced thin
> ½ cup chopped fresh parsley
> 1 green pepper, diced
> 4 cloves garlic, minced
> ½ tsp thyme
> 3 bay leaves
> 3 eggs
> ½ tsp Tabasco
> 2 sticks butter
>   bread crumbs
>   salt and freshly ground black pepper

Boil the eggplant halves until they're soft and tender, 15 minutes or more. Cool them and scoop out the insides, but leave a half inch wall of meat inside the rind to give it strength.

Dice the eggplant meats and set aside. Melt the butter in a Dutch oven, iron pot, or large skillet. Cook the green pepper, scallions, parsley, garlic, thyme, and bay leaves until the vegetables are soft and transparent. Remove the bay leaves. Add the shrimp and ham, and cook for 10 minutes more. Season with salt, black pepper, and Tabasco. Add the diced eggplant meats to the mixture in the pot. Mix thoroughly and cook slowly for a half hour. Remove from the fire, let it cool awhile, and then mix in the beaten eggs. Add enough bread crumbs to absorb the excess moisture in the dressing. Fill the eggplant shells with the mixture. Top with bread crumbs, and dot with butter. Bake in a preheated 350° oven for 15 to 20 minutes or until the tops are browned.

SHRIMP-STUFFED ARTICHOKES
(Serves 6 or more)

Shrimp-stuffed artichokes are a contribution to Creole cuisine by cooks of Italian descent. You won't find this dish in large fancy restaurants. It's too informal for them, and making it is too much work. If stuffed artichokes were made to bring in the cost of the time and labor it takes to make them, their price would be astronomical. The ingredients themselves are expensive enough.

> 6 large artichokes
> 2 lb shrimp, boiled, peeled, and finely diced (4 lb in the shell) or use whole tiny "titi" shrimp

1 lb grated Romano cheese
1 lb grated Parmesan cheese
2 loaves stale French bread, torn in pieces
½ can flat fillets of anchovy
3 cups olive oil
12 cloves garlic, coarsely chopped
1 large onion, coarsely chopped
4 scallions with 2″ of their green leaves,
   coarsely chopped
1 cup parsley sprigs
1 tsp basil
½ tsp thyme
½ tsp oregano
1 tsp Tabasco
   salt and freshly ground black pepper

Put through the fine blade of a grinder the pieces of French bread, the fillets of anchovy, the garlic, onion, scallions, and parsley. Place the ground mixture in a large mixing bowl and add two cups of olive oil, the grated cheeses, the finely diced shrimp, basil, thyme, oregano, and Tabasco. Season well with salt and black pepper. Using a large kitchen spoon, mix all the ingredients thoroughly until they form a heavy, coarse-textured paste.

Wash the artichokes and cut off their stems so they sit flat and upright. Take a knife and cut half to three quarters of an inch off the top of each artichoke. This requires a really sharp knife and a deft, neat cut. Now comes the stuffing operation: Take an artichoke and loosen its leaves by pressing down on the top and folding the leaves outward. Starting with the outside leaves and working toward the center, take approximately a teaspoon of stuffing and press it down tight at the bottom of each leaf. Keep going around and around until

each edible leaf has a bite of dressing at the bottom of it. By the time you reach the choke in the center (it's not necessary to remove the choke), your artichoke will be twice as big as when you started and two or three times heavier. When you have finished stuffing, wrap two or three loops of string around the outside of the artichoke and tie it. This will tighten the artichoke up a little and keep it from falling apart.

When you've repeated this operation with six artichokes you'll be pretty damn tired and you'll cuss me for having gotten you into this, but remember how good the end results will be.

Artichokes will turn black if cooked in aluminum or tin pans or in iron pots. Cook them in enamel or stainless steel pans or oven-proof glass dishes. An enamel turkey roasting pan is ideal. Pour a cup of olive oil and a cup of water in the bottom of the pan, and place the artichokes in it. Cover with a loose sheet of foil, bake in a slow to moderate oven for 2½ to 3 hours, every half hour removing the pan and spooning olive oil over each artichoke to keep it moist. Add more water and oil to the pan if necessary as the cooking progresses.

How do you tell if your artichoke is authentic? It should be oily, garlicky, shrimpy, cheesy, strident, and strong. Artichokes done this way are so rich that it takes a very hungry man to eat a whole one. It's a good idea to share them. They can be eaten warm, but the flavor improves if they are allowed to age overnight in the refrigerator and are served cold the next day.

To store them in the refrigerator or freezer, wrap them tightly in heavy-duty aluminum foil to keep them from drying out.

GRILLED SHRIMP KEBABS
(Serves 6)

This dish requires a barbecue grill or Hibachi.

2 lb peeled shrimp
1 lb bacon
1 dozen cherry tomatoes
1 16-oz can pineapple chunks (or 2 cups
  fresh pineapple chunks)
1 dozen small fresh mushrooms
2 green peppers, cut in 1″ squares
½ cup chopped parsley
½ cup vegetable oil
½ cup fresh lemon juice
  grated peel of ½ lemon
½ cup soy sauce
1 tsp salt
½ tsp black pepper

Place in a mixing bowl the oil, lemon juice, soy sauce, grated lemon peel, parsley, salt, and black pepper, and mix well. Add the peeled shrimp, pineapple, mushrooms, and green pepper, and mix well. Let it marinate for one hour, stirring now and then. Cut the bacon slices in half and fry until ¾ done but still limp. Mount everything on skewers, alternating shrimp with cherry tomatoes, pineapple, mushrooms, green peppers, and folded bacon. When the skewers are filled, lay them on well-greased wire grills and place over the hot coals for five minutes, basting them with the marinade now and then. Turn them over, baste some more, and cook for five minutes more, or until the bacon is crisp.

NOTE: When placing objects on a kebab skewer, always leave a little space between them so the heat can circulate. Otherwise something may come out raw.

Chapter 5

The Crab: Incredible Crustacean

The blue crab, also called Atlantic crab (and by the scientists *Callinectes sapidus*), is one of nature's greatest gifts to Louisiana and other states bordering on the Gulf of Mexico. From April to November they crowd into Lake Pontchartrain and into brackish bayous and streams. The commercial crabbers catch them by the thousands, and even amateur crabbers catch a lot of them.

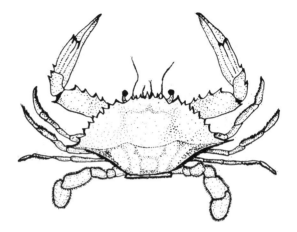

LET'S GO CRABBING!

Whether crabbing is a sport or not we'll leave to the authorities to decide, but it can provide a lot of fun for the whole family. Everyone from the three-year-old tot to the eighty-five-year-old grandmother can be an expert crabber. Crabbing is economical, and it's highly practical too, because it puts on the table some of the world's best seafood. Boiled crabs, stuffed crabs, crab gumbo—these are gourmet's delicacies, yet here in New Orleans they're eaten by everyone. Creoles and Cajuns have developed hundreds of different ways of cooking crabs.

The best places to go crabbing are seawalls, rockpiles, piers, bridges, and trestles. There are two basic methods of catching them: with a baited line and dipnet, and with a baited dropnet. Using the first method, you simply tie a piece of tough meat, a meaty soupbone, or a fish head to the end of a stout cord and throw it into the water. The hungry crab will grab hold of the bait and start eating, and if it's really hungry, it will let you tow it in, first along the bottom and then, as you get closer in, up toward the surface of the water. Watch out, though, because the crab will drop off if you drag it all the way to the surface. When you get it almost to the surface, you scoop it up quickly with a long-handled dipnet and deposit it in a basket or other receptacle. The typical crabber sets out a dozen or more of such baited lines and moves from line to line reaping the harvest.

Round dropnets are more efficient crab catchers. You tie the bait to the center of the dropnet, which you then lower into the water until it lies flat on the bottom. The crabs sidle up to feed on the bait, and you haul them up quickly before they have a chance to crawl up over the side of the net. The expert crabber keeps a half dozen or more nets in the water simultaneously, both to catch more crabs and to keep busy. The individual nets shouldn't be disturbed too frequently or any crabs that may have been approaching them may be scared away. It's after the crab has had a sample taste of the bait that it becomes most catchable. The crab catcher learns patience and finesse, if nothing else. A good afternoon's catch may be a whole basketful of crabs.

A rectangular wire box trap measuring about $3' \times 3' \times 2'$ and available at hardware stores is the most efficient crab catcher of all and can be left unattended. You bait the trap and leave it in the water overnight. When you take it out the next morning, it may have a couple of dozen crabs in it.

For an adult, crabbing is an easygoing and relaxing pastime. For children it's a different matter, a form of conquest over a fearsome adversary. The sixtieth crab is just as exciting as the sixth. My grown children often remind me that one of the greatest pleasures of their childhood was to go crabbing with me on a nice summer day.

A note of warning: A big lively crab can snap a lead pencil in two with its powerful claws, so it behooves you not to get in the way of those pincers. The natives know how to pick crabs up by the flippers, but beginners should stick to handling them with the net until they learn more about the critters' habits.

For those who don't have the time or inclination to go crabbing, live crabs can be purchased in fish markets all over New Orleans. Seafood dealers who will ship crabs or crabmeat by air express to distant cities are listed in the "Shopping Mart" in the rear part of this book.

Hermann B. Deutsch, apostle of crabfat. (Courtesy of *New Orleans States-Item*)

THE FABULOUS STORY OF CRABFAT

My friend the late, great Hermann B. Deutsch—known as "Mr. Hermann"—was a columnist for the *New Orleans States-Item* and one of the finest gourmands and food writers New Orleans ever had. Mr. Hermann's favorite subjects were crabfat and Pass Manchac catfish. He could turn out reams and reams of copy on these two beautiful subjects, and the way he described them would make you drool. He wrote on a wide variety of subjects—politics, sociology, New Orleans history—and he was pretty much what Harold Ickes called himself, an old curmudgeon. He could be a surly old he-bear when he wanted to. Although he was upper Midwest German, everybody loved him because he had so thoroughly Creole-ized himself that he could have passed for a Marigny de Mandeville. And when he began rhapsodizing on Creole food, he held his audience spellbound. He could take hold of an idea of minuscule importance and make it

sound as if it should be made an appendix to the gospels. Like crabfat, for instance.

Now just wot the hell is crabfat? Well, when the feeding is good the wise old crabs, especially the females, know that leaner days may be a-comin' soon. They store up a creamy substance in the corners of their top shells and in the body cavity, and this stuff, my friends, is *crabfat*. According to Mr. Hermann, it's the closest thing we have to the nectar of the gods on Olympus, and I certainly agree. When you're eating boiled crabs and remove the top shell, always dig into the corners of the shell with your index finger or the point of a knife, and extract every bit of the crabfat hiding there. As you eat it, savour it well and think pleasant thoughts about the good things in life.

The body cavity of the crab also has some crabfat all beautifully mixed up with the crab's yellow liver (like the green tomalley of a lobster), which has a delightfully acidic flavor. If you want to make one of the world's best hors d'oeuvres, spread a little bit of crabfat and crab

LOUIS ARMSTRONG

I WISH I COULD SHIMMY LIKE
MY SISTER KATE

Wish I could shimmy like my Sister Kate,
She shivers like jelly on a plate,
My mammy want to know last night
Why all the boys treat Sister Kate so nice,
Every boy in our neighborhood
Knows she can shimmy and it's understood.
I know I'm late but I'll be up to date,
When I can shimmy like my Sister Kate.

This song provides an example of how difficult it can sometimes be to trace the authorship of early jazz tunes. Louis Armstrong wrote *Sister Kate* when he was about 20 years old and sold it to A. J. Piron, the musician-publisher, for $50. Piron published it with his own name on it, and it became one of the most famous jazz hits of the early 1920s. Several well-known jazz bands cut records of it, but not Louis—he was pretty damn mad about it!

BUCKET'S GOT A HOLE IN IT

Bucket's got a hole in it,
Bucket's got a hole in it,
Bucket's got a hole in it,
It won't hold no beer.

Run and tell the lady next door,
Run and tell the lady next door,
It won't hold no beer,
It won't hold no beer.

Keep a-knockin'
But you can't come in,
Keep a-knockin'
But you can't come in,
Keep a-knockin'
But you can't come in.

Come around tomorrow night
And try me again,
Come around tomorrow night
And try me again.

Traditional

This traditional song was a favorite of all the early jazz bands. Joe Oliver cut a record of it, and so did Louis Armstrong. The lyrics given here are the oldest set we could find. Clarence Williams did a version of it with about a dozen verses.

Satchmo

Drawing by Emily Davis

The greatest jazzman of them all, New Orleans's gift to the world, her Number One Son, Louis Armstrong. Someday there will be a bronze statue of Satchmo in the center of the park the city is now building as his memorial.

On New Year's eve of 1913, when twelve-year-old Louis and some friends fired off an old gun, they put Louis in the Waifs' Home. Louis knew how to play cornet, so when the director of the home organized a band, he gave Louis an old battered cornet to play. They marched in holiday parades and gave concerts on special occasions. By the time

Louis left the home, he could play that cornet almost like a professional. Sometimes Bunk Johnson and Joe Oliver let him hide behind the piano at Pete Lala's and play along with them, and he quickly absorbed the style of those great masters. He and Sidney Bechet, the future great of the soprano saxophone, often played together. When Joe Oliver left for Chicago, Louis took his place at Lala's. After Oliver got established in Chicago, he sent for Louis to come up and play with his band. Joe Oliver's Creole Jazz Band was the hottest thing in Chicago, and it made jazz history.

Louis served a loyal apprenticeship with Joe Oliver. He was willing to play second cornet to the "king" because he knew he was learning plenty. Along the way he married Lil Hardin, the band's piano player, and she taught him to read music, something few other New Orleans jazzmen could do. There came a time, though, when Louis equaled and surpassed Oliver, and there was no holding him back.

He and Lil organized a small recording band called Louis Armstrong's Hot Five. The series of records they made for Okey made them famous all over the country, and jazz connoisseurs regard those records as the epitome of small jazz band music, perfect ensemble playing. The large bands that came along later could never achieve their freedom of spirit or their inspired improvisation.

The rest is musical history. Billed as the world's best trumpet player, Louis played with other bands and with his own groups, went on tours, and gave concerts all over the world. There were movies, radio, TV, and lasting fame. He was New Orleans's ambassador to the world, but he liked to come home as often as he could.

liver on a common saltine cracker. It's a transcendent treat that Brillat-Savarin himself would enjoy. Discard the crab's intestine, the little white wormlike thing in the crab's body cavity. It's edible and many crab fanciers do eat it, but it has a rubbery texture. The females often have red coral (eggs) in their body cavity. This is also a great delicacy and should be eaten.

The crabfat is the crab's own built-in sauce. When you're eating boiled crabs, always spread a bit of the crabfat on each bite. It brings out the flavor of the meat.

If you make a pot of Creole Gumbo with crabs but leave out the crabfat, it won't be fitten to eat. After digging out all the fat from the shells and adding it to the gumbo pot, crush the shells and place them in a small pot. Cover with water, boil vigorously for twenty minutes, and then strain the liquid into the gumbo pot. This way you'll have extracted every bit of the crabfat, and your gumbo will be glorious.

CRABFAT HORS D'OEUVRES

It's a safe bet that the Earl of Sandwich, who invented the sandwich, never made one as good as this:

Trim the crust from two thin slices of bread and toast it. Spread each slice with a very, very thin layer of homemade mayonnaise, spread one slice with a quarter inch layer of crabfat, top it with the other slice, and cut the sandwich into triangles. I tell thee truly, I could sit all night devouring these tidbits and washing them down with the best wine I could get my hands on—a good Chablis, a Clos Vougeot, or even a Romanée Conti or Lafite-Rothschild. It would have to be the best. And every now

and then I'd raise my glass and toast the ghost of my old friend Hermann B. Deutsch, the apostle of crabfat.

You have been forewarned: Never throw away the crabfat if you want to dine like a Creole.

THE RITUAL OF BOILED CRABS

The favorite way of cooking crabs in New Orleans is to boil them. Eating boiled crabs is almost a ritual, an established institution. It's great sport on an idle afternoon to sit around eating boiled crabs and washing them down with beer. Driving around town you'll see large signs in front of the fish markets, "Fat Boiled Crabs, Ready to Go." Or in a small neighborhood restaurant you'll often see a sign in the window, "Boiled Crabs Today." Boiled seafood is so popular in New Orleans that any little restaurant that gets a good reputation for boiled crabs and boiled shrimp has it made and can operate successfully just by selling those two items.

But it's still more fun to boil your own crabs. Here's how it's done.

BOILED CRABS
(Serves 6, maybe)

36 live crabs
**3 3-oz pkg "Crab Boil" spices (or 1 pkg
mixed pickling spices)**

3 coarsely chopped large onions
6 ribs celery with the leaves, coarsely
chopped
1 small bunch parsley
1 lb salt
4 tbsp cayenne
2 lemons, sliced

Estimate how much water it will take to cover the crabs, put it in a large pot, and add all the ingredients except the crabs. Boil this stuff vigorously for half an hour to make a good rich liquor. Dump the crabs into the pot, making sure they're all live and kicking. Don't worry! It doesn't hurt them. A crab has a very rudimentary nervous system and a vocabulary limited to a hiss, which should leave you with a clear conscience. If necessary, add enough hot water to the pot to completely cover the crabs.

After the water returns to the boil, cook them for 25 to 30 minutes (20 minutes is OK on smaller quantities). When they're done, the smell that comes from the pot is just like that of boiled corn on the cob. Fish the crabs out and cool them. (If you have more crabs to cook, you can use the broth in the pot over and over. The stronger it gets, the better the crabs will taste.) You can serve them hot, or you can let them cool to room temperature and then chill them in the refrigerator to be served cold. And now I'll tell you how to eat them.

HOW TO EAT BOILED CRABS
(A little melodrama in seven acts)

Act I. Lay the boiled crab on the palm of one hand, and grasp the legs in a firm grip between the palm and the side of the hand. Place the other hand over the top of the crab, grasp the shell by the point, and pull upward gently on the point. The shell will lift right off.

Act II. With a knife (or just your fingers) scrape off the "dead man's fingers," or gills, and discard. Dispose of the gizzard, the small cellophanelike bag behind the eyes at the top of the body cavity. Next break off and discard the mouth parts at the front and the "apron," or genitals, on the bottom of the shell. Everything that's left is edible. The creamy yellow stuff in the body cavity is the crab's liver. Like the tomalley of a lobster, it's a great delicacy and should be spread like mayonnaise on lumps of white crab meat to serve as "sauce."

Act III. Don't just pull off the crab's shell and throw it away, because it's often a treasure house of delicious stored-away crabfat. Dig into the corners of the shell with your index finger to bring out the lumps of yellow fat. As with the liver, use it as a sauce on the white meat. It has a sharp acid flavor that contrasts beautifully with the meat's blandness.

Twist off the claws, crack them with the handle of a table knife, and eat the meats.

Act IV. When you get the crab's body cleaned off, you'll find that it's composed of two partitions or sections, one on each side, with the shell of each section tapering to a sort of crown. Take a small sharp knife and cut off the top of each crown.

Act V. After cutting off the crowns, you'll have a perfect cross section of the crab's body, showing the meat in all the compartments as clearly as a draftsman's drawing. Break the body into two halves, and then, using the legs

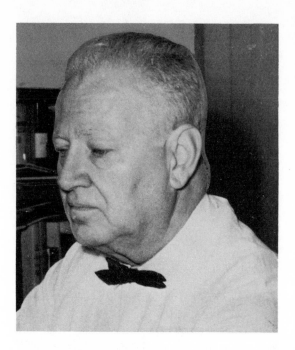

Charles "Pie" Dufour. (Courtesy of *New Orleans States-Item*)

as handles, break each half into segments. Holding each segment by the leg attached to it, bite off the meat. The large chunks of meat attached to the flippers at the back, called "flipper lumps," are highly prized by expensive restaurants for lump crabmeat cocktails and other dishes. This meat sells for eight to ten dollars a pound. Just look how much money you're saving by boiling and picking your own crabs!

Crack the small legs with your teeth and suck out the meat. (Your dentist won't approve, especially if you have bridgework or dentures!) A good crab eater is very conscientious about it. He takes his time and doesn't waste the slightest bit of meat.

Act VI. Wash down boiled crabs with voluminous quantities of good cold beer.

Act VII. Pleasant dreams!

There are two schools of thought on whether to use a knife in eating boiled crabs. The purists say nay, but others say yea. When my friend Charles "Pie" Dufour, music and drama critic, *arbiter elegantiarum* of things Creole, columnist for the *New Orleans States-Item*, first read my little seven-act melodrama, he wrote in his column, "I'll never give up my method of doing it. For one thing I wouldn't use a knife to get into a crab without feeling I was taking advantage of the poor dead thing. I do use a knife, but only the back of it to crack the claws with a sharp whack which generally permits the whole meat to show itself. But to dig into a crab with a knife, that ain't cricket."

On the other hand Charles Faget of Westwego has designed a little stainless steel

Charles Faget's crab knife.

weapon he calls "The New Orleans Crab Knife." 'Tis said that an adept worker in a crabmeat packing plant using this knife can clean out a crab in 30 seconds, and that even an untrained amateur can do it in three or four minutes. The knife is shown here, and the dealer's name and address are given in the rear of this book. A brochure giving instructions is furnished with the knife.

The crux of the matter is time. If you're in no hurry and eating boiled crabs just for the fun of it, forgo the knife. But if you're picking out a goodly quantity of meats for cooking, try the fast method of the packing plants, Charlie Faget's knife.

THE BOILED SEAFOOD DINNER, A NEW ORLEANS TRADITION

One of the grandest of New Orleans traditions is the boiled seafood dinner, an informal down-to-earth affair featured by small neighborhood restaurants that don't mind the muss and fuss involved. The dinner, usually for groups of 8 to 12 people, features large platters piled high with boiled crabs, boiled shrimp, and when they're in season, boiled crawfish. On the side there may be pickled marinated crabs, pickled oysters, fried softshell crabs, fried trout, and perhaps catfish and hush puppies.

As you drive out the River Road above New Orleans and come to Oak Street, you'll see a triangle of green grass at the intersection. Here once stood the Triangle Seafood Restaurant, of blessed memory. It was just a small neighborhood bar and restaurant, but its owners,

Mr. and Mrs. John Palmisano, served the best boiled seafood dinners in New Orleans. Whenever we had distinguished out-of-town visitors and wanted to show them something that was authentically New Orleans, we always took them to the Triangle for the Boiled Seafood Dinner, and no one was ever disappointed. The Palmisanos were very modest folks who never hankered for fame, but it came along anyhow, and they endured it for a few years, accommodating all comers. Then all of a sudden they became old and tired and just locked the place up and quit, much to the sorrow of their host of admirers.

One of the Palmisanos' most memorable dishes was their marinated crabs. It was a trade secret and we never did get their recipe, so the following method will have to do. The marinade must be very sharp and very, very garlicky. Small fat crabs are the best for marinating, but any kind will do in a pinch.

MARINATION

MARINATED CRABS I

3 dozen live crabs
3 pkg "Crab Boil" spices
1 cup salt

MARINADE
2 cups olive oil
1 cup mayonnaise
1 cup sour cream
1 cup wine vinegar diluted
  with 1 cup water
1 cup white wine
2 medium onions, chopped

6 scallions with 1″ of their green leaves, thinly sliced
1 green pepper, diced
2 ribs celery, diced
16 cloves garlic, coarsely chopped
6 Trappey's (or other) red hot pickled peppers, minced
½ cup fresh lemon juice
1 tbsp mixed pickling spices
2 tbsp salt
1 tsp freshly ground black pepper
1 tsp cayenne

Boil the crabs with three 3-oz packages of "Crab Boil" spices and a cup of salt in water to cover for 20 minutes. Cool the crabs and remove their top shells, saving any crabfat in the corners of the shells for the marinade. Remove the claws and crack them so the marinade can penetrate. Save any crabfat and coral in the body cavity of the crab for the marinade. Remove the gills, "apron," and mouth parts. Break the body into two halves, leaving the legs on. They're now ready to marinate. Mix thoroughly all the ingredients of the marinade. Place the crab body halves and the claws in a large enamel pan or stainless steel pot (an enamel turkey roasting pan is ideal), and pour the marinade over them. (The Triangle used gallon glass jars with screw tops to marinate and store their crabs.) Cover the container and marinate the crabs in the refrigerator for two or three days, stirring them around thoroughly now and then, so that all the crabs will get a good soaking. Serve them cold as a side dish for the Boiled Seafood Dinner or as an appetizer for another dinner. If completely covered with marinade, they'll keep for a week in the refrigerator. Add more vinegar-water mixture if necessary.

MARINATED CRABS II

1 dozen boiled crabs
1 cup olive oil
⅓ cup wine vinegar
4 cloves garlic, finely minced
1 tsp dry mustard
1 tsp horseradish
1 tbsp Worcestershire sauce
   juice of 2 lemons
1 rib celery, finely chopped
1 small green pepper, diced
1 medium onion, finely chopped
3 scallions with green leaves, thinly sliced
2 tbsp parsley, finely chopped
   salt and freshly ground black pepper

Remove the crab claws and crack them, but don't pick out the meats. Remove the top shells, and clean out and save all the crabfat in the corners of the shells. Now take a crab body and clean off the gills. Remove the crabfat from the body cavity and save it. Break off the mouth parts and sand bag, and remove the "apron" (genitals) on the bottom of the shell. Break the crab body into two halves, leaving the legs on.

Mix the olive oil, vinegar, garlic, mustard, horseradish, Worcestershire, crabfat, and lemon juice. Add all the chopped vegetables, and season with salt and pepper. Place the sauce in a large bowl or porcelain-enamel pot. Place the crabs and cracked claws in the sauce and toss them around. Marinate in the refrigerator for at least 24 hours, stirring them around now and then. Covered with sauce, they'll keep for a week in the refrigerator, and the older they get, the better they taste.

Beer goes better than wine with this dish, because the sharp acid flavor of the sauce can damage the taste of a fine wine.

MARINATED CRABMEAT

(Serves 6 as appetizer)

1 lb crabmeat
⅓ cup olive oil
⅓ cup dry white wine
½ tsp Tabasco
1 cup homemade mayonnaise
2 cups thinly sliced celery (use the tender inner stalks)
  salt to taste

In a mixing bowl combine the olive oil, wine, Tabasco, salt, and mayonnaise. Add the crabmeat and celery, and toss gently. Refrigerate for at least an hour. Serve on romaine or escarole lettuce leaves.

NOTE: You can substitute boiled peeled shrimp, cooked peeled crawfish tails, Maine lobster, spiny Florida lobster, or African rock lobster tails in this recipe and still have a delicious dish.

STUFFED CRABS

(Serves 6 to 12)

One of the favorite ways of cooking crabs in New Orleans is to stuff them. Small neighbor-hood restaurants do this best. The crabmeat dressing also makes an excellent stuffing for redfish, flounders, small striped bass, and other baking fishes.

Depending on their size and fatness, it takes about two crabs to produce enough meat to stuff one crab shell. Picking the meats out of boiled crabs is a tedious chore, but it's a labor of love, and as a bonus you get the crabfat. And you save a helluva lot of money since picked frozen crabmeat in the stores sells for four or five dollars a pound.

If you can't get fresh live crabs, you can make the dish with frozen crabmeat, but since you won't have the shells to stuff, you'll have to cook it in individual casseroles or pastry shells. It won't be as attractive as the real item, of course, but it will be very, very tasty.

24 live crabs (or 2 lb crabmeat)
12 crab shells
½ cup chopped parsley
1 green pepper, finely chopped
2 cloves garlic, finely minced
1 medium onion, chopped
3 cups bread crumbs
1 stick butter (or more)
2 tbsp sherry
  salt and freshly ground black pepper to taste

Boil 24 live crabs and pick out their meats. On an average it takes about 12 crabs to produce a pound of meat. Save all the crabfat.

Melt the butter in a skillet, and cook the onion, green pepper, garlic, and parsley until soft and transparent. Add the sherry, salt, and black pepper. Add the bread crumbs, crab-meat, and crabfat, and mix well. If it's too dry, add more melted butter. Divide the mixture into 12 parts and fill the crab shells. Bake in a 350° oven until the tops are browned. Before serving, brush the tops with melted butter and sprinkle with a few drops of sherry.

CRAB THERMIDOR
(Serves 4 to 6)

1½ lb flipper lump crabmeat
½ cup grated onion
½ cup fresh mushrooms, chopped
½ cup minced fresh parsley
½ cup grated mild American cheese
¾ stick butter
3 tbsp flour
1 tsp dry mustard
¼ tsp cayenne
½ pint cream
½ pint fresh milk
½ pint evaporated milk
1 oz Cognac (or other brandy)
1 oz sherry
1 tsp salt
½ tsp black pepper
   Parmesan cheese

You can use plain frozen crabmeat or the meat and crabfat from 18 boiled crabs, but the flipper lumps are best. If you use boiled crabs, you can save the shells and stuff the final mixture into them instead of using casseroles.

In a small skillet melt a quarter stick of butter, add the onion, mushrooms, and brandy, and cook until the mushrooms are soft. Stir in the parsley and set aside.

In a large skillet or heavy saucepan melt a half stick of butter, add the flour and dry mustard, and blend well. Remove from the fire, add the fresh milk, just a little at a time at first, and stir it in thoroughly. Add the evaporated milk and stir some more. Add the cream and stir again. Return to the fire, add the cheese, cayenne, sherry, salt, black pepper, the onion mixture, and if you have it, crabfat. Cook slowly, stirring constantly until all the cheese has dissolved and the mixture has thickened. Add the crabmeat and cook for two to three minutes longer, stirring very gently so as not to tear the crabmeat apart. Spoon the mixture into crab shells, if available, or into toasted pastry shells or individual casseroles. Sprinkle with Parmesan and place under the broiler flame until the Parmesan is lightly browned. Serve piping hot.

LUMP CRABMEAT AND CRAWFISH CARDINAL
(Serves 6 as an appetizer)

Like all great Creole cooks, Warren Le Ruth of Le Ruth's Restaurant likes to discover the affinity between things, and there is a great affinity between lump crabmeat and crawfish tails. Here's a perfect appetizer.

½ lb lump crabmeat
1 lb cooked and peeled crawfish tails
2 scallions, chopped fine
½ stick butter
¼ cup dry white wine
¼ cup tomato sauce
1½ cups thick bechamel sauce (white sauce)

FREDDIE KEPPARD

WAY DOWN YONDER IN NEW ORLEANS

Guess! Where do you think I'm going when
the wind starts blowing strong?
Guess! Where do you think I'm going when
the nights start growing long?
I ain't going East, I ain't going West, I ain't
going over the cuckoo's nest
I'm bound for the town that I love best,
where life is one sweet song.

Chorus
Way down yonder in New Orleans
In the land of dreamy scenes
There's a Garden of Eden, that's what I mean
Creole babies with flashing eyes
Softly whisper with tender signs.
Stop!
Oh won't you give your lady fair
A little smile,
Stop!
You bet your life you'll linger there a little
while.
There is heaven right here on earth
With those beautiful queens
Way down yonder in New Orleans.
They've got angels right here on earth
Wearing little blue jeans
Way down yonder in New Orleans.

Drawing by Emily Davis

Freddie Keppard (1889–1933) was "the King"
of Storyville cornetists after Buddy Bolden's
departure and until Joe Oliver reached his
prime. Keppard played with the Olympia
Band. In the early days this band was the
chief competitor of Buddy Bolden's Band.

Keppard played at many cabarets in The
District. In 1911 he and other members of
the Olympia formed the Original Creole
Band and went on a vaudeville tour, spreading the gospel of the new New Orleans
music. They could have been the first band
to make a jazz record, but when Victor
approached them in 1916, Freddie Keppard
refused. "Why should we put our stuff down
on records and make it easy for people to
steal it?"

Keppard was a big man with tremendous
volume. He was also a heavy drinker, and
when he got a load on and started playing,
he could drive everybody out of the building. But he could also play soft and sensuous,
and that's why he was everybody's favorite.

¼ **cup crawfish fat (from the shells of the**
boiled crawfish)
salt and red pepper to taste

Melt the butter and cook the scallions until
soft. Add the white wine and tomato sauce,
and cook five minutes. Add the bechamel
sauce and return to the boil. Add crabmeat,
crawfish, and crawfish fat. Season to taste with
salt and pepper. Return to the boil, stirring
gently. Serve piping hot in preheated small
casseroles.

CRABMEAT LAFITTE
(Serves 6 as appetizer)

The Andrew Jackson Restaurant on Royal
Street in the French Quarter features this
delicious crabmeat appetizer.

1 **lb lump crabmeat**
1 **stick butter**
2 **scallions with their green leaves,**
chopped
¼ **cup white onion, chopped**
2 **oz sherry**
½ **tsp black pepper**
6 **toast slices, trimmed**
dash paprika
salt to taste

Cook the white onion and scallions in butter
until limp. Add the crabmeat and seasonings,
and blend together until warm. Add the sherry
and simmer. Spoon onto toast and overlay
with Hollandaise sauce (see below). Sprinkle
paprika on top and serve at once.

HOLLANDAISE SAUCE
The Hollandaise for the recipe above should
be made before the crabmeat is prepared, and
it should be kept warm.

4 **egg yolks**
1 **oz tarragon vinegar**
¼ **tsp salt**
1 **stick butter**
3 **dashes Tabasco**

Add the vinegar to the egg yolks, and beat
until light. Put in the top of a double boiler and
cook slightly. Add butter slowly, beating con-
tinuously until the mixture is firm. Add a little
hot water if the sauce is too heavy and thick.
Stir in the Tabasco and keep the sauce warm
until it's ready for use.

CRABMEAT FAR HORIZONS
(Serves 1)

The Caribbean Room of the Pontchartrain
Hotel, owned by E. Lysle Aschaffenburg and
his son Albert, is recognized as one of the
finest Creole restaurants in New Orleans. Their
original contributions to the cuisine have been
many, and one of their best appetizers is Crabmeat Far Horizons.

5 **oz fresh white lump crabmeat**
1 **cup light cream**
¼ **tsp Coleman's prepared mustard**
12 **capers**
1 **pinch salt**
1½ **tsp butter, melted**

1½ tbsp Hollandaise sauce (or an egg yolk)
   Italian bread crumbs

Combine the cream, mustard, capers, and salt in a thick aluminum pan, bring to a short boil, and add the melted butter. When the mixture starts to thicken, add the Hollandaise sauce (or egg yolk). Add the crabmeat and fold it in lightly to avoid breaking the crabmeat lumps. When consistency is right, spoon into a pastry shell or serving dish. Sprinkle with Italian bread crumbs, and dot with small lumps of butter.

Place the shell in a 350° oven for about five minutes, or place under a broiler flame until golden. Serve at once.

CRAB CHOPS
(Serves 4 to 6)

Crab chops lying on a plate look very much like pork or lamb chops. Crab chops are a very old New Orleans specialty, and the idea behind them is that they served as a substitute for meat chops during the Lenten season. However, one can easily forget that they started out as a deception, because when the taste buds are hankering for them, crab chops are more delicious than meat.

12 fat crabs (or 1 lb frozen crabmeat)
 ½ stick butter
 ½ cup flour
 1 cup milk
 3 eggs, beaten
 2 tbsp finely chopped fresh parsley
 2 scallions (white part only), finely minced
 ⅛ tsp cayenne
 ⅛ tsp mace
 1 tsp Worcestershire sauce
   bread crumbs
   cracker crumbs
   salt and freshly ground black pepper

Boil the crabs 20 minutes and pick out their meats, saving the crabfat. Break off and save six of the small pincer claws. Melt the butter in a skillet, and cook the scallions and parsley until soft. Add the flour, blend well, and cook for a short while. Remove from the fire and add the milk a little at a time, stirring well. Stir in two beaten eggs. Return to the fire and add the cayenne, mace, Worcestershire sauce, salt, and black pepper. Cook slowly, stirring constantly until the mixture thickens. Add the crabmeat and crabfat, if any. Add enough bread crumbs to the mixture to give it body so it can be shaped and molded into "chops"— like pork or lamb chops. Place the chops on a tray and chill them in the refrigerator for at least three or four hours to harden them, and overnight is even better. When ready to cook, dip each chop in bread crumbs, then in beaten egg, and then in cracker crumbs. Place in a fry basket and fry in deep hot fat (375°) until golden brown. (If you don't have a basket and deep fat fryer, you can cook them in ½" of fat in a regular skillet, browning on both sides.) Drain them on paper towels, and keep the first chops warm until the whole batch is cooked. Stick a crab claw (or a frilly toothpick) in the small end of each chop to resemble a protruding bone. You may want to serve a Hollandaise sauce or a sharp cream sauce over these chops, but that's just gilding the lily, because the chops are so good they don't need embellishment.

CRABMEAT CANAPES

Try serving this dilly of a canapé at your next cocktail party.

1 lb crabmeat, flaked
¾ cup Monterey Jack cheese, grated
¼ cup sour cream
½ cup homemade mayonnaise
3 small scallions (white part only), finely minced
1 tbsp white wine
1 tbsp fresh lemon juice
¼ tsp Tabasco
    salt and freshly ground black pepper
    Melba toast or squares of toast

Mix the first eight ingredients together, stirring gently so as not to tear the crabmeat apart. Season to taste with salt and black pepper. Spoon the mixture onto Melba toast or small toast squares. Place the canapés on a cookie sheet in a preheated 350° oven, and leave them in just until they're heated through. Do not overheat or they will disintegrate and fall apart. Sprinkle with paprika. Great with a dry martini!

This mixture also makes a good appetizer for a dinner at which you want to impress a distinguished visitor from Pawtucket.

ITALIAN CRAB-STUFFED EGGPLANT

(Serves 4 or 8)

2 large eggplants
1 lb crabmeat
½ lb cooked ham (or ¼ lb prosciutto or country ham), diced
3 tbsp olive oil
1 tbsp chopped parsley
4 scallions with 3″ of their green leaves, finely chopped
1 small green pepper, finely chopped
3 cloves garlic, minced
½ tsp basil
¼ cup Marsala (or Madeira)
    bread crumbs as needed
    Parmesan cheese
    salt and freshly ground black pepper to taste

Cut the large eggplants in half, cover with water, and boil for 20 to 30 minutes or until soft. Scoop out the eggplant meats, leaving about a half-inch layer of meat to reinforce the thin peeling. Mash the eggplant meats up and set aside. Heat the olive oil in a skillet, and cook the green pepper, scallions, parsley, and garlic until soft. Add the ham, eggplant pulp, Marsala, basil, a teaspoon of Parmesan cheese, and salt and black pepper. (If you're using prosciutto or country ham, go easy on the salt.) If necessary, add bread crumbs to give the stuffing body, but not too many. Mix in the crabmeat gently. Stuff the eggplant shells, and top with bread crumbs mixed with Parmesan cheese. Bake in a preheated 350° oven until they're heated through and the tops are browned. Serve a good red Chianti with this. If the eggplants are very large and the portions too voluminous for only four servings, you can cut the stuffed eggplant halves into quarters and serve eight people—maybe (some New Orleanians have big appetites).

CRABMEAT MARINIERE BRENNAN

(Serves 3 or 4)

1½ cups crabmeat
 1 cup finely chopped scallions
 1 stick butter
 3 tbsp flour
 2 cups milk
 ½ tsp salt
 ¼ tsp cayenne
 ⅓ cup dry white wine
 1 egg yolk, beaten
   paprika

Melt the butter in a skillet, and cook the scallions until tender. Blend in the flour and cook slowly three to five minutes, stirring constantly. Stir in the milk until smooth. Add salt, cayenne, and wine, and cook about 10 minutes more. Add the crabmeat and heat through. Remove from heat and quickly stir in the egg yolk. Spoon into eight-ounce casseroles, and sprinkle with paprika. Heat under the broiler flame for a moment, and serve piping hot.

STUFFED CRABS AU GRATIN

(Serves 6)

Crabmeat has a great affinity for cheese and cheese sauces, but it must be a mild cheese so that it doesn't overwhelm the crab's flavor. This is a good cheesy stuffed-crab formula.

24 live crabs (or 2 lb crabmeat)
12 crab shells
 ¾ cup grated Swiss or Gruyere cheese
 1 cup chopped fresh mushrooms
 ½ tsp powdered mustard
   pinch of nutmeg
 1 cup milk
 1 cup cream
 2 tbsp flour
 ⅓ stick butter
   salt and freshly ground black pepper

Melt the butter in a skillet, add the flour, and mix well. Remove from the heat and add the milk little by little, stirring constantly. Add the cream the same way. Return to the fire and add the grated cheese, and cook and stir it until it becomes a smooth mixture. Add the mushrooms, mustard, nutmeg, salt, and pepper. When the sauce has thickened, place a layer of it in the bottom of each crab shell, fill the shell with crabmeat, and cover the top with another layer of the sauce. Bake in a moderate oven until lightly browned on top. This is ambrosial enough for the gods on Olympus. Wash it down with a Chassagne-Montrachet or some other treasure of a white wine.

If frozen crabmeat is the only kind you can obtain, you can put this mixture into toasted pastry cups or individual casseroles, and it will still be delicious.

CRABMEAT AU GRATIN EN CASSEROLE

(Serves 2 to 4)

 1 lb crabmeat lumps or chunks

**2 scallions with 3″ of their green leaves,
finely sliced**
¼ cup sauterne
2 tbsp sherry
**1 cup au gratin sauce (see recipe above)
toasted trimmed bread
Parmesan cheese**

Combine the first five ingredients, cover the bottom of a casserole dish with toast slices, and place the crab mixture on the toast. Sprinkle with Parmesan cheese. Bake in a pre-heated oven for 10 to 15 minutes, or until the top is brown.

HOT CRABMEAT HORS D'OEUVRES

If you want to make a good impression at your next cocktail party, you can put the mixture above in miniature pastry shells. (You can buy these small shells at quality stores or make your own.) Sprinkle Parmesan cheese on top of the· filled shells, and bake in a moderate oven until the cheese is browned. The number you make depends, of course, on the number of your guests, but they'll probably like it so well that you'll be kept running back and forth between the oven and the living room, so cook up plenty.

CRAB CAKES

Cajuns and Creoles alike dote on crab cakes, and they have dozens of different ways of making them. The method here, a basic one, can be embroidered on as you see fit.

1 lb crabmeat
¼ stick butter
1 small onion, grated
3 tbsp flour
¾ cup cream
1 tbsp chopped parsley
1 clove garlic, minced
1 tsp Worcestershire sauce
½ tsp powdered mustard
**2 egg yolks
dash of Tabasco
salt and freshly ground black pepper**
**1 egg, beaten
bread crumbs**

Melt the butter in a skillet, and cook the onion, parsley, and garlic until soft and translucent. Add the flour and stir it in well. Mix the cream with the Worcestershire sauce, mustard, egg yolks, Tabasco, and salt and pepper. Stir this mixture into the skillet and mix well, cooking and stirring a short while longer. Add the crab-meat and stir it in gently so as not to break it up. Remove from the fire.

After the mixture cools, shape it into small cakes. Dip the cakes in beaten egg and then in bread crumbs, and fry in hot fat until browned. Be careful not to fry too long or the flavor will be destroyed. Serve with homemade tartar sauce, homemade mayonnaise, or a mild tomato sauce—no ketchup, please! Wash these cakes down with a Portuguese Mateus rosé or, even better, a white Portuguese vinha verde (green wine). The term "green" refers not to color but to the wine's youth. It's still ferment-ing in the bottle, and it goes "pop" when you pull the cork.

CRABMEAT IMPERIAL
(Serves 6)

This recipe is called "Imperial" because you have to be rich as Croesus to buy lump crabmeat. For family consumption it's better to use plain frozen crabmeat. Or better yet, boil 24 live crabs, pick out their meats, and put the crabfat in the sauce. You can also save six of the crabshells and bake the mixture in them.

2 lb lump crabmeat (or plain frozen crabmeat)
¼ stick butter
1 small green pepper, finely diced
¼ cup chopped pimento
¼ cup grated onion
1 tbsp Creole mustard (or dry mustard)
½ cup homemade mayonnaise
2 eggs, beaten
salt and freshly ground black pepper to taste

Melt the butter in a skillet, add the green pepper, onion, and pimento, and cook until the pepper is soft. Add salt and black pepper. In a mixing bowl combine the beaten eggs, mayonnaise, and mustard, and mix well. Stir in the cooked vegetables. Add the crabmeat and mix it in gently so as not to tear the lumps apart. Place the mixture in six individual casserole dishes, pastry shells, or crabshells, and bake in a preheated 350° oven for 15 minutes. You'll feel royal, regal, imperial as you eat this—especially if you have a bottle of Clos Vougeot to go with it.

CRABMEAT LOUIS
(Serves 4)

1 lb crabmeat
1 large head (or 2 small) romaine lettuce
1 cup homemade mayonnaise
½ cup tomato sauce
juice of ½ lemon
1 tbsp capers
¼ tsp cayenne
salt and freshly ground black pepper

Remove the coarse ribs of the lettuce leaves, and finely shred the green part of the leaves. Mix the mayonnaise, tomato sauce, lemon juice, capers, cayenne, salt, and pepper. Add the shredded lettuce to this mixture. Add the crabmeat and mix it in gently so as not to break it up. Serve in four individual salad bowls.

LUMP CRABMEAT REMOULADE

Among epicures and gastronomes, lump crabmeat with remoulade sauce is considered the ultimate appetizer, as good as or even better than shrimp remoulade—and that's saying a lot. Use the same sauces as given earlier for shrimp remoulade.

It's really a toss-up as to which remoulade, the white or the red, goes best with lump crabmeat. Try both and let your tastebuds be your guide.

CRABMEAT REMICK
(Serves 4)

1 lb lump crabmeat (or plain crabmeat)
1 cup homemade mayonnaise
½ cup chili sauce
1 tsp dry mustard
¼ tsp cayenne
melted butter
lemon juice
bread crumbs
Parmesan cheese
salt and freshly ground black pepper

Divide the crabmeat into four portions and place in four well-buttered individual casseroles or pastry shells. Sprinkle the top of each casserole with a tablespoon of melted butter and a half teaspoon of lemon juice. Combine the mayonnaise, chili sauce, dry mustard, and cayenne, and mix well. Season with salt and pepper. Mix bread crumbs and Parmesan cheese, and sprinkle a layer over each casserole. Bake in a preheated 350° oven for 10 minutes, or just until heated through and lightly browned on top.

CRABMEAT RAVIGOTTE
(Serves 12 as appetizer, 6 as dinner)

2 lb crabmeat
½ cup scallions, sliced thin
1 cup chopped fresh mushrooms
1 tbsp chopped fresh parsley
¼ cup Cognac (or other brandy)
¼ cup white wine
1 cup light cream
1 stick butter
1 tbsp cornstarch
¼ tsp Tabasco
¾ tsp salt
¼ tsp freshly ground black pepper
2 tbsp lemon juice
pastry cups (or toast)

Melt the butter in a skillet, and add the scallions and chopped mushrooms. Cook slowly until soft. Add the cornstarch and mix in well. Stir in salt, pepper, Tabasco, and chopped parsley. Pour the brandy in a corner of the skillet, and when it's hot, flame it. When the flame dies, add the white wine and lemon juice, and mix well. Add the cream and cook over very low heat until the mixture thickens. Add the crabmeat and stir it in very gently so as not to break it up.

In a moderate oven, bake the pastry shells four to five minutes, or until they are three quarters done. Fill the shells with the crabmeat and sauce, and bake three to four minutes more, or just until heated through and the shell crusts are browned. Just before serving, sprinkle with paprika and chopped parsley.

This is a perfect appetizer when served in pastry shells. For a full dinner serve it on toast, or line the bottoms of individual casseroles with toast, and spoon the crabmeat and sauce over it. Run them under the broiler a moment to glaze the surface.

As a substitute for crab in this dish, you can use Maine lobster or spiny lobster from Florida.

CRABMEAT-STUFFED MUSHROOMS

1 lb crabmeat
25–30 large fresh mushrooms
¾ stick butter
3 cloves garlic, put through a garlic press
2 tbsp finely chopped fresh parsley
3 scallions with 3″ of their green leaves,
    finely chopped
4 tbsp finely chopped mushroom stems
½ cup unseasoned bread crumbs
½ cup dry white wine
    salt and freshly ground black pepper to
    taste
    mild Swiss cheese, grated

Clean the mushrooms. (*Note*: Never wash mushrooms. Simply wipe them off with a damp cloth. When you wash a mushroom, its gills become filled with water, making it difficult to sauté properly.) Remove the stems of the mushrooms and chop finely. Set them aside for use in the filling. Melt a half stick of butter in a skillet, and cook the mushroom caps just until tender. Do not overcook them. Set aside and save the butter stock. In another skillet melt a quarter stick of butter and add the chopped stems, garlic, parsley, and chopped scallions. Stirring constantly, cook over a low fire until the vegetables are soft and transparent. Add the crabmeat and white wine, and mix in gently. Add the butter the mushrooms were cooked in, and season to taste with salt and pepper. Add a half cup (more if needed)

of unseasoned bread crumbs to make the filling more solid. Remove the skillet from the fire, cool a little, and stuff the mushroom caps with the mixture. Cover a cookie sheet with aluminum foil, and place the stuffed caps on it. Sprinkle a little grated mild Swiss cheese on top of each mushroom. (Don't use a strong cheese, because it will overwhelm the crab's flavor.) Place in a moderate oven until they're heated through and the cheese is melting. Serve piping hot with Piper Heidsieck, perhaps.

CRAB-STUFFED AVOCADO
(Serves 4)

2 ripe avocados
½ lb crabmeat
3 tbsp olive oil
1 tbsp wine vinegar
½ cup thinly sliced celery heart
1 tbsp finely chopped chives or
    scallion leaves
1 tbsp minced stuffed olives
1 tbsp finely chopped fresh parsley
1 tbsp finely chopped green pepper
1 tbsp lemon juice
¼ cup homemade mayonnaise

Beat the oil and vinegar together in a mixing bowl. Add the celery, chives, olives, parsley, and green pepper. Add crabmeat and mix gently. Add lemon juice and enough mayonnaise to bind the ingredients together. Chill thoroughly. When ready to serve, cut the avocados in halves. Fill with crabmeat, and serve on lettuce leaves.

CRABS IN THEIR SHELLS STEWED IN A BROTH

(Serves 4)

This is a very old Cajun method of cooking crabs.

12 live crabs
1 stick butter
2 tbsp flour
1 32-oz can plum tomatoes, drained and chopped, and their juice
2 ribs celery, chopped
2 medium onions, chopped
4 scallions with their green leaves
2 cloves garlic, minced
½ cup chopped parsley
1 green pepper, chopped
½ tsp thyme
¼ tsp mace
¼ tsp cayenne
4 cloves
4 allspice
1 bay leaf
½ cup Burgundy
salt and freshly ground black pepper

Wash the live crabs well, avoiding their pincers as they jump around. Place them in a pot and cover with water. After the water comes to the boil, parboil the crabs for only 10 minutes, just to make the crabs easy to clean. Remove the crabs and let them cool. Save the crab water in the pot.

Melt the stick of butter in a large skillet, saucepan, or Dutch oven, add the flour, and blend it in. Add the onions, scallions, garlic, celery, and green pepper, and cook until the vegetables are soft and transparent. Add the parsley, thyme, mace, cayenne, cloves, allspice, bay leaf, wine, tomatoes, and their juice. Season to taste with salt and black pepper, and add a cup of the crab water. Mix well and simmer for one hour, or until the acidity of the tomatoes is reduced. Stir it frequently, and don't allow it to stick to the bottom of the pot and scorch.

While the broth is cooking, dress the crabs. Break off the claws and crack them. Lift off the top shell, clean the crabfat out of the top shell and the body cavity, and add it to the sauce. Clean off the dead man's fingers, the mouth parts and sand bag, and the "apron" (genitals) on the bottom of the crab. Leave the legs on. Break the crab's body into two halves, and then take a knife and cut the halves into quarters. This will give you 48 crab pieces. When the sauce is done, add the crab pieces and claws to it. Add just enough crab water to cover everything. Stir and mix well. Cover and cook at a slow boil for 30 minutes, stirring now and then. You'd better place an asbestos pad under the pot to keep it from scorching. Serve it in large soup bowls, 12 crab pieces and 6 claws to the bowl plus the sauce. It's the messiest job in the world to eat this with your bare hands, but that's how the Cajuns do it, and it's delicious! You won't find any prissy restaurant serving this dish, because it ruins their nice clean tablecloths.

Serve an imported red Burgundy or a Beaujolais or a Côte Rôtie with it. Or an Italian Valpolicella. The wine authorities are going to be mad at me for insisting that reds go better than whites with many Creole-Cajun seafood dishes, but it's a fact.

FRIED HARD-SHELL CRABS

(Serves 4)

You'll never find fried hard-shell crabs in a restaurant today, but this method of cooking crabs was very popular 100 years ago at the famous lakeshore restaurants of Milneburg and the West End. Many of these restaurants were built on pilings out over the water, and Lake Pontchartrain was so crowded with crabs that all a cook had to do was go out on the back porch and put his traps in the water. These restaurants helped promote jazz when it was in its infancy in the early part of the century, as witness the song on the next page.

12 fat live crabs
 1 egg
 1 cup milk
   corn flour
   lard
   cayenne
   salt and pepper

Wash the live crabs and parboil them for 10 minutes to make them easy to shell and clean. Cool them. Remove the claws, crack them, and set aside. Remove the top shells and discard. Clean off the gills, apron, mouth parts, and sandbag from each crab's body. Break the body in half, and then cut the halves into quarters. Beat an egg and add it to a cup of milk. Highly season corn flour with cayenne, salt, and black pepper. Heat three inches of

lard in a deep frypan with basket to 375°. (In the days before thermometers, the old timer floated a wooden kitchen match in the fat, and if the match lighted, the fat was ready for cooking.) Dip the crab pieces in the egg-milk, and then dredge in the flour, shaking off all excess flour. Arrange them in the bottom of the fry basket and cook for eight to ten minutes, or until they're golden brown. Drain on paper towels and serve piping hot on preheated dinner plates. Garnish generously with fresh parsley sprigs.

CHARLESTON!

SHE CRAB SOUP

(Serves 6)

This is not a Creole dish. It originated in Charleston, South Carolina, and Charlestonians are as jealously proud of their crab soup as New Orleanians are of their gumbo. But making it comes so close to the methods of Creole cookery—and we have such an abundant supply of crabs—that the recipe is not at all out of place among New Orleans crab dishes.

It's called She Crab Soup because only female crabs are used. Females usually have red coral eggs secreted in their body cavity, and when creamed, coral is an essential flavoring element of the soup. This recipe comes from Mrs. Julia Dougherty, a member of an old Charleston family.

12 live fat female crabs with their coral
    and crabfat (or enough crabs to produce
    1 lb of meat)

LEON RAPPOLO

MILENBERG JOYS

Now there's a tune,
A brand new tune,
'riginated down in Dixieland.
Eliza Green, the shimmie queen,
Says that it's just grand,
And every night, with all her might
She does a dance that's hard to beat,
The way she syncopates don't leave nothing
   out,
you should hear this baby shout.

Chorus
Rock my soul with the Milenberg Joys
(spoken) Stomp it!
Rock my soul with the Milenberg Joys
Play'em, daddy, don't refuse,
Separate me from the weary blues.
Hey! Hey! Hey!
Sweet boy, syncopate your mamma all night
   long,
With that Dixieland strain,
(spoken) Turn it on,
Play it down, then do it again,
(spoken) Won't be long now,
Every time I hear that tune,
Good luck says, I'll be with you soon,
That's just why I've got the Milenberg Joys.

As Jelly Roll Morton originally wrote it, this song was called *The Golden Leaf Strut*. Rappolo, Mares, and the New Orleans Rhythm Kings did a new version and called it *Milenberg Joys*. Milneburg* was a resort on the shore of the Lake Pontchartrain at the foot of Elysian Fields Avenue. There were seafood restaurants, picnic grounds, and pavilions where dances were regularly held, giving employment to many New Orleans musicians. A weekend excursion to Milneburg could be a real joy. The Pontchartrain Railway had a track down the middle of Elysian Fields and ran a regular small train called "Smoky Mary." The first small car of the train had barred windows and locks on the doors, and on the trips back from the lake the drunks were thrown in there to keep them from molesting the other passengers.

* For reasons now unknown, the publishers of the song misspelled the name of the resort town.

Rhythm King

Leon Rappolo (1902–1943) was the greatest white clarinet player to come out of New Orleans, and although his career was short, he carved himself a permanent niche among the great men of jazz. He came from a large family of musicians—classical legitimate musicians—and they were all a bit taken aback when Leon started blowing a hot bluesy clarinet of the type played in Storyville dance halls. But there was no holding him back, and he soared like Daedalus on silver wings toward the hot sun. He played at first with the Brunies boys, Abbie and George, at the Halfway House near Lake Pontchartrain. They had all grown up together, and while they were still kids, they had spent as much time as possible in Story-

ville listening to and absorbing the styles of great Negro musicians like Joe Oliver. Leon went to Chicago and fame as a member of the New Orleans Rhythm Kings. In the early 1920s the members of that band composed and made records of several jazz tunes that became immediate hits. The New Orleans Rhythm Kings became a household word all over the country, and everybody was playing and singing their music. Among their hits were *Tin Roof Blues, Farewell Blues,* and *Milenberg Joys.* Of course they were derived from older traditional blues, but the Rhythm Kings gave them their personal stamp, and Rappolo's clarinet solos were outstanding.

Rappolo was the first jazzman to discover the benefits (or was it deficits?) of smoking grass, and this quickly became a part of the jazz mystique. His music and lifestyle were imitated by the younger musicians, such as "Bix" Beiderbecke, who also burned his candle at both ends—and also burned out early.

The high life in Chicago caused Rappolo to have a mental breakdown, probably what would be called schizophrenia today. He returned to New Orleans and continued to play with the Brunies band at the Halfway House, but his illness grew progressively worse. Like his great predecessor, Buddy Bolden, the father of jazz, Leon Rappolo spent the last years of his life in a hospital for the mentally ill.

Jazz was a stern taskmaster.

1 pint milk
1 pint half-and-half cream
¼ stick butter
1 small onion, grated
¼ tsp ground mace
1 tsp Worcestershire sauce
2 large ribs celery, finely chopped
¼ cup crushed saltine crackers
2 pieces lemon peel
 salt and freshly ground black pepper to taste
 sherry

Boil the live crabs and pick out the meats, saving all the coral and crabfat. Cream the coral and crabfat together, and set the mixture aside.

Put the milk, half-and-half, mace, lemon peel, onion, celery, and Worcestershire sauce in a heavy pot, and heat slowly. *Do not allow it to boil.* When it's hot, add the crabmeat, coral-crabfat mixture, and butter, and season to taste with salt and pepper. Continue to heat, stirring constantly. Add the cracker crumbs to thicken the soup. Allow it to "set" for a few minutes so that the elements can get themselves together. Place a tablespoon of sherry in the bottom of each preheated soup bowl before ladling the soup in. Sprinkle on a little finely chopped parsley and a dash of paprika for garnish.

I've kitchen-tested this soup in my "laboratory" several times and can vouch for the fact that it's mighty good.

NOTE: If you can't find live she crabs in the shell, use a pound of frozen crabmeat and chop up the yolks of two hard-boiled eggs as a substitute for the coral.

CRABMEAT SALAD WITH CREOLE CREAMED CHEESE
(Serves 6)

This recipe was developed to use Creole Creamed Cheese, which is probably the most delicious dairy product in the bright lexicon of Creole cuisine. It comes from that ancient product, clabber. Clabber is produced when milk is allowed to sour and turn into curds and whey. Very similar to yogurt, it's the very same curds and whey that Miss Muffet ate as she sat on a tuffet. To make Creole Creamed Cheese, the curds and whey are placed in a cloth bag, and the whey is allowed to drain away. After it has drained for 24 hours, a mound of the semisolid curd is placed in the center of a container, and fresh cream is poured around it. It's on sale in 11-ounce packages in the dairy section of grocery stores all over New Orleans and South Louisiana. It's delicious when sprinkled with salt and pepper, or some sprinkle it with sugar, or it can be served with Kadota figs or other fruit preserves or with fresh fruit, such as peaches or strawberries. But it's also a terrific salad dressing, as you'll discover.

1 lb crabmeat
1 11-oz pkg Creole Creamed Cheese
1 large ripe avocado, peeled and diced
1 large Creole tomato, peeled and chopped (or 1 cup fresh tomato of another type)
1 small green pepper, chopped

3 scallions with 3″ of their green leaves,
   finely sliced
   juice of ½ lemon
1 inside heart rib celery, minced
½ tsp Tabasco
   salt and freshly ground black pepper to
   taste

Open the 11-ounce container of Creole Creamed Cheese and add a teaspoon of salt and the Tabasco to it. Mix well so that the curd, cream, salt, and Tabasco are blended. Place the crabmeat in a mixing bowl, and add the diced avocado, chopped tomato, green pepper, scallions, celery, lemon juice, and black pepper. Pour the Creamed Cheese over everything, and mix gently so as not to tear the crab and avocado pieces apart. Adjust the salt. Serve on a bed of fresh garden lettuce, Bibb or romaine or escarole. No good Creole cook would stoop to serving a nice dish like this on tasteless iceberg lettuce. If available, put a ring of crisp fresh watercress around the edge of the salad.

NOTE: If you can't find Creole Creamed Cheese, you can substitute a pint of heavy soured cream or a pint of plain yogurt in this recipe, and the results will be excellent.

SOFT-SHELL CRABS— GASTRONOMIC DELIGHT

The fried or broiled soft-shell crab is the ultimate expression of the Creole-Cajun cooking genius. It is the *ne plus ultra* of all Louisiana seafoods, the supreme gift Father Neptune places on the altar of gourmandise. Epicures everywhere agree on this. The eating of soft-shell crabs originated in New Orleans and South Louisiana. The Indians taught the early settlers how to use them. With modern transportation and refrigeration, New Orleans has now taught the rest of the nation to appreciate them. Fine restaurants in Boston, New York, and Chicago feature Lake Pontchartrain soft-shell crabs. They're packed while alive and shipped by air express. They arrive in faraway kitchens, still alive, only a few hours after leaving the water. When soft-shell crabs are quick-frozen, they can be shipped even greater distances and kept for longer periods of time. Freezing makes what was formerly a seasonal delicacy readily available year-round.

But the true gastronome believes that live fresh crabs are the most toothsome. In some New Orleans markets and restaurants soft-shell rabs can be obtained at very reasonable prices, but in periods of scarcity they become a luxury, and the price skyrockets.

Contrary to what some inland landlubbers may think, the soft-shell crab is not a separate species. It's just the same old blue crab at the molting stage. Like many reptiles and other crustaceans, crabs outgrow their shells. As a crab grows, its shell gets too tight for comfort, so it busts out and grows a larger shell. For a few hours after it sheds its old shell, the crab is soft and almost helpless—the soft-shell phase. When a hard-shell crab is about to molt, its body swells up inside the shell and splits it. It can then crawl out the back door of the shell. A crab that is preparing to molt is called a "buster," or "shedder." These are the crabs that are most highly prized by crab fishermen and by the epicures who eat them, because a crab taken in its "busting" stage can be removed from the water while its new shell is at the peak of softness. If allowed to remain in the water, the new shell will become leathery in a short while, and within a few hours it will be hard again. It is truly one of nature's miracles.

Before busting, a shedder always looks around for a safe place to hide, because after it has left its shell and is soft, it's completely helpless, an easy prey to predators, fish and other crabs (crabs are extremely cannibalistic). To cash in on this urge to hide, the crab fishermen sink "trot lines" into the bayou. A trot line is a long rope with leafy tree branches tied to it at intervals. The fisherman in his boat goes down the line lifting out the branches and shaking out the "busters" into the bottom of the boat.

An even better method is used by the professional crabbers, who harvest all types of crabs. One fine spring afternoon we watched a real Cajun crabber, Oreste LeBlanc, practice the art of crab sorting on the wharf behind his house on Bayou Barataria near Lafitte. He had two wooden slatted tanks, about twelve feet long and four feet deep, sunk into the water next to his wharf with their tops exposed. As he was unloading hard-shell crabs into one tank, he watched for crabs that were about to become busters—a good crabber can spot them almost by intuition—and he put those into the other tank. He kept a very close watch on the second tank, so that whenever a "buster" had completely shed its shell, he was ready to lift it out as quickly as possible and pack it in Spanish moss in a shipping container. Packed in this manner and refrigerated, the crabs could be kept alive for twenty-four hours, time enough to get them to the market,

into kitchens, and on the table. A refrigerator truck passed by every few hours to haul his crabs to the market.

To hedge his bets, Oreste LeBlanc had a walk-in freezer in which he could stash away his "busters" whenever the market for fresh, live soft-shell crabs became irregular. Speaking with undisguised pride about his freezer unit, he said, "She damn expensive machine, but she save my skin sometime. In old day my pappa have to throw away thousan' of dollar worth good soft-shell crab when the market bad."

My friends and I bought a full box of 48 live soft-shell crabs from Oreste. We rushed them back to New Orleans and had a sybaritic feast at the Skyscraper that night.

LOVE STORY

While speaking of soft-shell crabs—just in case anyone might be interested in the subject, the lovelife of crabs is unique in the annals of courtship. It's not very romantic; behaviorists could use it as proof that the caveman approach to love-making may be a normal technique. In the springtime the male crabs are always the first to migrate inland from deep water. They hang around like drugstore cowboys on a street corner waiting for the females to come in. When the ladies arrive in a rushing tidal wave of femininity, the males go crazy. Each male dashes around looking for a female who is about to "bust," and when he finds her, he leaps on top of her and pins her down, holds her there until her shell splits and she crawls out the back door of the shell and lies there soft and unable to move. Then the male grabs the helpless creature and rapes her. For a brief span, to protect his seed deposit the male proves himself to be a real cavalier (or is it male chauvinist?) and hovers over the female for several hours, protecting her from predators, until her shell has hardened and she is safe.

The female crab has the last laugh; when she is impregnated one time it lasts for a lifetime (up to 12 years). She carries the basic coral eggs around inside her body cavity and can fertilize her own eggs whenever she has the urge. This egg hoarding practice is not safe in the vicinity of Charleston, S.C., where the coral is highly prized as an ingredient for She Crab Soup.

TO CLEAN SOFT-SHELL CRABS

Soft-shell crabs should not be cleaned until just before they're cooked. Otherwise they'll deteriorate rapidly. Wash the crabs, lift the corners of the top shell gently, and remove the gills (dead man's fingers). Cut off the mouth part, and remove the sand bag from just behind the eyes. Remove the "apron" on the bottom of the shell. The crab is now ready for cooking.

FRIED SOFT-SHELL CRABS

Season milk with salt and freshly ground black pepper. Soak the crabs in the milk for 15 minutes. Remove and drain on paper towels. Roll the crabs lightly in yellow corn flour, and shake off the excess flour. Heat lard in a deep-fry pan to 365°. Fry the crabs until light golden brown and crisp, about five or six minutes. The crabs should float on the surface of the fat while cooking, so don't overcrowd the pan. Lift them out with a slotted spoon or spatula, and drain on paper towels. Serve on preheated plates, piping hot, along with lemon wedges or fresh homemade tartar sauce.

BROILED SOFT-SHELL CRABS

This was a favorite method of cooking busters in the olden days. Melt a half pound of butter and place it in a bowl, season with salt, freshly ground black pepper, and a dash of cayenne. Dip the crabs in the butter, and then dust lightly with yellow corn flour. Place them on a cookie sheet and broil them approximately 10 minutes, turning them over midway. Serve with lemon wedges or homemade tartar sauce.

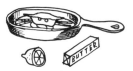

SOFT-SHELL CRABS SAUTEED IN BUTTER
(Serves 2)

2 large or 4 small soft-shell crabs
1 stick of butter
** juice of 1 lemon**
** milk**
** corn flour**

Melt the butter in a skillet large enough to hold the crabs. Dip the crabs in milk and then in corn flour, and shake off the excess flour. Place them in the skillet and cook slowly. (Slow frying in butter is the best method for cooking seafood, because it does not burn out the flavor.) When the crabs are brown on both sides, place them on preheated serving plates. Turn the heat up high, and add the lemon juice to the butter in the skillet. As it foams up, scrape and stir back in the flavor some brown particles clinging to the sides of the skillet. When the butter has lightly browned, pour the sauce over the crabs, and serve immediately.

SOFT-SHELL CRABS SAUTE MEUNIERE AMANDINE

(Serves 2)

  2 large or 4 small soft-shell crabs
  2 sticks butter
  **¾ cup sliced natural or blanched almonds
      (¼ lb)**
  juice of 2 lemons

Melt the butter in a skillet large enough to hold the two crabs. Dip the crabs in milk and then in corn flour. Shake off the excess flour. Place them in the skillet and cook them slowly. When the crabs are nicely browned on both sides, place them on hot plates and keep them warm. Raise the heat and add the almonds and lemon juice to the butter in the pan. Scrape the bottom and sides of the skillet to release any browned particles clinging there. These delicious bits are the soul of the meunière sauce. When the almonds are a very light golden brown, pour the sauce over the crabs on hot serving plates, and serve at once.

   The secret of all amandine dishes lies in the handling of the almonds. Always use sliced natural or blanched almonds, not slivered

almonds. Since the almonds take longer to cook than the other elements in the sauce, it's best to give them a precook. Melt butter in a skillet and slowly cook the almonds, stirring constantly, just until they are golden yellow, no more. Remove from the skillet and set aside. When added to the lemon and butter, they should cook only until they're a very light brown. Dark brown almonds have an unpleasant bitter flavor.

BRENNAN'S BUSTERS BEARNAISE

(Serves 3)

  **9 busters (soft-shell crabs), cleaned
      and dried**
  1 egg, beaten
  1 cup milk
  ½ cup butter (1 stick)
  6 buttered toast triangles
  1½ cups Bearnaise sauce
  1 tbsp chopped parsley

Make a batter with the egg and milk. Dip the busters in the batter, drain, dredge in flour, and fry gently in butter until golden brown. Mount on toast triangles and cover with Bearnaise Sauce. Sprinkle with chopped parsley.

BEARNAISE SAUCE
  ½ cup dry white wine
  1 tbsp wine vinegar
  1 tbsp minced onion
  ½ tsp chopped parsley
  ⅛ tsp freshly ground black pepper
  3 egg yolks
  1 stick butter, melted

One of New Orleans' most famous restaurants, Brennan's, was founded in 1940 by Owen Brennan, an Irishman with a flair for French and Creole cooking. The restaurant got its start in the Old Absinthe House on Bourbon Street and then moved to its present location in the historic Patio Royal-Morphy building on Royal Street. Unfortunately, Owen died of a heart attack just before the restaurant moved to its new location. His widow and his three sons, "Pip," Jimmy, and Ted, carried out the program that Owen had outlined, and the restaurant became nationally famous. "The Brennan Cookbook" by Hermann B. Deutsch is a classic in the field of Creole cookery. Among the seafood dishes they have made popular are Busters Bearnaise, Crabmeat Marinière, Shrimp Victoria, Redfish Perez, and Pompano Grand Duc. They have revived the Madame Bégué type of luxury breakfast, and "Breakfast at Brennan's" has become as famous a phrase in New Orleans as "Dinner at Antoine's."

Heat the wine and vinegar in a small saucepan. Add the minced onion, parsley, and black pepper (no salt). Boil down over a hot fire until reduced to a paste. Cool, strain into a saucepan, and beat in the egg yolks. Place over very low heat and add the melted butter slowly (as in making Hollandaise), stirring until the mixture has the consistency of Hollandaise.

SOFT-SHELL CRAB WITH LUMP CRABMEAT (CRABE AVEC CRABE)

(Serves 2)

This is one of the grandest and most delicious dishes to come out of New Orleans. Putting lump crabmeat on top of a soft-shell crab is like gilding the lily with 24 karat gold leaf. But it works! One of the greatest virtues of the dish is its simplicity. It has no frills and frou-frou.

4 medium-sized soft-shell crabs
½ lb lump crabmeat

½ stick butter
juice of 1 lemon
vegetable oil or fat
milk
corn flour

Dip the crabs in milk and then dredge in the corn flour, carefully shaking off the excess flour. Using a French frying skillet with a wire basket, heat the oil or fat to 365°. Place the crabs in the frying basket, and fry briefly until they're a light golden brown. Set the fried crabs aside and keep them hot. Melt the butter in a skillet, and add the lump crabmeat and lemon juice. Cook just long enough to heat the crabmeat through, stirring very gently so as not to break up the lumps of meat. Preheat two serving dishes, put two fried crabs on each plate, and cover with the crabmeat lumps and the butter-lemon sauce in the pan. Serve with it a good Chablis, Pouilly Fuissé, or Le Montrachet. Good enough for a state dinner in honor of the Prime Minster of Afghanistan.

Chapter 6

Hymn of Praise
to the Oyster

Oysters! The very name is magic, evoking visions of Arabian nights, halcyon days, Lucullan banquets, love feasts, orgies. Oysters have propensities for romance, connotations of fulfillment, promises of joy. They're the food for lovers and honeymooners. They renew the flagging ardors of the middle-aged and promote connubial rapport for all ages at all times. Oysters are a miracle.

"Eat oysters—Love longer," those bawdy signs the National Oyster Growers Association places in fish markets all over the country, are not just a figment of the oyster growers' imaginations to increase consumption. For thousands of years it has been known that oysters are one of the world's best aphrodisiacs, producing vigor,

vitality, and muscular stamina. Serious nutritional scientists have recently been digging into this subject, and they find that the wholesome results are obtained because oysters contain significant amounts of zinc and magnesium, two minerals necessary for a healthy metabolism (and perhaps a healthy libido).

Louisiana produces more oysters than any state in the Union, and the natives of the state, along with hordes of visitors, consume more oysters than any other people anywhere else. Most oysters are eaten raw on the half-shell, but the Creole-Cajun cuisine has so many good ways to cook oysters that you could eat them three times a day without becoming tired of them. The forty oyster recipes in this chapter **123** only scratch the surface of the delightful subject of oyster cookery. A whole volume could be written by someone with enough time, patience, and enthusiasm for the project.

Because there aren't enough oysters growing wild to supply the market today, they're carefully farmed and cultivated. The brackish bayous and salt marshes of southeastern Louisiana have just the right balance of fresh and salt water for the oysters to flourish. The state leases these shallow water bottoms to oyster growers, who seed them with "spat" (young oysters). When the oysters approach maturity, they're moved to new beds closer to the saltier waters of the Gulf, where they take on their characteristic salty flavor. An oyster grower has to move his oysters around four to five times before they're ready for marketing. A connoisseur will not eat an oyster if it's not good and salty. Sometimes an oyster grower, overeager for a fast buck, will ship his oysters to the market without giving them the saltwater phase of treatment. As a result, they'll be fat, flabby, gorged on fresh water, and taste-less. This practice damages the whole oyster industry.

Some Cajuns grow oysters, but most of the oyster farming and marketing is in the hands of people of Yugoslavian descent, whose ancestors came to Louisiana in the nineteenth century from Dalmatia, a province on the Adriatic coast. Since ancient Roman times, the Dalmatians have been cultivators of shellfish (as well as spotted dogs who love to ride on firetrucks). If you see a New Orleanian whose name ends in "ich" it's a safe bet that he's a Yugoslavian and connected with the oyster business in some way.

The love life of oysters is nothing to get excited about; anchored as they are in one spot, they never get to see their mates. But they can really communicate. In the springtime they release some sort of excitant fluid into the water, and the females start spewing forth millions of eggs. The egg and the sperm meet in the water, and fertilization takes place. Only a small fraction of the baby oysters survive to become mature adults.

Oysters.

Oyster lugger landing on the levee at New Orleans, around 1910. (Courtesy of the Special Collections Division, Tulane University Library)

An oyster changes its sex two or three times during its lifetime. This helps prevent extinction by maintaining a balance of the sexes. How remarkable, an oyster may have a grandfather and a grandmother in the same individual!

HOW AN AMATEUR CAN OPEN OYSTERS SAFELY

Many people have injured themselves severely by trying to open an oyster the wrong way. Professional oyster openers have a heavy S-shaped anvil made of lead. It holds the oyster steady while the opener penetrates the sides of the shell with a special oyster knife. Learning the trick takes a good deal of time, practice, and the proper equipment. An amateur can more safely

attack an oyster through its hinge, and the two best tools are a small metal beer can opener and a screwdriver. The beer can opener should be the kind that punches triangular holes in the tops of cans. The curve of its point is perfect for fitting under the hinge of the oyster and providing strong leverage when it's pressed downward. Or the amateur can use a screwdriver that has the strength to pry open the oyster at the hinge without breaking. If you try to do this with a knife, the point can easily break, and you can stab yourself in the hand. Even if it doesn't break, the knife may slip and cut you. When using either the beer can opener or the screwdriver, you should keep a small paring knife handy for cutting the adductor muscle of the oyster. Here are the steps in sequence.

Lay the oyster on a flat surface, steady it with one hand, take the beer can opener (or the

screwdriver) in the other hand, and pry the oyster open at the hinge. You don't have to open it all the way. Just make a small slot between the shells. Slip the small paring knife through this slot, and sever the oyster's adductor muscle where it joins the inside of the top shell. The top shell will then lift right off. Next slide the knife under the oyster's body, and sever the muscle where it joins the bottom shell. Try not to waste any of the oyster's juice, which is the best part. Hold the oyster over a small pan when opening it in order to catch any of the juice that sloshes out. And here's a point to remember: At the point where the two hinges join, there often accumulates a little crumb of black mud with a foul smell and a bitter taste. Wipe it off with the point of the knife. Also wipe off with the flat of the knife blade any pieces of shell that may be scattered around the oyster. If an oyster has only a little juice, looks dry, and has gills that are stuck to the side of the shell, discard it as a doubtful specimen. Always serve raw oysters on the deep side of the shell. It can't slide off, and the shell holds the juice. Now that you know the ground rules of the game, you can really enjoy your oysters.

A VANISHED INSTITUTION

In the old days oyster bars were one of the most familiar sights in New Orleans. At any time of the day or night you could step up to the bar and have a dozen or two on the half shell. It was a

pleasure you could frequently enjoy because they cost only a dime a dozen in those days. New Orleanians never paid any attention to that "R" month stuff. They were so close to the source of supply that an oyster never had a chance to go bad. The oyster was always popular year-round.

Of all those oyster bars in New Orleans, only a few survive today. Among the best are the Acme Oyster House, at 724 Iberville Street, which usually has the saltiest oysters in town; and Felix's, across the street at 739 Iberville. The fact that they are nearly always crowded attests to the continuing popularity of the succulent bivalve.

Most old-time drinking saloons, in addition to their oyster bars, had free-lunch counters loaded with such dainties as baked red snapper, boiled shrimp and crawfish, pickled oysters, roast beef, boiled ham, etc., and if you bought a few drinks, you could step up and indulge yourself freely. There was plenty of competition among the saloons to see who could put on the biggest free-lunch spread.

OYSTERS ON THE HALF SHELL

Most oyster connoisseurs know that the best way to eat an oyster is raw on the half shell with just a little squeeze of lemon juice and a drop of Tabasco. The oyster is swooshed right down off the half shell along with the natural juice—nectar of the gods. Each oyster is then chased down

Salty oysters on the half shell. (Courtesy of Louisiana Wildlife and Fisheries Commission)

with a bite of saltine cracker. But the connoisseurs are only a minority. Maybe ninety percent of all oyster eaters like to dip their oysters in some kind of sauce, usually ketchup and horseradish. For their benefit, here are two recipes for oyster sauce.

OYSTER COCKTAIL SAUCE I

1 **bottle chili sauce (tomato)**
2 **tbsp horseradish**
1 **tbsp lemon juice**
¼ **to ½ tsp Tabasco**
  salt and freshly ground black pepper to taste

Mix all the ingredients well and chill. Serve in small individual cups. Many people like to pick an oyster up with an oyster fork, dunk it in the sauce, and then eat it. Actually, it's better to place a small dab of the sauce on top of the oyster and then swoosh it right off the shell. This way the oyster's juice becomes part of the sauce.

OYSTER COCKTAIL SAUCE II

In most New Orleans oyster bars, you'll see small (two-ounce) bottles of olive oil sitting in a row over behind the bar. They're for customers who want to make a New Orleans-style Italian oyster sauce. Free of ketchup, it's very tasty and doesn't overwhelm the flavor of the oyster.

ITALIAN OYSTER COCKTAIL SAUCE

1 **cup olive oil**
2 **tbsp horseradish**
  juice of ½ lemon
¼ **tsp Tabasco (or more)**
  salt and freshly ground black pepper

Mix the ingredients well, spoon a little of the sauce over each shucked oyster, and swoosh the oyster off the shell. Emily Post and Amy Vanderbilt would never approve of this swooshing business, but it's *de rigueur* in New Orleans, for both ladies and gents.

FRIED OYSTERS I

Frying oysters should be one of the simplest of all culinary tricks, but far from it. Very few cooks can do it just as it should be done. Millions of martyred oysters give their lives each year just to end up as hard brown lumps on dismal seafood platters. Like Charles Lamb's roast pig, the oyster is tender, sensitive, and helpless, and it should be handled with befitting care, taste, and discrimination.

To get the best results in frying oysters, you should use yellow corn flour of the type sold in Italian grocery stores (in Latin American stores it's called masa harina). Never use corn meal, because it's too coarse and will not cook thoroughly in the short time required to fry an oyster. The commercial "fish fries" found in the grocery stores are also too coarse. No batter is required for frying oysters, just the simple flour. The best fat for frying oysters is hog lard, and the next best is vegetable oil. It's good to use a deep-fry pan with a wire basket, though the basket isn't absolutely necessary, since they float on the surface. You can remove the oysters from the fat with a slotted spoon.

So here we go: Preheat the deep fat to about 260°. Season the flour well with salt and pepper. Select medium-fat oysters and drain them. Roll them lightly in the flour, shaking off the excess flour. Fry them in the hot fat for 2½ to 3 minutes, depending on their size. When done, the oyster will be a light golden brown, crisp on the outside but—most important—still juicy on the inside. If the oyster is cooked too long, the natural juices will evaporate, and the oyster will be robbed of its distinctive flavor.

Serve with lemon wedges, tartar sauce, or chili sauce, but please, never put ketchup on a nice tasty oyster.

FRIED OYSTERS II

There's always controversy about frying oysters! Although I disagree emphatically, some culinary artists insist that an oyster *does* need batter, and that cracker crumbs are better than corn flour. So here's one for them.

Add a beaten egg and a dash of Tabasco to a cup of milk and mix well. Dip the oysters in this mixture, then roll them in cracker crumbs, and shake off the excess crumbs. Fry them in deep hot lard until golden. Drain quickly on paper towels and serve at once. *De gustibus*!

THE "PO' BOY" OYSTER LOAF (ALSO CALLED "LA MEDIATRICE," THE PEACEMAKER)

Next to Louis Armstrong, New Orleans's greatest gift to the world is the "po' boy" sandwich. And what a miracle of a sandwich it is— much more delicious than those latecomers up North that are variously called submarines, heroes, and grinders. Originally po' boys were made with oysters, but today you can get them with roast beef, ham, and many other items. Back during the depression, when a dozen oysters cost only five or ten cents, you could get a big oyster po' boy for twenty cents (hence the name). Today the price is more likely to be $4.50, but it's still worth it.

The oyster loaf is also known as "La Mediatrice," or the peacemaker, because when a New Orleans husband came home in the wee hours with no excuse, he always brought a hot oyster loaf for two with him. Could any wife be angry at such a thoughtful spouse? So instead of boxing his ears, she shared the sandwich with him, and all was peace.

A little restaurant out on Magazine Street called Casamento's, which is unique among New Orleans oyster houses, is well known among gourmets. Very small—about 16 feet by fifty feet—it's probably the cleanest and neatest restaurant in America. The walls and floors are sparkling, spotless white tiles, and

Tin Roof Blues

TIN ROOF BLUES

I have seen the bright lights burning up and
*   down old Broadway,*
Seen 'em in gay Havana, Birmingham,
*   Alabama, and say,*
They just can't compare with my hometown
*   New Orleans.*

Chorus
Cause there you'll find the old Tin Roof
*   Cafe,*
Where they play the blues till break of day,
Fascinatin' babies hanging around
Dancing to the meanest band in town,
Lawd, how they can play the blues,
And when that leaderman starts playin low,
Folk get up and start to walk it slow,
Do a lot of movements hard to beat,
Till that old floor man says, "Move your
*   feet!"*
Lawd, I've got those Tin Roof Blues.

Tomorrow evenin' my train is leavin',
I'm going to my sweet mama tomorrow
*   evenin',*
Just like a breeze I'll blow—back to New
*   Orleans,*
Where jazzin' babies grow.

Every day my baby writes to me and says,
"Daddy, please don't you keep your mama
*   grievin',*
Tell me you'll soon be leavin', and please
Bring your dancin' shoes and come on home
*   to me!"*

"The Old Master" by Kenneth Burke

This song is a good example of how the early jazzmen stole one another's material. Originally called *Jazzin' Baby Blues*, it was composed by Joe Oliver, whose band played it frequently in Chicago. Leon Rappolo and the other members of the white New Orleans Rhythm Kings, also playing in Chicago, would come in to listen and learn from King Joe. They memorized *Jazzin' Baby* and brought it out with new lyrics and a new title, *Tin Roof Blues*, which became a hit. Joe Oliver was so mad he tore all the titles off his music after that, so those fellers couldn't tell what he was playing.

the table tops are white Carrara marble. Not only the kitchen but even the restrooms out back are lined with white tile.

The oyster bar up front serves good salty oysters on the half shell, but the real glory of the place is their oyster loaf, probably the best in New Orleans (or in the whole nation for that matter). They use long, thick slices of buttered and toasted Italian pan bread instead of the traditional French loaf, but more important, the oysters inside are cooked perfectly. Mrs. Mary Ann Casamento took me on a tour of the kitchen, where a handsome black lady cook, standing at a small six-burner stove frying the oysters, was so casual and calm that you couldn't believe there were forty people out front drooling and waiting for their oyster loaves. No rush, no muss, no fuss. As a restaurant owner myself, I know that's the only way to run a kitchen, but very few operators can achieve it. And Lord bless my soul, Mrs. Mary Ann showed me confirmation of what I had been preaching for twenty years, that the best way to fry oysters is to use yellow Italian corn flour and hog lard.

My own recipe for making an oyster po' boy for two—that is, the traditional double oyster loaf—calls for an 18-inch loaf of French bread. For one person, use a 10- or 12-inch loaf of bread and a dozen oysters.

PO' BOY OYSTER LOAF
(Serves 2)

2 dozen oysters
1 18″ loaf French bread
butter
corn flour
shredded lettuce (optional)
mayonnaise or chili sauce (optional)

Split the top crust off the loaf of bread about a half inch down. Scoop out a good bit of the soft bread inside the bottom, making a pirogue of it. Brush both the top and bottom pieces with butter and toast lightly under the broiler flame.

Roll the oysters in corn flour, fry in hot lard, and drain. Pile the oysters in the hollowed-out section of bread. If you like, you can cover with a layer of shredded lettuce and swab the inside of the top crust with homemade mayonnaise or chili sauce (but no damn ketchup, remember). Place the lid in position over the filled bottom section. Cut it in half, and it's ready for two peaceable people to eat.

OYSTER PAN ROAST
(Serves 1)

This is what New Orleanians, hurrying to work, often grab for a quick breakfast. But it's also good for lunch, supper, or a midnight snack.

1 dozen oysters and their liquor
¼ stick butter
1 tsp chili sauce
dash of Worcestershire
dash of Tabasco
salt and freshly ground black pepper

Melt the butter in a skillet, add the flavoring elements, and stir them in. Add the oysters and their liquor and cook them just until they're plump and their edges are curled. Place the oysters on slices of toast on a preheated serving plate, and pour the pan juices over them. Anyone who doesn't care for fried oysters will find pan roast oysters ideal for filling the po' boy oyster loaf.

PIGS IN BLANKETS
(An appetizer)

1 dozen oysters
6 slices bacon

Cut the bacon slices in half crosswise, and fry them in a skillet until three-quarters done but still limp. Wrap each bacon piece around an oyster and skewer with a sharp toothpick. Place the wrapped oysters in a broiler pan and broil them on each side until the bacon is browned and the edges of the oysters inside are curled. Bacon and oysters have a great affinity for each other. This dish makes an excellent appetizer or party hors d'oeuvre.

ABOUT OYSTER OMELETS

Batistella's used to have a small restaurant in one of the French Market buildings before the Disneyland remodeling drove all the nice old-time places away. Their sign out front boasted "We invented the po' boy sandwich." That's a big mouthful and very hard to prove, but since

their husky breakfasts featured hot biscuits, sausage, and blackstrap molasses, the place was always crowded with longshoremen in the early morning. And I was often there to eat their tasty oyster omelets. One morning as the cook was fixing my omelet, I suggested, "How 'bout crumbling up a strip of bacon in those oysters?" He did, and it was the best omelet I had ever eaten. It's still my favorite.

OYSTER OMELET
(Serves 1)

4 oysters, cut in quarters
1 slice bacon
2 eggs
1 tsp cream
salt and freshly ground black pepper

Fry the slice of bacon brown, drain it, and crumble it. Pour off most of the bacon fat in the skillet, add the chopped oysters, and cook for only two minutes. Add the crumbled bacon to the oysters, and set aside. Beat the eggs with the cream, and pour into a buttered skillet or omelet pan. Make the omelet in the usual manner, using the oyster-bacon mixture for filling.

OYSTERS EN BROCHETTE
(Serves 4 to 6)

36 oysters, shucked
12 slices bacon
36 thick slices fresh mushrooms

corn flour
2 sticks butter, melted
juice of 2 lemons
2 tbsp chopped parsley
cayenne
salt and freshly ground black pepper

Fry the bacon in a skillet until three-quarters done but still limp. Cut each slice into three pieces and set aside. Melt the butter in a saucepan, and add the lemon juice, cayenne, salt, and black pepper. (This is a version of the famous Maître d'hotel butter.) Dip the slices of mushroom in the butter sauce and coat them. Dip the oysters in the sauce and coat them. Sprinkle the oysters lightly with a thin coat of corn flour.

Use six small skewers. Fold a piece of bacon double and spear it on the skewer. Add an oyster, spearing it through the adductor muscle, or "eye." Add a slice of mushroom. Continue in this manner until you have six of each item on each skewer. There are several ways to proceed from here. You can grill the skewers on a barbecue grill or hibachi, broil them on a buttered cookie tin under the broiler flame (turning once), or fry them gently in butter in a large skillet. The important thing is not to overcook the oysters. Cook only until they are lightly browned and the bacon is crisp. Place six slices of trimmed toast on pre-heated serving plates, and unload the cooked pieces onto the toast. Heat what's left of the lemon-butter sauce in a saucepan, and add the chopped parsley. Pour equal amounts of this sauce over each serving.

OYSTER PIE
(VOL AU VENT)
(Serves 4 to 6)

Creoles and Cajuns have a special kind of pie called a *vol au vent*. A round hole two or three inches in diameter is cut in the center of the top crust to serve as a vent. The piece of removed crust is baked, too, and at the end is replaced in the hole.

2 unbaked pie crust shells
4 dozen oysters (about 2 pints) and
  their liquor
3 slices bacon
1 stick butter
3 tbsp cornstarch
2 scallions with 3″ of their green leaves,
  sliced thin
1 small onion, minced
½ small green pepper, minced
1 small rib celery, minced
4 fresh mushrooms, chopped
3 tbsp chopped fresh parsley
1 tbsp lemon juice
¼ tsp cayenne
1 oz Cognac
  salt and freshly ground black pepper to
  taste
  chicken broth or bouillon

Fry the bacon brown and crisp. Drain, cool, crumble, and set aside. Melt the butter in a skillet, add the cornstarch, and blend well. Add the scallions, onion, green pepper, celery, mushrooms, parsley, crumbled bacon, and

Cognac, and cook until the vegetables are soft and transparent. Add the cayenne and black pepper. Add the oysters and their liquor and cook for five minutes more, stirring well to mix thoroughly. Test for saltiness and add more salt if necessary. If the mixture is too thick and heavy, add some chicken broth, bouillon, or plain water. Place the mixture in a pie crust shell. Cut a hole two to three inches in diameter in the center of the top shell. (Save the cut-out circle and bake it, too.) Trim the edges of the pie, and then seal them by moistening and pressing down with the tines of a fork. Glaze the top by brushing with egg or milk. Bake in a preheated 400° oven for 30 to 45 minutes, or until the top is browned. Replace the baked circle of crust in the hole, and serve the pie piping hot.

OF ROCK SALT, SHELLS, AND SAUCES

In the golden age of the Creole aristocracy, when the sugar and cotton plantations were bringing in enormous wealth (1840s and 1850s), the sons of *la famille* were often sent to Paris to be educated and given "polish." Most of them were playboys, and they didn't learn much, but they acquired a rich patina of social graces (and disgraces) that would flavor Creole culture when they got back home. One can imagine a patois dialogue between a just-returned son and his father:

PERE: Alors, mon fils, mais qu'est que t'as gagné à Paris? (*Well, my son, and what did you learn in Paris?*)

SON: Eh bien, mon père, les livres ataient gros, mais j'ai dancé la Mazurka, jové aux craps, et j'appris la recette pour la sauce Mornay. (*Well, Papa, the books were pretty dull, but I learned to dance the mazurka, shoot craps, and make a Mornay sauce.*)

PERE: Très bien! C'est assez et mieux que j'ai fait à ton age. Visite la belle Celestine la dites: ce soir premier fois, Huîtres Mornay. (*Very good! That ought to be enough to get you by. Go into the kitchen and teach Celestine how to make that Mornay thing, and tonight we'll try it on some oysters.*)

The favorite way to cook oysters in New Orleans is to place the oysters on the half shell on a bed of rock salt, cover with a layer of sauce, and bake them in the oven. Some of these sauces are very old, going back to the early part of the nineteenth century.

The most famous dish of all is Oysters Rockefeller, invented (or developed) around 1900 by Mr. Jules Alciatore, owner of Antoine's restaurant and son of the founder. Mr. Jules, a creative genius, invented many of the seafood dishes that became New Orleans classics, such as Pompano en Papillote. Many food historians say that Mr. Jules got the idea for Rockefeller sauce from the green sauce that had been used for years to make Escargots Bourguignonne, but I'm inclined to disagree. I believe he got the idea from Oysters Florentine, a very popular Parisian dish that had been introduced very early to New Orleanians by some imported chef or by one of the returning "educated" sons. It's a very simple dish: a layer of spinach on an oyster shell, then an oyster, then a layer of Mornay sauce. I can well imagine Mr. Jules taking a piercing look at an Oyster Florentine and saying, "Throw out that Mornay, and put the oyster on the bottom and the spinach on top." And presto! Oysters Rockefeller were invented. He is said to have given the dish that name because it tasted so rich. Antoine's has never divulged the secret of their Rockefeller sauce, but your taste buds can tell that it's very simple, because it doesn't overwhelm the flavor of the oyster.

Nowadays there are as many Rockefeller sauces as there are restaurants, and they all taste different. At Antoine's it tastes like spinach, at Galatoire's it has a strong flavor of parsley, and at Chez Helene, the famous soul food restaurant, the Rockefellers taste so good that one is inclined to think they must put a little *gris gris* (voodoo potion) in the sauce.

In addition to the spinach and parsley that seem to be standard, some cooks load their Rockefeller sauces with green scallion leaves, green pepper, celery, lettuce, watercress, and even squash and mirliton, plus herbs and spices. I don't belong to that school of thought myself, but just to be fair to everybody, I'll give you some of those recipes.

Among the most famous of the rock salt–half-shell oyster dishes, one must list Oysters Rockefeller, Bienville, Roffignac, Florentine, and several Italian types, which use garlic generously. The old La Louisiane Restaurant (whose co-owner was an Alciatore) used a sauce made of ground walnuts, but the records don't reveal whether they were English walnuts or our native black walnuts, both of which have great culinary possibilities. The creative cooks of New Orleans are constantly coming up with new types and new names, but let's face it, the old classics are usually the best.

OYSTERS ROCKEFELLER
(Serves 4 as appetizer, or 2 as a full dinner)

Because I believe Rockefeller sauce should be kept very simple, with only spinach and a little parsley for the greens, I have developed the following recipe and used it in my own restaurant for several years without a complaint. On the contrary, pretty girls have rushed into the kitchen to kiss me, and that's a real chef's bonus, a spinachy kiss.

2 dozen oysters on the shell
1 large bunch fresh spinach
½ cup chopped parsley
1 stick butter
½ cup bread crumbs
2 tbsp Worcestershire sauce
¼ tsp Tabasco
1 tsp anchovy paste (or 2 fillets, chopped fine)
1 oz Pernod (or Herbsaint or Ouzo)
Parmesan cheese
rock salt

Wash the mud off the outside of the oysters in the shell. Open them and hold them over a mixing bowl to catch every bit of their juice. Wash the oysters in their own juice, removing any shell particles or sand, and set them aside. Strain the juice through triple cheesecloth and set it aside. Wash the deep halves of the oyster shells and set aside.

Wash and stem the spinach leaves. Melt the stick of butter in a skillet, and cook the spinach and parsley until soft. Add the bread crumbs, Worcestershire, Tabasco, anchovy paste, and Pernod. Mix well and cook for a couple of minutes longer for the elements to blend. Place this mixture in an electric blender and cream it. (Or if, as some gourmets do, you like a little texture in your Rockefeller sauce, beat it with an eggbeater instead of putting it in the blender.) Set aside.

Place a thick layer of rock salt in the bottom of each of four tin pie pans. Place six of the deep shells on the salt in each pan. Lay an oyster on each shell. Place these exposed oysters under the broiler flame for a minute, just long enough to make their edges curl slightly. Remove from the broiler and add a teaspoon of oyster juice to each oyster on a shell. Cover each oyster completely with the spinach sauce (about a tablespoon). Sprinkle just a pinch of Parmesan cheese on top of each. Bake them in a preheated 400° oven for about five minutes, or until thoroughly heated through. Remove from the oven and place under the broiler flame until the spinach is very lightly browned. Serve piping hot in the pan on the bed of rock salt. Caution the guests to let them cool a few minutes before attacking them.

This is a festive dish, and the sense of euphoria can be heightened by a good Champagne —Pol Roger, Piper Heidsieck, Mumm's Extra Dry, or whatever your conscience allows you.

About the pans: The old-fashioned nine- or ten-inch tin pans are the best. They last forever. The pans at Antoine's are so black from use that they seem to be fifty years old. Modern foil pans can be used, but they have to be handled very carefully or they'll fold and tilt and throw their contents on the floor.

About the salt: Rock salt or ice cream salt is the best. Morton's makes a good coarse kosher salt that works very well. Lacking these, you can use plain table salt. Salt serves two purposes: It keeps the shells from tilting and spilling their contents, and it retains heat and keeps the shells hot. Actually, the salt isn't absolutely necessary. A skillful cook can arrange the oysters in the pan and bake them without using any salt at all.

If you want to be thrifty, as many of the most famous restaurants are, it helps to know that rock salt can be washed and sterilized and used over and over again.

About the Pernod: Oysters Rockefeller was originally made with real absinthe, a licorice-flavored drink made from wormwood, which was a great favorite in France and in New Orleans. But because wormwood was a powerful narcotic, like opium, and very habit-forming, the drink was banned worldwide. Of the passable substitutes today—Pernod, Ouzo, and Herbsaint—Pernod is best. Don't overuse it, because its piercing flavor can damage a sauce if the cook is too generous.

NOTE: Many cooks make Rockefeller sauce in large quantities and freeze it in small packages so that it will be immediately available when unexpected oysters drop in.

OYSTERS BIENVILLE
(Serves 4 as appetizer, 2 as dinner)

Oysters Bienville are almost as good as Rockefellers, and in fact, some gourmets prefer them. Just to give both types a chance, many restaurants serve a "6 × 6," that is, 3 Bienvilles and 3 Rockefellers on the same pan. Brennan's even serves a 2 × 2 × 2, or 2 Rockefellers, 2 Bienvilles, and 2 Roffignacs.

Arnaud's Restaurant has always been a staunch proponent of Oysters Bienville, and connoisseurs have come from near and far to feast on them. A good many years ago, Mrs. Germaine Cazenave Wells, Arnaud's owner, game me her recipe, which runs like this:

2 dozen oysters on the half shell
4 scallions with 2″ of their green leaves, finely chopped (or 1 medium onion, finely minced)
3 tbsp flour
2 tbsp butter
½ cup chicken or fish broth
1 lb peeled shrimp, chopped
1 cup chopped fresh mushrooms
3 egg yolks
¼ cup white wine
½ cup cream
dash of Tabasco
salt and pepper to taste
rock salt
bread crumbs, paprika, and Parmesan cheese, mixed

Prepare the Bienville white wine sauce in advance, as follows: Cook the scallions in butter until golden, add the flour, browning it slightly, add the broth, and stir. Add the mushrooms and the chopped shrimp, stir, and cook for a couple of minutes. Beat well together the egg yolks, the wine, and the cream, and put them into the sauce, stirring rapidly to prevent curdling. Add the Tabasco, salt, and pepper. Cook slowly 10 to 15 minutes.

While the sauce is cooking, place rock salt on four tin pie pans. Place six oysters on the deep side of their shells on top of the salt in each pan. Bake until the oysters are about half done (7 minutes). Spoon the Bienville sauce over the oysters, covering each oyster well with a layer of it. Sprinkle with mixed bread crumbs, paprika, and Parmesan cheese. Bake in the oven until light brown, and serve at once. A fine Chablis is the wine the French like best with oysters. It goes very well with Oysters Bienville, named in honor of that stalwart son of France who founded New Orleans.

OYSTERS ROFFIGNAC
(Serves 4)

In the days before the Civil War, one of the best restaurants in New Orleans was Roffignac's, at the corner of Royal and St. Peter Streets, catty-corner across from the Skyscraper (there's a supermarket on the spot now). The restaurant was owned by the family of Count Louis Philippe de Roffignac, a French refugee who was mayor of New Orleans in the 1820s. They invented Oysters Roffignac, one of the earliest of the oysters-in-the-shell-with-sauce dishes served in the city.

2 dozen fresh oysters in their shells
½ lb peeled boiled shrimp (about a lb raw shrimp in the shell)
6 scallions with 2″ of their green leaves, thinly sliced
8 fresh mushrooms, chopped
2 cloves garlic, put through a garlic press

1 stick butter
2 tbsp cornstarch
1 tbsp paprika
¼ tsp cayenne
1 tbsp lemon juice
¼ cup dry red wine
    salt and freshly ground black pepper to
    taste

Wash the mud off the outside of the oysters in the shell. Open them, holding them over a bowl to catch every bit of their juice. Wash the oysters in their own juice, removing any shell particles or sand, and set them aside. Strain the juice through triple cheesecloth, and set it aside. Wash the deep halves of the oyster shells, and set them aside.

Boil a pound of fresh shrimp in the shell for three minutes. Peel, chop them in quarter-inch pieces, and set aside.

Melt the butter in a skillet, add the cornstarch, and stir well to blend. Add the scallions, garlic, chopped mushrooms, paprika, cayenne, lemon juice, wine, oyster juice, and salt and black pepper. Cook slowly until the vegetables are soft. Add a little fish stock or chicken broth if it's too dry. Stir in the shrimp pieces.

Place the mixture in an electric blender and chop. Don't cream it, though, because it should have a bit of texture to it.

Put a thick layer of rock salt in the bottom of each of four tin pie pans. Place one oyster on each shell, six shells to a pan. Run the exposed oysters under the broiler flame for a minute, just enough to heat them through and slightly curl their edges. Remove from the broiler, and cover each oyster completely with the sauce. Bake them in a preheated 400°

oven for about five minutes, or until thoroughly heated through, remove from the oven, and place under the broiler flame until the tops are lightly browned. Serve piping hot in the pan on the bed of rock salt. Caution the guests to let them cool a moment before trying to eat them because they're very hot.

OYSTERS FLORENTINE
(Serves 4)

This dish has been a long-time favorite among the epicures of Paris. Young Creole blades who went to school in Paris brought the idea back to New Orleans. In the world of cuisine, "Florentine" almost always means with spinach.

2 dozen oysters
½ stick butter
¼ cup flour
½ cup fish stock or chicken broth
2 egg yolks
¼ cup grated Swiss cheese
1 cup cream
1 bunch fresh spinach (or 2 pkg frozen)
    salt and freshly ground black pepper to
    taste

Melt the butter in a skillet, add the flour, and cook slowly, stirring constantly until thoroughly blended. Now mix in the fish stock or chicken broth. Beat the cream and egg yolks together and add them. Add the grated Swiss cheese. Cook over very low heat for 10 minutes more, stirring constantly. Season with salt and black pepper. This is a version of Mornay sauce, the classic French sauce for fish or shellfish. Cook a bunch of spinach in butter, and add salt and pepper to taste. Cream in the blender or with an eggbeater. Lay the deep halves of oyster shells on rock salt in pans. Cover the shells with a layer of spinach, place an oyster on top of each, and cook under the broiler flame for three to five minutes, or until the edges of the oysters curl. Cover the oysters with the Mornay sauce. Place under the broiler flame for a moment until the tops are glazed and lightly browned. Sprinkle with paprika and serve at once in the cooking pans.

OYSTERS CASINO
(Serves 4 as appetizer, 2 as full dinner)

2 dozen fresh oysters on the half shell
1 stick butter
6 slices bacon, cut in quarters
½ cup grated onion
½ cup chopped fresh parsley
1 cup diced green pepper
2 cloves garlic, minced
1 tsp anchovy paste (or chopped fillets)
  dash of Tabasco
  salt and freshly ground black pepper to
  taste

Fry the bacon pieces until they are three-quarters done but still limp, and set aside. Discard the bacon fat from the skillet. Melt the butter, and cook the green pepper, onion, parsley, and garlic. Add the anchovy paste. Season with Tabasco, salt, and black pepper. Place the oysters on the deep sides of their shells (along with their liquor if any is available)

on rock salt in tin pie pans. Cover each oyster completely with the sauce. Place a small piece of bacon on top of the sauce on each oyster. Bake in a preheated 400° oven until lightly browned and the bacon is crisp.

BAKED OYSTERS WITH WILD RICE
(Serves 2 to 4)

Wild rice, which is not a relative of domesticated rice, is a seed that grows wild on the margins of lakes in Minnesota and Michigan. Long ago the government gave the Indians a monopoly on the wild rice trade, and they're the only ones who may legally harvest it. It's very scarce and very expensive, and it's usually mixed with ordinary rice to bring its price down. However, on payday, when you want to splurge on something really good, use the wild rice pure and unadulterated, as instructed in this recipe.

2 dozen oysters on the half shell and their
  liquor
1 cup wild rice
¾ stick butter
½ green pepper, finely chopped
1 cup fresh chopped mushrooms
4 tbsp fresh parsley, chopped
¼ tsp Tabasco
¼ cup sherry
1 tbsp lemon juice
  salt and freshly ground black pepper

Wash the wild rice thoroughly to get rid of any trash that may be mixed in with it. Drain it.

NEW ORLEANS FUNERALS

Photo by Johnny Donnels

JUST A CLOSER WALK

Just a closer walk with thee,
Grant it, Jesus, if you please,
Daily walking close to thee
Let it be, dear Lord, let it be.

Through the days of toil that's near
If I fall, dear Lord, who cares?
Who with me my burden shares,
None but thee, dear Lord, none but thee.

When my feeble life is o'er,
Time for me will be no more.
Guide me gently, safely on,
To thy shore, dear Lord, to thy shore.

Traditional

The Second Liners

Even in French colonial days, it was a New Orleans custom to have a brass marching band in funeral parades. The Negroes adopted the idea from the Frenchmen, and it became something of a ritual with them.

After the Civil War, when musical instruments became more widely available, the Negroes formed brass marching bands all over the city, and no funeral in New Orleans was complete without music. The fraternal orders and burial societies all vied with one another to see who could give their members the best send-off. On the way from the funeral home to the cemetery, the bands played solemn hymns and dirges (Louis Armstrong said that Bunk Johnson could play a hymn so sad and beautiful that it would make everybody cry.) On the way back from the cemetery, the band would cut loose and play wild free stuff like *Didn't He Ramble* and *Muskrat Ramble*.

The groups of dancing kids and spectators who follow the band are called "The Second Line," and they're a tradition at all funeral parades, carrying umbrellas, beating on tambourines, blowing tin flutes, and generally making themselves seen and heard. Sometimes the Second Liners get so wild and rambunctious that many funeral home directors have been talking about cutting them out of the picture, but the custom is so well established that they can't do much about it. Shucks, a jazz funeral parade wouldn't be no fun without the Second Liners!

Photo by Johnny Donnels

Bring four cups of water to a boil, and add a half stick of butter and a teaspoon of salt. Add the wild rice and stir. Turn the heat very low, cover the pot, and cook slowly for 45 minutes. Do not stir. At the end place the pot in a moderate oven, uncovered, for five to ten minutes to get rid of excess moisture.

Melt a quarter stick of butter in a skillet, and cook the green pepper, mushrooms, and parsley until soft and transparent. Season with Tabasco, a little salt, and black pepper. When the rice is cooked, mix the vegetables with it. Put a layer of the rice mixture on the deep bottom shells of the oysters, and place the shells on pans of rock salt. Lay an oyster on top of each shell. Spoon a little melted butter over each oyster. Mix the sherry and lemon juice with the oyster liquor, and spoon a little of the mixture over each oyster. Bake in a preheated 350° oven until the edges of the oysters curl. Dust with paprika and serve at once in the pans they were baked in.

OYSTERS BENEDICT
(Serves 2)

- **2 dozen oysters and their liquor**
- **¼ stick butter**
- **4 thin slices country ham (or cooked ham, prosciutto, or Canadian bacon)**
- **4 slices trimmed toast or Holland rusks**
- **1½ cups Hollandaise sauce**
  salt and freshly ground black pepper to taste

The slices of country ham must be thin. Cook the slices in a covered skillet very slowly for 20 minutes. Slow cooking brings out the full flavor

of the ham (other types of ham or Canadian bacon will not need to be cooked as long). Set the ham aside and keep it warm. Melt the butter in a skillet and add the oysters and their liquor. Season with pepper and, if necessary, a little salt (remember that the oyster liquor is salty). Cook over low heat until the oysters are plump and their edges curled. Place two slices of trimmed toast (or rusks) on each of two preheated serving plates. Lay a slice of ham on each piece of toast. Place a dozen oysters on the ham on each plate. Pour a little of the pan juices over the oysters. Spread ¾ cup Hollandaise sauce on top of the oysters of each serving. Serve at once, piping hot. This makes a terrific breakfast, but it's regal enough to serve at a state dinner.

OYSTERS A LA POULETTE
(Serves 2 to 4)

In Creole cookery the term *à la poulette* always means with eggs, although "poulette" literally means pullet, or chicken.

- **2 dozen oysters and their liquor (about a pint)**
- **2 scallions with 3″ of their green leaves, chopped very fine**
- **1 clove garlic, put through a garlic press**
- **2 tbsp chopped fresh parsley**
- **3 egg yolks, beaten**
- **½ stick butter**
- **3 tbsp flour**
- **½ cup cream**

⅛ tsp each ground cloves, ground
  allspice, mace
¼ cup sherry
  salt and freshly ground black pepper
4 slices trimmed toast or Holland rusks

Melt the butter in a skillet, stir in the flour, and cook slowly for about 10 minutes to get rid of a "floury" taste, stirring constantly. Add the scallions, parsley, garlic, cloves, allspice, mace, some black pepper, and a little salt. Add the oysters and their liquor. Cook slowly until the oysters are plump and their edges curled. Cut the heat very low. Mix the egg yolks, cream, and sherry together in a small mixing bowl. Add a tablespoon of the hot skillet sauce to the bowl and stir rapidly. Then empty the bowl into the skillet, stirring rapidly again to prevent curdling. Don't boil again, just heat through, or your "poulettes" will become scrambled eggs. Place the oysters on toast or Holland rusks, and pour the pan sauce over them.

OYSTERS AND ARTICHOKES CASSEROLE
(Serves 6)

4 dozen oysters and their liquor
4 large artichokes
½ stick butter
3 tbsp cornstarch
2 tbsp chopped parsley
2 scallions with 2″ of their green leaves,
  finely sliced
1 clove garlic, minced
¼ tsp basil
¼ tsp thyme
  dash of Tabasco

½ cup heavy cream
¼ cup sherry
  salt and freshly ground black pepper
  pastry shells
  bread crumbs
  butter

Boil the artichokes in salted water for an hour, or until soft and tender. Remove from the pot and cool. Scrape the artichoke leaves, saving the pulp. Chop the artichoke bottoms into quarter-inch cubes, and set aside. Melt the butter, add the cornstarch, and make a light roux, stirring 15 minutes over a low flame. Add the parsley, scallions, and garlic, and cook until soft. Add the artichokes, basil, thyme, Tabasco, and black pepper. Add the oysters and their liquor (if the oysters are large, cut them in half). Cook until the edges of the oysters curl. Add the cream and the sherry. Adjust the salt. Divide the mixture into six portions, as required. Place in pastry shells or individual casseroles, sprinkle with bread crumbs, dot with butter, and bake in a preheated 400° oven until the tops are browned.

MARSHALL'S OYSTERS EN CASSEROLE
(Serves 2 to 4)

Walter Stauffer McIlhenny, the president of the company that makes Tabasco, gave me this recipe. Some wizard named Marshall invented the beautiful dish. (He must have been in his cups and just goofing around. That's how most great dishes are discovered.) Here the common saltine cracker reaches a pinnacle of fame it will probably never know again.

2 dozen oysters
12 saltines
½ stick butter
3 tbsp olive oil
½ cup onion, chopped
2 cloves garlic, minced
2 hard-boiled eggs, sliced
1½ cups heavy white sauce
¾ cup fresh mushrooms, chopped
¼ tsp Tabasco
    sharp Cheddar cheese, grated

¼ cup grated onion
1 stick butter, melted
½ cup light cream
1 cup cracker crumbs
1 tsp Worcestershire sauce
1 tbsp lemon juice
    Tabasco
    salt and freshly ground black pepper
    paprika

Put saltines, butter, olive oil, onion, and garlic in a casserole in preheated 300° oven. Bake and stir until the crackers are golden brown. While the saltines are toasting, cook the eggs hard and make the white sauce. Drain the oysters, and put the liquor in the white sauce for added zip. When the saltines have reached a rich golden brown, fold all the other ingredients, including the oysters, into the white sauce, and add it to the things already in the casserole, mixing gently. Sprinkle a layer of sharp Cheddar over the top, raise the oven to 350°, and bake until the cheese melts, or the edges of the oysters curl. It tastes great! Just as a variation, we once tried old-fashioned thin-split beaten biscuits as a substitute for the saltines. It was difficult but still very tasty.

Place a layer of two dozen oysters in the bottom of a greased shallow baking dish. Sprinkle with half the melted butter, half the parsley, half the onion, half the cracker crumbs, and half the seasonings. Repeat with another identical layer of everything. Sprinkle the top generously with paprika. Pour the cream in at the corners, being careful not to wet the crumb topping. Bake in a preheated 375° oven for 20-25 minutes, or until firm and the top is browned.

OYSTERS "JOHNNY REB"
(Serves 4 to 6)

1 quart oysters, drained (about 4 dozen)
¼ cup fresh parsley, chopped

OYSTER STEW I (VERY PLAIN)
(Serves 1)

The purists believe that the best oyster stew is the very plain one—only oysters, milk, and a little butter to cook the oysters in. Here's how it's done.

1 dozen oysters
¼ cup oyster liquor
1 cup milk
2 tbsp butter
    salt and freshly ground black pepper to taste

Melt the butter in a skillet and add the oyster liquor. Cook the oysters slowly in this fluid, stirring them around and turning them over. Cook only until the oysters are plump and their edges curled. Meantime, be heating the milk in a small saucepan. Bring it to just this side of the boiling point, but don't boil. Add the oysters and pan juices to the milk, and cook one minute longer to blend. Serve in a preheated soup bowl. Add black pepper, taste it, and if necessary, add salt. Sometimes the oyster liquor is so salty that no more salt is needed.

This stew is not only one of the tastiest, healthiest dishes in the world but also a famous cure for hangover or impotence.

However, not everybody likes oyster stew so plain. There are dozens of ways of making it, and I'll give you a few here. They may sound alike, but the flavor of each is a little different.

OYSTER STEW II
(Serves 1)

Substitute cream for milk in the recipe above for a richer stew with more body.

OYSTER STEW III
(Serves 2)

2 dozen oysters (if small, use 3 dozen; about 1½ pints)
½ cup oyster liquor
6 scallions with 2″ of their green leaves, sliced very thin

½ stick butter
1 quart milk (or 1 pint milk and 1 pint cream)
⅛ tsp ground thyme
salt and freshly ground black pepper
paprika
chopped parsley or chives

Melt the butter in a saucepan, and cook the scallions until they're soft and transparent. Add the thyme. Add the oysters and their liquor, and cook gently until their edges curl. Meanwhile, heat the milk (or milk-cream) in a separate saucepan to just this side of the boiling point, add to the oysters, and cook just a minute longer. Add black pepper, and adjust the salt. Ladle into two preheated soup bowls, dividing the oysters equally. Sprinkle a pinch of chopped parsley (or chopped scallion leaves or chives) and a dash of paprika on top of each bowl.

OYSTER STEW IV
(Serves 2 to 4)

2 dozen oysters (about a pint)
½ cup oyster liquor
3 tbsp butter
2 tbsp cornstarch
2 cups milk
2 tbsp grated onion
⅛ tsp thyme
⅛ tsp cayenne
2 bay leaves
salt and freshly ground black pepper to taste

Cut the oysters into quarters and set aside.

Melt the butter in a saucepan, add the cornstarch, and blend. Add the onion, thyme, cayenne, and bay leaves. Add the oysters and the oyster liquor. Season with black pepper and cook for 10 minutes. Meanwhile, heat the milk in another saucepan but don't boil it. Add it to the oyster mixture, and cook for five minutes longer over low heat, stirring and blending thoroughly. Remove the bay leaves. Adjust the salt. Serve in preheated soup bowls. Garnish with finely chopped green scallion leaves (or chives or parsley) and a dash of paprika.

OYSTER STEW V
(Serves 2 to 4)

  2 dozen oysters and their liquor (about a pint)
  1 small onion, grated
  1 stalk celery, grated
  ½ small clove of garlic, put through garlic press
  1 pint light cream
  ¼ stick butter
  1 tbsp flour
  2 tbsp sherry
  ⅛ tsp cayenne
  salt and freshly ground black pepper

Melt the butter in a skillet, add the flour, and stir until well blended. Add the onion, celery, and garlic, and cook for five minutes. Add the cayenne. Add the oysters and their liquor. Cook, stirring until the oysters are plump and

their edges are curled. Add the cream slowly, stirring vigorously to keep it from curdling. Mix in the sherry. Serve in preheated soup bowls. For garnish, float a small lump of butter on top of the stew in each bowl, along with a pinch of chopped parsley and a dash of paprika.

OYSTER-BEEF STEW
(Serves 4 to 6)

This dish was popular in New Orleans a hundred years ago, and it's as good now as it was then.

  4 dozen oysters (2 pints) and their liquor
  1 lb tender beefsteak, cut in ½″ cubes
  1 16-oz can beef broth (more if necessary)
  1 stick butter
  ¼ tsp cayenne
  ½ cup chopped fresh parsley
  salt and freshly ground black pepper
  nutmeg, mace, thyme
  flour

Put some flour in a paper bag, and season it with salt and pepper. Trim all the fat from the beef cubes, put them in the bag, and shake well. Remove and shake off excess flour. Melt the stick of butter in a stew pot or Dutch oven, add the beef, and sear it on all sides. Lower the heat and add the beef broth and a cup of water to the pot. Simmer for an hour or more, skimming it now and then and stirring from the bottom of the pot to keep it from sticking. Add the cayenne. Season with a pinch each of thyme, nutmeg, mace, and black pepper. Add the parsley. Toward the end, add the oysters and their liquor, and cook for 10 minutes more, or until the oysters are plump and their edges curled. Serve in preheated soup bowls with chopped green scallion tops generously sprinkled on top.

OYSTER BISQUE
(Serves 4)

We must not forget that the Gulf Coast of Mississippi, Alabama, and Florida is Creole country, too. Iberville established the first French colony in the Mississippi Valley in 1703 when he built Fort Maurepas at the site of the present Ocean Springs, Mississippi, across the bay from Biloxi. This is great oyster and shrimp country. A good many years ago, Mrs. Trilby French Steiner took over an antebellum mansion at Ocean Springs and transformed it into one of the best Creole restaurants on the Gulf Coast. Her specialty, of course, is native seafoods. She called it—what else?—Trilby's. Twenty years ago she gave me her recipe for Oyster Bisque, and I still have it tacked to my kitchen wall.

1 quart shucked oysters (4 to 5 dozen)
    and their liquor (about a pint)
1 pint half-and-half cream
3 tbsp flour
½ stick butter
    Tabasco
4 tbsp sherry
    salt and freshly ground black pepper
    to taste

Melt the butter, add the flour, and make a light roux. Add the cream slowly and stir until very smooth. As the mixture thickens, add a little oyster liquor, and keep adding the liquor until it's medium thick. Add salt, black pepper, and a dash of Tabasco, but be careful with the salt because the oyster liquor may be very salty. At the last, add the oysters, which have been put through the medium blade of the grinder (or you can chop them by hand). As a final touch, add the sherry. Cook for 10 minutes more. Serve in preheated soup bowls.

CREOLE OYSTER SOUP
(Serves 2 to 4)

1 pint oysters and their liquor (about 2
    dozen)
¼ stick butter
2 tbsp flour
1 inside rib celery, finely diced
1 cup light cream
1 small onion, minced
½ small green pepper, finely chopped
1 tbsp fresh parsley, chopped
2 bay leaves
    pinch each of thyme and cayenne
    salt and freshly ground black pepper

Melt the butter in a saucepan, add the flour, and cook slowly, stirring five minutes to make a light roux. Add the celery, onion, green pepper, parsley, bay leaves, thyme, and cayenne. Cook, stirring constantly, until the vegetables are soft and transparent. Season with a little salt and black pepper (remember that the oyster liquor is salty). Add the oyster liquor. Chop the oysters and add them. Simmer until the oysters are cooked, about 10 minutes. Remove from the fire, and add the cream slowly, stirring rapidly to prevent curdling. Remove the bay leaves. Return to the fire and heat thoroughly but don't boil. Serve in preheated soup bowls garnished with a pinch of chopped parsley, a little piece of butter, and a dash of paprika.

OYSTER-MUSHROOM SOUP
(Serves 4 to 6)

1 quart oysters (about 4 dozen) and their liquor (about a cup)
½ lb mushrooms, sliced
¼ stick butter
2 tbsp flour
1 cup milk
1 cup cream
2 scallions with 3″ of their green leaves, finely chopped
1 tbsp parsley, chopped
salt and freshly ground black pepper to taste

Cook the oysters and their liquor in a saucepan over low heat until the edges curl. Melt the butter in a skillet, add the flour, blend well, and cook slowly for five minutes. Add the scallions and parsley, and cook until they're wilted. Season to taste with salt and pepper. Add the mushrooms, and heat them just through. Add the milk and cream slowly, stirring constantly, and cook until the mixture

thickens a little, but don't boil it. Add the cream sauce to the oysters and their liquor in the saucepan. Heat thoroughly without boiling, and serve at once in preheated soup bowls.

CREOLE OYSTER-ARTICHOKE SOUP
(Serves 8 as full dinner, 16 as appetizer)

4 pints oysters (about 8 dozen) and their liquor (about a pint)
2 16-oz cans artichoke hearts
1 stick butter
8 tbsp flour
4 small cloves garlic, minced
6 tbsp finely chopped parsley
1 cup scallions with their green leaves, finely sliced
1 cup chopped fresh mushrooms
¼ tsp mace
¼ tsp thyme
¼ tsp cayenne
1 pint half-and-half cream
1 pint fresh milk
1 pint evaporated milk
½ cup sherry
chicken broth, if needed
salt and freshly ground black pepper to taste
cornstarch, if needed

In a Dutch oven, melt the butter, add the flour, and cook slowly to make a russet brown roux. Add the scallions and garlic, and cook until limp. Add the mushrooms, parsley, mace, thyme, and cayenne. Chop the artichoke hearts and add them to the pot. Cook for 10 minutes, stirring now and then. Add the fresh milk, half-and-half, evaporated milk, and oyster liquor. Cook over low heat for 10 minutes, stirring frequently. Add the sherry. Cut the oysters into quarters, add them to the pot, and cook over low heat 10 to 15 minutes more. Season to taste with salt and black pepper. It should be very salty and zesty. It should also be thick and creamy, so if it lacks body, mix some cornstarch with cold water, and add it to the pot as a thickener.

NOTE: The artichoke flavor will be more pronounced if fresh artichokes are used to make this soup. Boil six artichokes for an hour. Scrape the pulp from the leaves, finely chop the artichoke bottoms, and add these to the soup instead of the artichoke hearts.

A WILD OYSTER SOUP
(Serves 6)

3 pints oysters (about 6 dozen) and
  their liquor
2 large fresh artichokes
1 lb fresh green Italian-type asparagus
  spears
1 lb fresh mushrooms, chopped
2 scallions with their green leaves, minced
2 cloves garlic, minced
½ cup fresh chopped parsley
1 stick butter
4 tbsp cornstarch

1 pint or more light cream (or half-and-
  half)
½ tsp thyme
¼ tsp cayenne
  sherry
salt and freshly ground black pepper to
taste

Cover the artichokes with two quarts of unsalted water, and boil for an hour or until tender. Remove and cool. Save the water. Boil the asparagus spears and mushrooms in the same water for 20 minutes. Remove and cool, and again save the water, which by now is on the way to being a damn tasty soup stock. Scrape the artichoke leaves, saving the pulp. Finely mince the bottoms of the artichokes and set aside. Cut the hard bottoms off the asparagus and discard. Finely mince the top parts of the asparagus and set aside. Also set the chopped mushrooms aside.

Make a light russet-colored roux by melting the butter in a skillet, adding the cornstarch, and stirring constantly over a low flame for 15 to 20 minutes. (This is how the great Escoffier made roux, using cornstarch instead of flour.) When the roux is golden, add the scallions, garlic, and parsley, and cook slowly and constantly until the vegetables are soft and transparent. Add the artichoke pulp, the chopped artichoke bottoms, the asparagus, and the chopped mushrooms, thyme, cayenne, and black pepper. Add two cups of the vegetable cooking water to the pot, and then cook and stir for 15 minutes until it's a good pulpy mess but still has plenty of texture. Dump this mixture into a Dutch oven or stew pot, add the rest of the vegetable cooking water, stir well, bring to the boil, and then lower the heat to medium. Add the oysters whole and their liquor (if the oysters are very large, cut them in half). Cook until the edges of the oysters curl. Stir in the cream and add more cream if the soup is too thick. Heat well but don't boil again. Adjust the salt. Place a tablespoon of sherry in the bottom of each preheated soup bowl, and ladle in the soup. Serve with plenty of hot crunchy French bread on the side. This is one of those rich Creole soups that make a full meal. Serve a good white wine with it.

OYSTER-HOMINY SOUP
(Serves 4)

If you had dined at the St. Charles Hotel or the St. Louis Hotel a hundred years ago, they would probably have served you oyster-hominy soup with pride. The dish had humble beginnings. The Indians taught the earliest settlers how to make it.

2 dozen oysters (a pint and a half) and
   their liquor
4 slices bacon
1 small green pepper, chopped
1 small onion, minced
3 scallions with 3″ of their green leaves,
   thinly sliced
1 rib celery, chopped fine
2 tbsp chopped parsley
½ stick butter
2 tbsp flour
1 16-oz can chicken broth (more if
   necessary)
1 16-oz can hominy
   salt and freshly ground black pepper

Fry the bacon in a skillet until brown and crisp. Drain on paper towels, crumble, and set it aside. Add to the bacon grease in the skillet the green pepper, celery, onion, and scallions, and cook until the vegetables are soft and transparent. Discard the grease. Put this mixture in a stew pot or Dutch oven, and clean the skillet. Melt the butter, add the flour, and cook slowly, stirring constantly until well blended. Add the chicken broth and parsley, blend well, and add this mixture to the stew pot. Simmer for half an hour, adding more broth if the mixture is too thick. Season with salt and black pepper. Go easy on the salt, because both the oyster liquor and the broth are salty.

Add the oysters and their liquor. Cook for 10 minutes more, or until the edges of the oysters curl. Meanwhile, heat the hominy in another saucepan. When ready to serve, spoon the hominy into four preheated soup bowls, and ladle the soup and oysters over the hominy in equal portions. Sprinkle with finely chopped green scallion leaves.

NOTE: This dish has a much better flavor if homemade hominy is used. Instructions for making hominy are given in Chapter 2.

CREAM OF OYSTER SOUP
(Serves 6)

When you buy your oysters at the fish market, ask the fishmonger to give (or sell) you three cups of oyster liquor.

1 pint oysters (about 2 dozen)

3 cups oyster liquor
3 scallions with 3″ of their green leaves, chopped
¼ stick butter
2 tbsp flour
    dash of Tabasco
    salt and freshly ground black pepper
    sour cream

Melt the butter in a saucepan, add the flour, and blend well, cooking and stirring constantly for five minutes to make a light roux. Add the scallions and cook until they're wilted. Chop the oysters and add them to the pan. Add the oyster liquor, a dash of Tabasco, and some black pepper. Mix well and simmer slowly for 30 minutes. Remember that the oyster liquor is salty, so taste the soup and add more salt only if necessary. Strain through double cheese-cloth, and serve in preheated bouillon cups with a small dollop of sour cream floating in each cup. An excellent way to get a fancy dinner off to a good start.

NOTE: It would be a damn shame to throw away the oysters you strained out. You can freeze them and use them to flavor some future dish.

OYSTER CHOWDER

(Serves 6)

1½ quarts oysters
2 cups oyster liquor
¼ lb salt pork, cut in small cubes
3 medium onions, chopped
2 large potatoes, diced
2 tbsp flour

1 quart milk
1 pint evaporated milk
    salt (if necessary) and freshly ground black pepper

Fry the salt pork in a soup pot, adding a little water to keep it from getting browned. When the pork is almost done, add the onions and a little more water, and cook until they are soft. Then add the potatoes and just enough water to cover, and simmer until the potatoes are done. Cut the oysters into quarters, and add them to the pot along with the oyster liquor. Dissolve the flour in a little milk, and add it to the pot, stirring it in well. Cook for 10 minutes longer. When ready to serve, add the milk and the evaporated milk, and heat the chowder through, but don't boil it. Add some black pepper and salt if necessary (both the salt pork and the oyster liquor are salty). Serve in pre-heated soup bowls with pilot crackers or common crackers or, best of all, that old southern favorite, beaten biscuits.

STRICTLY FOR THE BIRDS— OYSTER STUFFING

Everybody who has ever had it swears that oyster dressing is the only real stuffing for the Thanksgiving or Christmas turkey. It adds that final festive touch.

But in New Orleans you don't have to wait for Thanksgiving or Christmas. Oyster dress-ing, an everyday affair, is used to stuff a wide variety of birds, both domesticated and wild: chickens, Rock Cornish game hens, ducks, geese, quail, doves, snipe, woodcock, and just about anything else you can name. Or baked in a casserole, it can be served as a side dish at almost any kind of dinner.

OYSTER STUFFING

(For a 10-pound turkey)

1 **quart oysters and their liquor**
1 **stick butter**
1 **medium onion, chopped**
3 **scallions with their green leaves,
   finely sliced**
½ **cup finely chopped celery**
¼ **cup chopped fresh parsley**
½ **green pepper, chopped**
2 **cloves garlic, minced**
6 **chicken livers and 6 gizzards (or the
   giblets of the turkey)**
1 **bay leaf**
¼ **tsp thyme**
¼ **tsp mace**
¼ **tsp cayenne**
1 **8-oz loaf stale French bread
   salt and freshly ground black pepper**

Boil the chicken livers and gizzards (or turkey giblets) for a half hour. Remove, cool, and chop them fine. Save and set aside the broth.

Melt the butter in a saucepan or Dutch oven. Cook the scallions, onion, celery, green pepper, parsley, and garlic until the vegetables are soft and transparent. Add the bay leaf, thyme, mace, cayenne, salt, and black pepper. Add the chopped livers and gizzards (or giblets). Mix well and simmer for 20 minutes, adding giblet broth if needed. Remove the bay leaf, and set the mixture aside.

Chop the oysters coarsely, and place them in a saucepan with their liquor. Cook until the oyster pieces are firm. Remove them with a slotted spoon and add to the vegetable mixture. Break the stale French bread into small pieces and drop them into the oyster liquor in the saucepan to moisten. Add a little of the giblet broth if you need more moisture. Knead it to a paste. Mix the bread and vegetable-oyster mixture together gently. Stuff your bird with the dressing, filling the cavity only three-quarters full, because the stuffing will expand when the bird is being roasted. Any leftover dressing may be baked in a casserole.

Substitutions: You can substitute a package of commercially prepared seasoned stuffing in cubes (such as Pepperidge Farm's) for the stale French bread. In upstate Louisiana they use corn bread to make their stuffing. And where rice is grown in the southern part of the state, cooked rice instead of bread is used in stuffing.

To add crunch: Toast a cup of pecan halves until golden, chop them up, and add to the dressing. Or pan-fry a cup of sliced almonds in butter until golden, and add them to the dressing.

For added zip: Rub your bird inside and out with Cointreau liqueur, and add half a cup of it to your stuffing. If you're looking for real luxury, then you can substitute Grand Marnier for the Cointreau.

A word of caution: Do not use commercial poultry seasonings that are highly flavored with sage in your oyster dressing, because the sage overwhelms the flavor of the oysters.

ACADIAN OYSTER STUFFING

½ **lb Andouille sausage, chopped fine**

Oyster cannery at Henderson
Point. (Lino-cut by the author)

2 pints oysters and their liquor (about 4
  dozen)
6 chicken livers
6 chicken gizzards
1 cup fresh mushrooms, chopped
1 medium onion, chopped
½ green pepper, chopped
3 scallions with their green leaves,
  thinly sliced
3 ribs celery, finely chopped
½ cup fresh parsley, chopped
2 cloves garlic, minced
1 stick butter
1 tbsp Worcestershire sauce
¼ tsp cayenne
½ tsp thyme
2 bay leaves
1 7-oz pkg seasoned stuffing in cubes (such
  as Pepperidge Farm's)
  salt and freshly ground black pepper

Boil the giblets 30 minutes. Remove and chop.

Save the broth. Melt the butter in a saucepan
or Dutch oven. Chop the sausage fine and
cook in the butter for 10 minutes. Add the
chopped giblets, mushrooms, onion, green
pepper, celery, scallions, parsley, garlic, Worcestershire, cayenne, bay leaves, thyme, salt,
and black pepper. Add the oyster liquor and,
if necessary, some of the giblet broth. Simmer
this mixture for 45 minutes. Remove the bay
leaves. Cut the oysters in halves or, if they're
large, in quarters, add them to the pot, and
continue to simmer for 10 minutes more. Add
the cube stuffing and mix well. Add a little
broth if it's too dry. Stuff your bird, filling the
cavity only three-quarters full.

Variations on the theme: Various types of
Creole-Cajun sausages can be substituted for
the Andouille: red or white Boudin, Chaurice,
Saucissons, and Creole smoked sausage. Or
you can use Italian sausage, Spanish chorizo,
Portuguese linguica, Polish kielbasa, or plain
breakfast sausage.

Chapter 7

Hail to the Crawdad!

The crawfish, also known as crawdad, mud-bug, and crayfish, is the pride of Acadiana and all the marshland country of southern Louisiana. Like the shmoos, they are a sort of manna from nature—self-reproducing, self-sustaining, easy to capture, and very pleasing to the palate.

In the little Cajun town of Breaux Bridge on Bayou Teche, there is a historical marker proclaiming that, in honor of the town's centennial year of 1958, the Louisiana State Legislature officially declared it "La Capitale Mondiale de l'Ecrevisse," the Crawfish Capital of the World. It was no hollow accolade, either, because within a fifty-mile radius of the town, more crawfish are produced than in any other

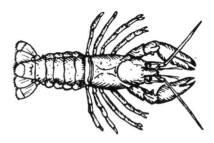

area of the world—twenty million pounds a year, to be exact. And that figure will go up and up as commercial crawfish farming increases. Rice farmers have discovered that their flooded rice fields make perfect crawfish farms. At the height of the harvesting season, one field can produce 1,500 pounds of crawfish a day and that ain't hay! In the not too distant future, frozen Louisiana crawfish tails may be available in supermarkets all over the country. Before that can be true, however, the catch will have to be vastly expanded, because Louisianians love their own crawfish so much that they eat more than three-fourths of the present annual catch themselves, leaving only a trickle for the outsiders. Some live crawfish are flown by air express to European centers, where they command enormous prices. A girl from Sweden told me that she paid a dollar apiece for Louisiana crawfish in Stockholm, where they're called langoustines, or lobsterettes. They're nibbled very slowly, no doubt because of the price!

Breaux Bridge used to have an annual Crawfish Festival in the spring of each year, but the affair became so popular (tens of thousands of crawfish-hungry people would descend on the small town) that the municipal facilities were completely overtaxed. The town fathers decided to have the festival biennially, but even then there were never enough crawfish to go around. During the festival there was never a motel room available within fifty miles of Breaux Bridge.

Some of the restaurants of the area have become nationally famous for their crawfish dishes. Among them are Thelma's of Breaux Bridge, Broussard's in New Iberia, Don's in Lafayette, Bilello's in Thibodaux, and Gino's in Houma. But even though they're not famous, nearly all the small Cajun restaurants scattered throughout the area serve excellent crawfish dishes. They have to since most of their customers are locals who demand a high standard of excellence in the cooking of their crawfish.

Crawfish look like small lobsters, and actually the flavor is similar to that of lobster—but better. This is why Maine lobster growers fear their competition and hope they'll never achieve a national market. There are several different species of crawfish, all growing together side by side. When they're alive, their colors are variable—green, yellow, beige, red, deep maroon, almost black—but they all have a deep red color when boiled. Like crabs, crawfish have to be boiled before the meat can be extracted. There is great variability in the size of crawfish, but the average is about the size of a man's thumb. The tail meat and the fat and liver (tomalley) inside the heads are the edible parts. Also extremely variable is the amount of shelled meat in relation to the weight of crawfish in the shells. This variability makes it very difficult to specify quantities required in recipes. What's true today may be different in a week or two. But the Cajuns don't worry about this problem. They just never write down recipes.

Going crawfishing, like crabbing, is fun for the whole family, and the kids usually end up catching more crawfish than the grown folks. Crawfish live in rivers, bayous, sloughs, ponds, flooded swampy areas, and even roadside ditches. Their season lasts from February to May, that is, when there's always plenty of water around. Crawfish always seem to be hungry and eager to be caught. A kid can tie a piece of meat to the end of a string, toss it in a ditch, draw the crawfish to the surface, and scoop them up with a dip net. It's easy to fill a bucket in a short while. Drop nets of the type used to catch crabs but with smaller mesh are also popular. The professionals use large traps built of chicken wire. Baited with meat, these can catch and hold hundreds of crawfish.

And after you've caught your crawfish comes the joy of feasting.

NOTE: Since crawfish live in the mud, they should always be soaked for about 15 minutes in clean water to give them a bath. Add some salt to the soaking water, and its laxative effect will purge the crawfish of mud in their stomachs. After this initial soaking, place them in a colander under cold running water to give them a good rinse.

BOILED CRAWFISH
(Serves 8 to 12)

  1 40-lb sack of live crawfish
12 unpeeled onions, chopped
  1 whole bunch celery with green leaves, chopped
12 lemons sliced
  2 bunches parsley, chopped
  1 dozen scallions with their green leaves, chopped
  4 whole heads unpeeled garlic, chopped
  6 3-oz pkg "Shrimp Boil" spices
  3 oz cayenne
  1 bottle red wine
  4 lb salt
  4 oz black pepper
  5 lb small red new potatoes, unpeeled (optional)

If you don't have an extra large stock pot, you can use a 30-gallon garbage can as described in the section about the Chimney Sweepers Shrimp Boil (Chapter 4).

Fill the can a third full of water, and add all ingredients except the crawfish and new pota-toes. Bring to the boil and cook at a rolling boil for 30 minutes to make a good rich liquor. Soak the crawfish in salted water in the sink for 15 minutes to clean and purge them. Then rise them well. Discard any crawfish that are dead. When they've all been thoroughly soaked and rinsed, add them to the boiling liquor in the pot, and then add the new pota-toes. The liquor should cover everything com-pletely, so add hot water if it doesn't. It may take 20-30 minutes to return to the boil. Then boil for 15 minutes. Cut off the heat. Eat one of the crawfish to test for doneness, and if it doesn't taste done or spicy enough, let the whole batch soak in the hot spicy liquor for a few minutes longer. Since eating boiled craw-fish can be a messy business, don't serve them in the living room if you have Aubusson car-pets. Cover a large table with a thick layer of newspapers, pile the steaming crawfish in the center, and let the guests stand around and feast. If you've opted for the little red new potatoes, you'll find them a great accompani-ment. They're hot and spicy, and they taste like no potato you've ever eaten in your life. Serve plenty of cold beer or chilled white or red wine. (Do you know that lightly chilling a red Beaujolais takes off the "bite" and makes it excellent for a seafood situation such as this?)

HOW TO EAT BOILED CRAWFISH

There's lots of disagreement about the best way to eat boiled crawfish, but here's a gener-ally accepted method. Break the head and the tail apart. Put the head to your lips and give it a good suck to get those nectarlike juices inside (but be careful not to suck anything down your windpipe). Peel the tail by grasping each side of the shell with your thumbs and cracking it open. Lift out the meat, devein it (you don't have to devein a shrimp, but you *do* have to devein a crawfish), plop it in your mouth, and gleefully devour it. It melts on your tongue, caresses your taste buds, and is 10 times better than Maine lobster. Lift off the carapace, the top shell of the head. Run your thumbnail down the cavity of the bottom shell, and it will come out with a lump of yellow liver and crawfish fat. Suck it off your thumb. M-m-m, better than caviar! Crack the claws with your teeth, and suck out the meat and juice (they're very thin and won't damage your bridgework). And thus it goes. A true crawfish connoisseur can keep it up for a couple of hours and eat 10 or 15 pounds—which after all is only a pound or two of meats.

NOTE: A smart cook who intends to make Crawfish Bisque with stuffed heads at some time in the future will go around and gather about 100 of the top shells lying around and wash them and freeze them for future use.

CRAWFISH CARDINALE
(Serves 4)

The dish known as "Ecrevisses Cardinale" is said to have been invented by Antoine's many years ago. The "Cardinale" comes from the fact that, though not really the deep red of a cardinal's hat, the dish is pink. It didn't take much doing to invent it as the formula is very simple.

We're not exactly sure of Antoine's method, but here's a recipe that works well.

1 lb peeled crawfish tails
¼ cup crawfish fat, if available
½ stick butter
3 tbsp flour
1 cup half-and-half cream
1 medium onion, grated
2 tbsp tomato paste
2 tbsp brandy
2 tbsp white wine
¼ tsp cayenne
¼ tsp nutmeg
  salt and white pepper

Melt the butter in a saucepan, and cook the grated onion for three or four minutes. Add the flour and blend well. Add the cup of cream a little at a time, stirring constantly. Cook the mixture over low heat, stirring constantly until it thickens. Add the tomato paste, brandy, white wine, cayenne, and nutmeg. Add the crawfish and their fat and mix well. Season to taste with salt and white pepper. Cook for 10 minutes more, stirring constantly. Serve in pre-heated individual casseroles or in pastry cups.

CRAWFISH-LUMP CRABMEAT CARDINALE
(Serves 6 as appetizer)

Mr. Warren Le Ruth, the owner-chef of Le Ruth's Restaurant in Gretna, likes to pile luxury on top of luxury, as witness his famous crab-on-crab dish (lump crabmeat on top of soft-shell crabs). In the following recipe he

TRADITIONS

Copper repoussé sculpture by the author

DIDN'T HE RAMBLE!

Didn't he ramble,
Didn't he ramble!
He rambled all around,
In and out of town.
Didn't he ramble,
Didn't he ramble!
He rambled till the butcher cut him down.

My grandpa was so long,
He nearly touched the sky.
An eagle went up to build its nest,
The young ones stayed and cried.

My grandpa was in the market,
His feet was in the street,
A lady came passing by, she said,
Look at that market meat.

Chorus
Didn't he ramble,
Didn't he ramble!
He rambled all around,
In and out of town.
Didn't he ramble,
Didn't he ramble!
He rambled till the butcher cut him down.

Traditional

SAINTS GO MARCHING IN

Oh, when those stars refuse to shine,
Oh, when those stars refuse to shine,
I want to be within that number,
Oh, when those stars refuse to shine.

Oh, when that sun begins to shine,
Oh, when that sun begins to shine,
I want to be within that number,
Oh, when that sun begins to shine.

Oh, when those Saints go marchin' in,
Oh, when those Saints go marchin' in,
I want to be within that number,
Oh, when those Saints go marchin' in.

Traditional

Dick Allen of the Tulane Jazz Archives says that *Didn't He Ramble* goes back to a sixteenth century English folksong called *The Stag*. It was one of the only songs anyone ever heard George Washington singing. It's now the traditional song the funeral band plays on the way back from the cemetery.

Warren Le Ruth, owner-chef of Le Ruth's Restaurant in Gretna and one of the leading seafood chefs of New Orleans.

mixes crawfish tails and lump crabmeat, and the result is sublime.

1 lb cooked, peeled, and deveined crawfish tails
¼ cup crawfish fat
½ lb lump crabmeat
2 scallions, chopped fine
½ stick butter
¼ cup white wine
¼ cup tomato sauce
1½ cups thick bechamel sauce (see below) salt and cayenne to taste

Cook the chopped scallions in butter. Add the white wine and tomato sauce, and reduce for five minutes. Add the bechamel sauce and return to the boil. Add the crabmeat, crawfish, and crawfish fat. Return to the boil, stirring very gently so as not to break up the crab lumps. Season with salt and cayenne. Serve in small preheated individual casserole cups or in small pastry cups.

BECHAMEL SAUCE
½ stick butter
4 tbsp flour

1 cup cream
½ cup milk
pinch of nutmeg
white pepper
salt

Melt the butter in a small saucepan, and add the flour. Cook slowly for five minutes, stirring constantly. Pour in the milk and cream a little at a time, and keep stirring until the mixture has thickened. Add a pinch of nutmeg, and season to taste with white pepper and salt.

CRAWFISH ETOUFFEE I
(Serves 4)

If you're traveling through Acadiana and you pass by a small roadside restaurant with a big crudely lettered sign out front reading "A-2-FAY" (a very close approximation of the pronunciation of the word "étouffée"), you'd better stop and go in and sample their version of this dish. Most of these small Cajun restaurants are very honest and conscientious, and they'll give you a good run for your money in Cajun crawfish cooking. Some of them, such as Thelma's in Breaux Bridge and Bilello's in Thibodaux, have become quite famous.

Etouffée means "smothered," and that pretty well describes what the delicious blanket of sauce does to the crawfish.

2 lb crawfish tails, boiled, cleaned, and
    deveined, and their fat (about 20 lb live
    crawfish)
1 large onion, chopped
2 scallions with their green leaves,
    chopped
2 ribs celery, finely chopped
1 small green pepper, chopped
2 cloves garlic, minced
1 stick butter
2 tbsp flour
2 cups water
    cayenne
    salt and freshly ground black pepper to
    taste

Melt the butter in a saucepan, add the flour, and cook over low heat, stirring constantly, to make a light brown roux. Add the onion, scallions, celery, green pepper, and garlic, and cook until the vegetables are soft. Add the crawfish fat and water. Season with cayenne, salt, and black pepper. Simmer for 15 minutes, stirring now and then. Add the crawfish and simmer for 10 minutes longer. Let it "set" for half an hour before serving. Serve in preheated soup bowls over a bed of hot steamed rice. For garnish, sprinkle chopped green scallion leaves on top.

CRAWFISH ETOUFFEE II
(Serves 6)

2 cups crawfish tails
½ cup crawfish fat
1 stick butter
3 tbsp flour
3 scallions with 3″ of their green leaves,
    thinly sliced
1 medium onion, chopped
2 cloves garlic, minced
2 tbsp chopped fresh parsley
½ cup tomato sauce (puree)
½ tsp grated lemon peel
1 tbsp lemon juice
1 cup hot water
1 cup fish stock or chicken broth
¼ cup sherry
¼ tsp cayenne
¼ tsp thyme
1 oz brandy
    salt and freshly ground black pepper to
    taste

Melt the butter in a saucepan and add the flour. Cook over low heat, stirring constantly, for 20 minutes to make a russet brown roux. Add the onion, scallions, garlic, and parsley, and cook until the vegetables are soft and transparent. Add the tomato sauce, lemon peel, cayenne, thyme, lemon juice, crawfish fat, hot water, and brandy. Cover and cook slowly for 20 minutes. Add the sherry, then the crawfish tails. Stir in the fish stock or chicken broth. Serve in preheated soup bowls over beds of hot steamed rice. Garnish with fresh chopped parsley or finely chopped green onion or scallion leaves.

CRAWFISH ETOUFFEE III
(Serves 5 to 6)

This is a very simple version of étouffée that almost anybody can make. And it's especially easy if you can buy frozen crawfish tails.

2½ lb crawfish tails
1 stick butter
3 tbsp flour
2 large onions, finely chopped
¼ cup fresh chopped parsley
    salt and freshly ground black pepper to taste
¼ cup sherry (optional)

Melt the butter in a saucepan or Dutch oven, add the flour, and blend well for four or five minutes over low heat. Add the onions and mix well. Cover with water by a half inch, and boil gently for 45 minutes until the onions are almost dissolved. Scrape the bottom of the pan now and then to make sure it is not scorching or sticking. If your pot isn't thick, put an asbestos pad under it. Add the tails (and crawfish fat, if you have it). Season to taste with salt and black pepper. (Although the Cajuns don't often add sherry, you may add a quarter cup at this stage if you wish.) If the gravy is too

thick, add enough hot water to thin it to the desired consistency. Simmer for 20 minutes more. Add the parsley and serve over beds of rice in preheated soup bowls.

COWBOYS AND CRAWFISH

The Wild West wasn't the only part of America that produced cowboys. In the early days the prairie region of southwestern Louisiana was great cattle-raising country, and wherever you find cows, you'll find cowboys. The Cajun cowboys of Louisiana were a breed apart, famous for their wild and carefree ways, independent and proud as the gauchos of Argentina. Like the gauchos, they were handy with sharp knives, and they loved gunplay, with all the noise and smoke. But most of all, they loved horses and horsemanship. They developed the Louisiana Quarter Horse, now a famous breed, which gets its name from the fact that it was run on short, quarter-mile race tracks.

When the rice farmers took over the region, many of the cowboys migrated to the West, where you can find Cajun names on headstones in Tombstone, Amarillo, Fort Dodge, and other cowboy centers.

Just about the only legacy the Cajun cowboy has left us is tasso, a form of jerky dried beef. Since he had no refrigeration, he usually carried a chunk of this stuff around in his saddlebags to eat as needed. It's much better than plain jerky beef, though, because at the time of curing it's rubbed down with a wide variety of fragrant herbs, spices, and other unguents. Like Andouille and Boudin sausages, tasso is still sold in a few small neighborhood groceries throughout the Acadian country. If you live far away and can't run around the corner to an Acadian grocery store you can substitute dried jerky beef, pemmican, plain old corned beef brisket—or pastrami if you're rich enough.

CRAWFISH-TASSO ETOUFFEE

(Serves 6)

    1 lb crawfish tails
    1 lb tasso
    2 large onions, chopped
    4 scallions with their green leaves,
       finely sliced
    4 cloves garlic, minced
    1 small green pepper, chopped
    1 16-oz can tomatoes, drained and
       chopped
    ½ small can tomato paste
    2 lb fresh okra (or 3 pkgs frozen)
    ½ stick butter
    3 tbsp flour
    ½ tsp cayenne
       salt and freshly ground black pepper

Cut the tasso into chunks, cover with water, and soak overnight. The next day boil it gently for two hours, or until it's soft and tender. Take it out, cut it up into dice, and set aside. Save the broth.

Melt the butter in a large skillet, add the flour, and blend well, cooking over low heat for five minutes and stirring constantly. Add the onions, scallions, green pepper, and garlic, and cook until the vegetables are very soft and disintegrating. Add some tasso broth if necessary. Add the tomatoes and the tomato paste.

Wash the fresh okra, and cut it into quarter-inch slices, discarding the tops and stems. Add to the skillet and continue cooking until the okra loses its gummy consistency. If your skillet is overloaded at this point, transfer everything to a stewpot. Add the diced tasso and crawfish tails (and crawfish fat if you have any). If your tasso broth is too salty, dilute it with water and add two cups of the diluted mixture to the pot. (Use the broth straight if it's not too salty. It can also be used in place of water in steaming the rice.) Cook at a simmer for 20 minutes more. Season with salt, black pepper, and cayenne. Ladle over hot steaming rice in preheated soup bowls. And never forget those Cajun cowboys!

CRAWFISH STEW

(Serves 4 to 6)

This staple Cajun dish is eaten day in and day out during the crawfish season, and the Cajuns never seem to get tired of it. Down at New Iberia in the heart of Acadiana, there's a small Cajun restaurant called Broussard's. It's off the beaten track, and you have to wander through back streets to find it. During the crawfish season, of course, they specialize in crawfish dishes. One night they served me a bowl of crawfish stew that was one of the best dishes I've ever eaten—absolutely ambrosial, fit for the gods on Olympus. There must have been a hundred tiny crawfish tails in that one bowlful, and I sympathized with the person who'd had to peel them. Our host, Mr. Broussard, offered to give me the recipe, but we were so busy talking about the mystique of crawfishes that I forgot to get it. However, here's another one that's very good.

20 lb live crawfish (or 2 lb crawfish meats)
    crawfish fat
½ cup butter
5 tbsp flour
2 large onions, minced
1 large green pepper, minced
2 ribs celery, chopped fine
1 16-oz can tomato sauce (puree)
¼ tsp cayenne
    salt and freshly ground black pepper

Soak the live crawfish in cold salted water for 15 minutes. Pick out and discard any dead ones, and rinse the rest in a colander under the faucet. Place them in a pot and cover with hot water. Turn the heat high, and when the water comes to the boil, cook the crawfish for 10 minutes. Remove from the pot, cool, peel, and devein the tails. Save the fat from the heads.

Melt the butter in a large skillet or Dutch oven, add the flour, and make a golden brown roux. Add the onions, green pepper, and celery, and cook until the vegetables are soft

and transparent. Add the tomato sauce. Add the crawfish and their fat and mix well. If the mixture seems to need moisture, add a cup and a half of hot water. Cover and simmer for 30 minutes, stirring now and then and scraping the bottom of the pot to make sure it's not sticking. Season with cayenne, salt, and black pepper. Serve in preheated soup bowls, garnishing with chopped green scallion tops or chopped parsley. Serve hot steamed rice on the side.

A PIE IS A PIE IS A PIE . . . .

Back in the halcyon days of my youth, when I was a student at LSU, the fraternity that adopted me called me "the permanent pledge," because I was such a playboy and my grades were so low that they were never allowed to initiate me. Some of the guys in that frat became real wheels. Wade O. Martin, Jr., served several terms as Secretary of State of Louisiana, Lansing Mitchell became a federal judge, and Oma Bates was a hero in World War II. Maybe even I could have been some kind of a wheel if I hadn't been such a freewheeler.

Wade "Chup" Martin owns a 350 acre farm down at Henderson, in St. Martin Parish, where he alternates raising crawfish, rice, and soybeans. (The soil is so rich and the climate so mild down there that you can keep something growing year-round.) At the peak of the crawfish season he harvests 2,500 pounds a day, and brother, that ain't hay.

With so much stock around it's only natural that Mrs. Julie Martin is one of the best crawfish cooks anywhere.

And not only that—she knows how to make a good pie crust. Incidentally, I've never known an amateur male cook who could make a decent pie crust. So if that's one of your problems, it's safer to run to the supermarket and buy frozen pie crusts or pastry shells, some of which are very good and not to be sniffed at. But when all the chips are down, it's the homemade item that tastes best. The pie crust dough in the recipe below can be used to make the pastry shells called for so often in this book.

CRAWFISH PIE

(1 pie)

THE PASTRY DOUGH

4 cups sifted all-purpose flour
½ tsp salt
½ lb unsalted butter, chilled and cut into ¼″ bits
½ lb lard, chilled and cut into ¼″ bits
ice water

Combine the sifted flour and salt, and sift together into a large chilled mixing bowl. Drop in the butter bits and lard. Working quickly, use your fingertips to rub the flour and fat together until the mixture looks like flakes of coarse meal. Pour eight tablespoons of ice water over the mixture all at once, and gather the dough into a ball. If the dough crumbles, add up to four more tablespoons of ice water, a teaspoon at a time until the particles adhere. Dust lightly with flour, wrap the dough in waxed paper, and chill for 30 minutes.

Place the dough on a lightly floured table, and press into a rectangular shape about an inch thick. Dust a little flour over and under it, and roll it out into a strip about 21 inches long and 12 inches wide. Fold the strip into thirds to form a three-layered rectangular packet. Repeat the rolling out and folding process three times more, ending with the dough in a layered packet. Wrap the dough tightly in waxed paper, and refrigerate for at least an hour. If you don't need it immediately, you can keep the dough in the refrigerator for three or four days before using it.

THE PIE FILLING

10 lb live crawfish
4 tbsp butter
2 cups onion, finely chopped
1 cup scallions with 3″ of their green leaves, finely chopped
½ cup celery, finely chopped
½ cup green pepper, finely chopped
3 cloves garlic, minced
¼ cup unsifted flour
1 tbsp tomato paste
½ cup parsley, finely chopped
½ tsp cayenne
¼ tsp salt
butter, softened

Soak the live crawfish in cold salted water for 5 minutes, and then rinse thoroughly in a colander set under cold running water. In a heavy eight- or ten-quart pot bring four quarts of water to a boil. Drop the crawfish in and boil briskly, uncovered, for five minutes. Drain the crawfish and shell and devein them. Save as much of the yellow fat as possible. Place the crawfish meat and fat in a bowl and set aside.

In a heavy skillet melt four tablespoons of butter over moderate heat. Add onions, scallions, celery, green pepper, and garlic, and stirring frequently, cook until soft, about five minutes.

Remove the skillet from the heat, and stir in the unsifted flour. When it's well incorporated, add tomato paste, parsley, cayenne, and salt. Empty the contents of the skillet over the crawfish meat and fat, and toss them together gently but thoroughly.

Preheat the oven to 350°. To assemble the pie, spread about a tablespoon of softened butter over the bottom and sides of a 9-inch pie pan. Cut off half the chilled dough, and on a lightly floured surface, pat the dough into a circle about an inch thick. Dust a little flour over it and under it, and roll it out from the center to within an inch of the far edge of the dough until the circle is a quarter-inch thick and 13-14 inches in diameter.

Place the dough in the pie pan, gently pressing into the bottom and sides of the pan and being careful not to stretch it. Cut the excess dough from the edges, leaving a one-inch overhang. Fill the pie shell with crawfish mixture. Roll out the remaining half of the dough into a 13-inch circle about a quarter-inch thick.

With a pastry brush dipped in cold water, lightly moisten the outside of the pastry shell, and place the top crust in position over the filling. Cut off the pastry even with the bottom crust, and crimp the top and bottom crusts together firmly. Cut two or three one-inch long parallel slits in the top of the pie as vent holes. Bake in the middle of the oven at 350° for 15 to 20 minutes, or until the crust is golden brown. Serve at once. And now I guess you good ole boys know how to bake a pie!

CRAWFISH-EGGPLANT PIE
(Serves 4)

1 lb boiled peeled crawfish and their fat, if any
1 stick butter
1 large eggplant, peeled and diced
1 small onion, grated
1 rib celery, grated
1 green pepper, minced
½ cup fish or chicken broth (or water)
½ cup bread crumbs
2 tbsp sherry
  salt and freshly ground black pepper
  Parmesan cheese

Melt the butter in a skillet, and cook the onion, celery, green pepper, and diced eggplant until soft, stirring now and then. Add the broth and sherry. Add the crawfish tails, crawfish fat, and bread crumbs. Season with salt and black pepper. Pour the mixture into a greased ovenproof glass pie dish. Sprinkle with Parmesan cheese and heat in a moderate oven just until it's bubbly and the Parmesan is melted. You can serve it at once, but it tastes even better if you set it aside, let it age awhile, and then reheat it.

CRAWFISH BISQUE, ONE OF THE RITES OF SPRING

Making crawfish bisque is high and holy Cajun ritual, one of the rites of spring, a vernal ceremony in praise of the crawdad. When you make crawfish bisque from scratch with fresh live crawfish, it's a hell of a lot of work, but your elbow grease will add savour to the dish. With the intensive crawfish farming that's underway nowadays, there's a more plentiful supply, and you can buy frozen crawfish tails, frozen crawfish fat, and frozen shells in many supermarkets. They're now also being shipped out to other parts of the country so that many more people can enjoy what was formerly a local delicacy. This freezing business has another convenience, of course. It makes the product available even in crawfish country during the months when live crawfish are out of season.

Here are two standard Cajun recipes for crawfish bisque, and you can choose the one that fits your needs. The first is for a relatively small bisque that serves six to eight people. The second recipe is for a whopping big batch that will serve a mob—thirty to forty—or provide enough crawfish bisque for freezing to keep you supplied for quite a spell. When frozen in individual plastic packets, it will always be immediately available if an archbishop or a distinguished foreign diplomat drops in for supper. Although high-class restaurants would never admit it, this is how they solve the problem of Bisque d'Ecrevisses. It would keep a restaurant kitchen in a state of permanent uproar if they tried to make fresh crawfish bisque every day. There wouldn't be space or time to cook anything else.

CRAWFISH BISQUE I

(Serves 6)

THE CRAWFISH

Soak 20 pounds of live crawfish in cold salted water for 15 minutes. Pick out and discard any

dead ones. After they have soaked, place them in a colander and run cold water over them to rinse them thoroughly. Place them in a pot and cover with hot water. Turn the heat high, and when the water returns to the boil, cook them for 10 minutes. Remove the crawfish from the pot, saving the liquor. Let the crawfish cool. Then break them in two, and peel and devein the tails. Open the heads, remove all the yellow fat, and save it in a small container. Break off and save the claws. Divide the meat into three parts, two thirds for the stuffing and one third for the bisque. Wash the top shells of the heads (about 48) for stuffing.

FOR STUFFING THE HEADS
⅔ of the crawfish tails
1 large onion, minced
3 scallions with 3″ of their green leaves, minced
4 cloves garlic, minced
2 tbsp parsley, chopped
1 small green pepper, minced
2 ribs celery, minced
¼ stick butter
1 cup bread crumbs (or more)
½ tsp cayenne
 salt and freshly ground black pepper
 flour

Grind the crawfish tails (or chop them very fine). Melt the butter in a skillet and cook the onion, scallions, garlic, parsley, green pepper, and celery until they're soft and transparent.

Add the ground crawfish meat. Season with cayenne, salt, and black pepper. Add a cup or more of bread crumbs to make the mixture into a stiff dressing, and stuff the heads. Roll the heads in flour, place them on a large greased cookie sheet, and bake them in the oven for just a few minutes until they're browned. Be careful not to scorch or burn them. (Some people prefer to roll the heads in flour and fry them brown in deep hot fat.) Set the browned heads aside.

THE BISQUE

Place the crawfish claws in the bottom of a pot, and crush them thoroughly with a pestle or the bottom of a thick bottle. Add the crawfish fat to the pot. Add 2½ quarts of the crawfish boiling water, and boil vigorously for 20 minutes to make two quarts of rich stock. Strain it through triple cheesecloth, and set it aside.

⅓ **of the crawfish tails**
½ **cup flour**
1 **stick butter**
3 **medium onions, finely chopped**
3 **ribs celery, minced**
1 **small green pepper, finely chopped**
2 **cloves garlic, minced**
½ **6-oz can tomato paste**
¼ **tsp cayenne**
¼ **tsp thyme**
2 **quarts crawfish stock**
¼ **cup scallion tops, chopped**
¼ **cup chopped fresh parsley**
  salt and freshly ground black pepper

Melt the butter in a skillet, add the flour, and make a dark brown roux. Add the onions,

celery, green pepper, garlic, and tomato paste, and cook for 15 minutes, or until the vegetables are very soft and falling apart. Add some stock, if necessary, to moisten. Season with cayenne, thyme, black pepper, and salt, and mix well. Add the crawfish stock and cook for 15 minutes. Add the crawfish tails. Add the stuffed heads, the chopped scallion tops, and the chopped parsley, and cook for 10 minutes more. Place a layer of hot steamed rice on the bottom of preheated soup bowls, and ladle the bisque and stuffed heads over it (about 6 to 8 heads in each bowl).

CRAWFISH BISQUE II
(Serves 30 to 40)

You should get about six willing helpers for this project. Peeling the crawfish alone would take one person a month of Sundays. That's why Cajuns have such large families—so there'll be plenty of crawfish peelers available.

THE CRAWFISH

Buy a 40- to 50-pound sack of live crawfish. If you don't have a large zinc washtub to clean them in, you can use your bathtub. (Shucks, don't be squeamish about your ole tub! My artist friend Ed Giobbi bleeds and leaches a hundred-pound tuna in *his* bathtub.) Put them in the tub and cover them with water. Pick out and discard any dead ones. Dissolve three boxes of salt in a pot of water, and add it to the tub. Let them soak for 15 minutes. The salt has a laxative effect and purges them of any excess mud they may have inside them. Stir them around to wash them well. Pull out

MESSIN' AROUND

What is all this noise I hear around here?
Please don't keep me in doubt, what is it all
    about?
Now honey, calm yourself and don't be
    angry with me
And right here on this spot something hot
    you'll see!

Chorus
That dance called "Messin' Around"
A dance that's new in the town;
It runs the Charleston way out of gas,
Don't even have to step and still it's full
    of pep,
Keep your doggies still, Mess Around until
    morning,
My grandma thinks it's nice
And grandpa, now, he's done it twice,
It is the easiest dance I've found
Let's go right now, Sure is a wow,
Messin' Around, Messin' Around
Dance they call "Messin' Around."

Daddy spent the night down in a cafe,
Came home at break of day.
Oh boy! How he did sway,
then mama met him at the door
With freezin'est bow
And said "Doggone your soul, get me told
    right now."

Chorus
Have you been Messin' Around,
Out with some other sweet brown?
Cause if you were, you can catch some air,
I tried to use you right,
But you stayed out all night,
Spose you got a thrill
Messin' round until morning,
Now, brother, you can go tight
And stay out just one more night
Then to some cabaret I'll be bound.
If you don't stop I'm goin' to hop,
Get a new man, with a sedan.
Then I'll start Messin' Around!

Photo by Johnny Donnels

Members of the Olympia Marching Band
take a rest. The Olympia Marching Band is
the oldest and most famous of the New
Orleans brass marching bands. Although it
has only eight to twelve members, they
can put on a good funeral parade, or play
for conventions, movies, and TV programs.
They've become something of a showcase
piece, and Alan Jaffe took them on a
tour of Europe. Until three or four years
ago, their bass drummer was 90-year-old
Booker T. Glass, one of the greatest of all
parade drummers. He said his legs were
O.K., but he didn't like totin' that forty-
pound drum on five-mile marches no more,
so he quit the "prades." He's still alive and
he'll play with the band on special occasions that don't require no marchin'.

the stopper and drain the tub, but be careful not to let excess debris stop up your drain pipe. Replace the stopper and cover the crawfish with cold water to rinse them. Rustle them around until they're very clean because the water they're boiled in will be used for stock. If the rinsing water gets very muddy, drain it out and rinse them again. There's nothing so fine as a well-laundered mudbug.

If you don't have a large enough stock pot to boil all of them at once, you'll have to divide them into batches of 15 to 20 pounds and cook them in shifts. (Or you can use a new 30-gallon garbage can, as described under Chimney Sweepers Shrimp Boil.) Place the washed crawfish in a pot, and pour on enough plain hot water to cover. Do not use salt or spices, because this water will become stock. Turn the heat high, and when the water returns to the boil, cook them for 10 minutes. Remove the crawfish from the pot and save the broth. Use fresh hot water for boiling each new batch. Save the broth after each boiling session until you have a total of two and a half gallons. Cool the crawfish. Break the crawfish in two, and peel and devein the tails. Open the heads, remove all the yellow fat, and save it in a small container. Break off and save the claws. Wash the top shells from the heads, and set them aside for stuffing. Depending on the phase of the season and the development of the crawfish, you'll have between 12 and 16 cups of peeled crawfish tails. Divide the meats into three parts, two thirds for the stuffing and one third for the bisque.

FOR STUFFING THE HEADS
⅔ **of the crawfish tails**
5 **large onions, finely chopped**
10 **cloves garlic, minced**

10 **scallions with 3″ of their green leaves, thinly sliced**
1 **cup fresh parsley, chopped**
5 **green peppers, finely chopped**
10 **ribs celery, finely chopped**
1 **lb butter**
3 **cups seasoned bread crumbs**
1 **8-oz loaf French bread**
1 **tsp cayenne**
   crawfish broth
   salt and freshly ground black pepper

Grind or chop the crawfish tails very fine. There's so much stuff to cook here that if you don't have an extra large skillet, you should divide everything in half and cook it in shifts. Melt the butter in a skillet, and cook the vegetables until they're soft and transparent. Add the black pepper. Tear the French bread into small pieces, moisten it with a little crawfish broth, and knead it with your fingers until it's a paste. Add enough kneaded bread and bread crumbs to the skillet to make the mixture into a stiff dressing, and stuff the heads with it. (It's easy for me to write this and easy for you to read it, but by the time you've finished stuffing those 250 crawfish shells, you're gonna be dog tahrd. That's one of the reasons I suggested that you get a half dozen helpers.) Roll the heads in flour, place them on a large greased cookie sheet, and bake them in the oven just a few minutes until they're browned, but be careful not to scorch or burn them. This will have to be done in shifts, too. Some people prefer to roll the heads in flour and fry them brown in deep hot fat, but I don't opt for this. God knows, a crawfish bisque is rich enough from the butter in it and doesn't need any more fat. Set the browned heads aside, and keep them warm.

THE BISQUE

Place the crawfish claws in the bottom of a large flat-bottomed pot, and crush them thoroughly with a pestle or the bottom of a thick bottle. Add the crawfish fat to the pot. Add two and a half gallons of the crawfish broth, bring back to the boil, and boil vigorously for 30 minutes. Strain through triple cheesecloth and set aside. This is now a truly beautiful broth.

⅓ **of the crawfish tails**
1½ **lb butter**
2 **cups flour**
5 **large onions, finely chopped**
6 **cloves garlic, minced**
10 **ribs celery, finely chopped**
5 **small green peppers, finely chopped**
1 **cup chopped fresh parsley**
1 **cup green scallion tops, finely chopped**
2 **6-oz cans tomato paste**
  bread
1 **tsp cayenne**
  crawfish broth (2½ gallons)
  salt and freshly ground black pepper
  thyme

You'll need a large skillet and a five-gallon soup pot. Making the roux is the crucial point of the whole operation, and if you goof off, you can spoil everything. So don't get impatient and turn the heat too high. You'll only burn or scorch the roux, and then you'll have to throw it out and start over again. Melt the butter in a large skillet or Dutch oven, add the flour, and then stir and cook slowly for 30 minutes or more, or until the roux becomes a rich russet brown, about the color of a pecan. Add all the chopped vegetables except the parsley and scallion tops. Add the tomato paste, and cook for 15 minutes, or until the vegetables are very soft and falling apart. Add some crawfish broth, if necessary, to moisten. Season with cayenne, thyme, black pepper, and salt, and mix well. Pour this mixture into the large soup pot, and add two and a half gallons of crawfish stock (if stock is insufficient, use water). Bring the mixture to the boil, lower the heat, and cook for 15 minutes. Add the crawfish tails. Add the stuffed heads, the chopped parsley, and the chopped scallion tops, and cook for 10 minutes more, or until everything is thoroughly heated through. Serve over a layer of rice in preheated soup bowls.

Serve your six helpers a good crawfish bisque dinner, and then freeze the rest of it. Keep a good count of your portions and mark the freezing containers clearly. A cup and a half of bisque with 6 to 8 heads makes one serving.

A good imported dry sherry goes beautifully with crawfish bisque.

FRIED CRAWFISH
(Serves 2 to 4)

This dish is the specialty of Mr. J. Burton Angelle, the director of the Louisiana Wildlife and Fisheries Commission.

1 **lb crawfish tails**
2 **eggs**
  milk
  flour
  salt and freshly ground black pepper
  to taste
  cayenne

Season the cleaned crawfish tails with salt and pepper. Season flour with salt, pepper, and cayenne. Beat the eggs and add a little milk. Dip each crawfish in the egg-milk mixture and then in the flour. Fry in deep hot fat just until lightly golden. Don't overcook. Fried crawfish make delicious hot hors d'oeuvres for a party, or they can be served as the main dish for a dinner.

CRAWFISH SALAD
(Serves 4)

Another of Mr. Angelle's specialties is crawfish salad.

 2 **cups boiled crawfish tails, diced**
 1 **cup celery, chopped**
 2 **hard-cooked eggs, chopped**
 2 **tbsp dill pickles, chopped**
 ½ **tsp Worcestershire sauce**
   homemade mayonnaise
   salt and freshly ground black pepper
   to taste

Combine all the measured ingredients thoroughly, and mix with fresh mayonnaise to the desired consistency. Season lightly with salt and pepper, and serve on a bed of shredded lettuce.

CRAWFISH-STUFFED GREEN PEPPERS
(Serves 5)

Mr. Angelle's wife, Shirley, dotes on crawfish-stuffed peppers. Here's her recipe.

 1 **lb crawfish tails, coarsely chopped**
 1½ **sticks butter**
 1 **large onion, minced**
 1 **green pepper, minced**
 1 **cup chopped celery**
 2 **cloves garlic, minced**
 1 **tbsp fresh chopped parsley**
 ½ **loaf stale French bread**
 1½ **tsp salt**
 ½ **tsp Tabasco**
 1 **egg, beaten**
 5 **medium green peppers, halved**

Melt the butter in a skillet, and cook the onions, green pepper, celery, and garlic until the vegetables are light brown. Add parsley, crawfish tails, and French bread, which has been soaked in water and squeezed out. Add salt and Tabasco and blend thoroughly. Remove from the heat, add the beaten egg, and blend.

Cut green peppers in half, and remove the seeds and membrane. Parboil in salted water for five minutes, and then drain. Pile the crawfish mixture into the pepper shells, garnishing with whole crawfish tails, if desired. Bake in a preheated 350° oven for 15 to 20 minutes.

Chapter 8

The Fishes — If It Swims, We Can Cook It!

SPECKLED TROUT, EVERYBODY'S FAVORITE

The speckled trout is Louisiana's own fish because it's more plentiful here than anywhere else. Its the delight of gourmets and seafood chefs and the darling of all who fish, whether for sport or business, because it's available year-round. Its meat is firm and white and of a delicate flavor. It can be fried, broiled, or poached, and it can be served with a wide enough variety of sauces to test the skill and ingenuity of any seafood cook. Speckled trout is served with pride in the finest restaurants.

The speckled trout is a beautiful iridescent fish, bluish-black or grayish silver with bronze overtones, with black spots along its upper side. When first taken from the water, it actually gleams. It is not a trout at all, actually, but a member of the squeteague-weakfish family, which includes croakers, drums, and redfish. Its average size of about a pound and a half makes it very popular in the fish markets. It scales easily and fillets beautifully.

Although the specks are present year-round, their prime season is May and June. Get out of bed in the dark and be ready to fish at the crack of dawn, when the fish are hungry. Use light tackle and cast them a bright spoon or a hook baited with live shrimp. The chances are pretty good that you'll have speckled trout for breakfast.

HOLD TIGHT, HOLD TIGHT

There is a peddler from Cincinnati
Who comes daily with his fishery,
Fish is what he sells,
Listen to him and hear him yell, FISH!

Chorus
Hold tight, hold tight, hold tight, hold tight,
Foo-ra-de-ack-a-sa-ki, want some seafood,
  mama,
Shrimps and rice, they're very nice.
Hold tight, hold tight, hold tight, hold tight,
Foo-ra-de-ack-a-sa-ki, want some seafood,
  mama.
Codfish and sauce and then, of course,
I like oysters, lobsters, too,
And I like my tasty bit of fish
When I come home from work at night
I get my favorite dish, Fish!
Hold tight, hold tight, hold tight, hold tight,
Foo-ra-de-ack-a-sa-ki, want some seafood,
  mama,
Shrimps and rice, they're very nice!

Hold tight, hold tight, hold tight, hold tight,
Foo-ra-de-ack-a-sa-ki, want some seafood,
  mama,
Shrimps and rice, they're very nice.
Hold tight, hold tight, hold tight, hold tight,
Foo-ra-de-ack-a-sa-ki, want some seafood,
  mama.
Codfish and sauce and then, of course,
I like kippers, mackerel, too,
And I like my tasty bit of fish
When I come home from work at night
I get my favorite dish, Fish!
Hold tight, hold tight, hold tight, hold tight,
Foo-ra-de-ack-a-sa-ki, want some seafood,
  mama,
Shrimps and rice, they're very nice!

This rollicking song is probably the most famous seafood song ever written. When it first came out in the late 1930s, both the Andrews sisters and Fats Waller made records that became nationwide hits. Oddly enough, the prudish censors of that day and time saw a lot of double meaning in the song (wal, mebbe there is a leetle bit) and refused to let the Andrews girls sing it on the radio. There were large billboards all over New Orleans (illustrated with crabs,

Want Some Seafood, Mama

"Early Morning Concert" by Francisco McBride. Jazz plays an intimate part in the lives of just about everybody in New Orleans.

shrimp, and oysters) proclaiming, "I want some seafood, mama, and cold Dixie Beer." It was the campaign that put Dixie on an equal footing with Jax, the other famous local beer, (the Cajuns call it Jacques beer). In those days the breweries of New Orleans produced some of the best beer in America, very appropriate to go with the best seafood in the country.

Some of the best traditional New Orleans bands still play *Hold Tight* today. You can't keep a good tune down.

Speckled trout.

SPECKLED TROUT AMANDINE GALATOIRE
(Serves 6)

This is the most popular fish dish in New Orleans. "Sauté meunière amandine" is a very old French classic cooking process. Mr. Jean Galatoire and his four nephews brought the method with them from France, and they made it famous. It has been widely imitated but never equalled, and it still tastes best at Galatoire's Restaurant on Bourbon Street.

I have hanging on my kitchen wall Mr. Justin Galatoire's personal recipe for the dish. He wrote it out for me eighteen years ago in a beautiful flowing antique script.

  6 trout fillets
  milk
  flour
½ lb butter
  juice of 2 lemons
¼ lb sliced almonds
  salt and pepper

Fillet three trout of about 2½ pounds each, dip the six tenderloins in cold milk, sprinkle with

flour, and season with salt and pepper. Melt the butter in a large skillet, and place the fish fillets in it, skin side up. Cook slowly until brown, then flip them over with a spatula, and brown the other side. Use a slow cook, not a hot fry, which would destroy the delicate flavor of the fish. Remove the fish, place on warm serving plates, and keep hot. Add the lemon juice and almonds to the butter in the pan. Raise the heat high and stir and scrape the bottom and sides of the pan to release any browned particles, which are delicious—the soul of the meunière. Stir until the almonds turn a light golden brown (don't let them get too brown or they'll be bitter). Pour this sauce over the fish fillets and serve immediately, piping hot.

NOTE: The secret of success with this dish lies in the handling of the almonds. They must be exactly the right tone of golden brown. Use sliced natural or blanched almonds, not slivered almonds. Prepare the almonds in advance by slowly cooking them in butter until they're golden yellow, and then set them aside. Add them later to the lemon-butter sauce in the skillet, and cook until golden brown. If you try to cook the almonds from scratch in the lemon-butter sauce, the butter may scorch and the lemon juice may evaporate before the almonds even start to brown, and you'll have a bad sauce.

TROUT AMANDINE LONGFELLOW
(Serves 1)

Longfellow House at Pascagoula, Mississippi, has its own delicious method of making trout amandine. Here it is.

Fillet a two-pound trout, remove the skin, and marinate the fillets for a few minutes in butter, paprika, salt, and freshly ground black pepper. Rub crushed almonds into the meat on both sides. Place the fillets on a buttered broiler plate, and broil under a medium fire, turning once. They're done when the meat flakes easily with a fork. Don't overcook.

Pour over the trout a sauce made of equal parts of butter, Sauterne, and lemon juice. Sprinkle with sliced toasted almonds.

NOTE: Toasted pecans, chopped, can be substituted for almonds in these amandine recipes, and the resulting sauce is delicious.

SUBSTITUTIONS: Haddock, redfish, flounder, or pompano fillets are delicious when cooked à la amandine.

TROUT FILLETS VERONIQUE I
(Serves 6)

Chef Justin Callens, one of New Orleans's greatest, gave us his recipe for Trout Veronique. The word "veronique" always means with grapes.

6 trout fillets
1 12-oz can white grapes
½ cup sauterne
4 tsp lemon juice
½ lb butter
1 tbsp chopped parsley
   salt and freshly ground black pepper

Poach the white grapes in the sauterne for five minutes. Melt the butter in a large skillet, and free it of foam. Cook the trout fillets gently for five minutes on each side (a little longer if they're large). While the fillets are on the fire, add the lemon juice and chopped parsley, and then add the grapes and sauterne. Raise the heat, cook on full fire for about two minutes more, and serve on hot plates.

TROUT FILLETS VERONIQUE II
(Serves 4)

When preparing this dish, make your Hollandaise sauce first. Keep it warm by placing the cooking pan in another pan of warm water (not hot water or it will cook).

4 fillets of trout
1 cup dry white wine
2 cloves
2 allspice
4 peppercorns
1 lemon slice
1 bay leaf
1½ cups Hollandaise sauce (see below)
1 12-oz can white grapes (or 1½ cups peeled white seedless grapes)

INSTANT BLENDER HOLLANDAISE SAUCE
2 sticks butter
4 egg yolks

2 tbsp vinegar
⅛ tsp cayenne
½ tsp salt

Melt the butter in a small skillet, and set it aside. Place the egg yolks, vinegar, cayenne, and salt in a blender, and mix them at the lowest speed. Pour in the butter slowly, blending all the while. When the mixture has absorbed all the butter and fluffed out, it's done.

Place the wine and a cup of water in a flat pan, add the cloves, allspice, peppercorns, lemon slice, and bay leaf, bring to the boil, and then cut the heat very low. Place the fillets in the pan. They should be covered by the liquid, so add hot water, if necessary. Poach for seven or eight minutes, not allowing the poaching liquid to bubble or boil. The fish are done when the meat flakes when tested with a fork. Be careful not to overcook them, or they'll fall apart. Lift the fillets from the water with a spatula, hold them over the pan to drain well, and place them on warm serving plates. Keep the fish warm while finishing the sauce. Remove the spices and lemon from the cooking water. Boil it down rapidly until it is reduced to about three quarters of a cup. Drain the grapes, add them to the cooking water, and heat through. Turn off the heat, and let the mixture cool a little. Add the Hollandaise sauce and stir it in rapidly. Ladle the sauce over the fillets, sprinkle with paprika and chopped parsley, and serve at once. It goes flat if allowed to get cold.

TROUT MARGUERY I

(Serves 4)

Marguery sauce is named for the Restaurant Marguery, one of the most famous Paris res-

taurants of the nineteenth century. Their chef, M. Mangin, is said to have developed the sauce.

Trout Marguery is another dish made famous by Galatoire's. I never did get the recipe from Mr. Justin Galatoire before he passed away. But anyway, it's so complex that he would probably not have had time to sit down and write it out. Here's one method of doing it.

4 trout fillets (from two 2½ lb fish)

MARGUERY SAUCE
½ stick butter
3 tbsp flour
1 cup milk
1 cup rich fish stock (see below)
1 cup cooked shrimp, peeled and chopped (or whole tiny "titi" shrimp)
1 cup fresh mushrooms, sliced and cooked in butter until wilted
salt and freshly ground black pepper to taste

POACHING INGREDIENTS
fish stock
2 cloves
2 allspice
1 bay leaf
4 peppercorns
1 lemon slice

This dish is prepared in three steps: first the fish stock, then the Marguery sauce, and finally the poaching of the fish.

When you buy your trout fillets, ask the fishmonger to give you the heads, backbones, tails, and trimmings of the fish to make fish stock. (If these aren't available, you can substitute chicken broth or bouillon for the fish stock.)

FISH STOCK

4 lb fish heads, bones, tails, trimmings
4 cloves garlic, minced
3 onions, coarsely chopped
1 cup parsley sprigs
1 lemon, sliced
2 cups dry white wine
¼ tsp ground cumin
½ tsp powered saffron (or 1 tsp of the stringy type)
½ tsp thyme
½ tsp basil
½ tsp freshly ground black pepper
4 tsp salt (or more)

If saffron is unavailable, substitute a tablespoon of turmeric (for color). Place all the ingredients in a large saucepan or pot, add about four quarts of water, and boil for 30 minutes. Strain through triple cheesecloth and set aside.

MARGUERY SAUCE

Melt the butter in a skillet, add the flour, and cook over low heat for five minutes, stirring constantly. Add the milk a little at a time, and keep stirring. Blend in a cup of fish stock. Cook slowly until the sauce thickens. Add the shrimp and the mushrooms, and mix well. Season to taste with salt and pepper, set aside, and keep hot.

THE POACHING

In a flat poaching pan large enough to hold the four fillets, place enough of the fish stock to completely cover the fish, add the cloves, allspice, bay leaf, peppercorns, and lemon slice. Bring to the boil, cut the heat very low, and put the fish fillets in the pan. Poach them gently (the liquid must not boil or bubble) for eight to ten minutes, depending on the thickness of the fillets. Be careful not to overcook or the fish will fall apart. The fillets are done when the meat flakes when tested with a fork. Lift the fillets from the water with a large spatula, holding them over the pan for a moment to drain well. Place them on warm serving plates, and cover each fillet with a blanket of the hot Marguery sauce. Slide the dishes under the broiler flame for a moment to glaze the top of the sauce. Decorate with parsley sprigs and serve at once. Dig out a dusty old bottle of Clos Vougeot, and chill it lightly. Be careful not to shake the bottle unnecessarily or you'll make the wine nervous. If you don't have a Clos Vougeot, Graves or Chablis will go well.

NOTE: Always strain your poaching liquid and add it to any other fish stock you may have left over. Cool it down to room temperature, place it in plastic containers, and freeze it. Then you'll always have fish stock available when it's called for. Good fish stock is indispensable in many seafood dishes.

TROUT MARGUERY II
(Serves 4)

Follow the recipe above, but instead of poaching the fillets, broil them in butter on individual metal sizzle platters. When the fish are done, cover with a blanket of the Marguery sauce, replace under the flame for a moment to glaze the sauce, and serve on the hot sizzle platters.

TROUT MARGUERY III
(Serves 4)

One school of thought on Trout Marguery holds that the trout should be baked and that the sauce should be Hollandaise, with crabmeat in addition to the shrimp and mushrooms. I can't vouch for this as a true Marguery, but it's a delicious concoction.

4 ½-lb fillets of trout (or 8 small ones)
1 stick butter
¼ cup dry white wine
1 cup shrimp, boiled, peeled, and chopped (or tiny whole "titi" shrimp)
1 cup crabmeat
1 cup fresh mushrooms, sliced and cooked in butter
   cayenne
   salt and freshly ground black pepper
2 cups Hollandaise sauce

Preheat oven to 350°. Melt the butter in a flat-bottomed oven pan, and add the wine. Season the fillets with salt, pepper, and a little cayenne, and lay them in the pan. Bake in the oven for 15 to 20 minutes, or until the fish flakes when tested with a fork. While the fish are cooking, make two cups of Hollandaise sauce. Heat the chopped shrimp, crabmeat, and mushrooms in a small saucepan, and add them to the Hollandaise sauce, stirring rapidly

to mix well. Place the trout fillets on preheated serving plates, put a blanket of the sauce over them, and serve immediately. The dish is so rich that the wine you serve should be very, very dry.

BROILED SPECKLED TROUT I
(Serves 4)

4 fillets from two 2½-lb trout (or 8 small fillets)
½ stick butter, melted
   salt and freshly ground black pepper
   cayenne
   Maître d'hotel butter or anchovy butter (see below)

Rub the fish fillets with melted butter, sprinkle with salt, black pepper, and a little cayenne. Butter individual metal sizzle platters, and place a fillet on each, skin side up. Broil for four minutes, flip each fillet over with a large spatula, and broil the other side. Squeeze a little lemon juice over it while it's broiling. The fish is done when it flakes easily when tested with a fork. Don't overcook. Spoon Maître d'hotel butter or anchovy butter over the fillets, and serve piping hot on the sizzle platters. (Or you can broil them on a flat broiler pan, and when they're done, transfer to warm serving plates, spoon the flavored butter over them, and serve at once.)

MAITRE D'HOTEL BUTTER
In spite of its fancy-sounding name, Maître d'hotel butter is nothing but lemon-butter sauce jazzed up with parsley, salt, and pepper.

1 lb butter
1 tsp salt
⅛ tsp cayenne
4 tbsp chopped fresh parsley
4 tbsp fresh lemon juice
    freshly ground black pepper

Let the butter get soft at room temperature. Cream it, add the other ingredients, and mix well. When ready to serve, melt two or three tablespoons for each serving of fish, and spoon it over the cooked fish.

NOTE: Chill whatever Maître d'hotel butter you have left over, and roll it into balls about the size of a golf ball. Wrap tightly in waxed paper and keep in the freezer until you need it again. In addition to being good with fish, it's great on steaks and chops.

ANCHOVY BUTTER
1 lb butter
1½ tbsp anchovy paste (or finely minced fillets)
1 tbsp grated onion
2 tbsp fresh lemon juice
¼ tsp cayenne
    freshly ground black pepper

Soften the butter and cream it with the remaining ingredients, mixing well. When ready to serve, melt two or three tablespoons for each serving, and spoon it over the cooked fish.

NOTE: Store any surplus anchovy butter as described above for Maître d'hotel butter. In addition to being good on fish, steaks, and chops, anchovy butter makes a great hors d'oeuvre when spread on crackers.

BROILED SPECKLED TROUT II
(Serves 1)

This is the ideal way to broil tender young speckled trout weighing three quarters of a pound to a pound. The head and tail are left on for good looks, and lying on the platter, the trout looks like a double fish with a single tail—a visual effect much favored by high-class restaurants.

Starting at the very front of the head, split the fish down the back with a sharp knife, being careful not to cut all the way through. Cut down the body to within a half inch of the tail. Fold the fish open like the pages of a book. Clean out the entrails and the black stomach lining, and remove the backbone and ribs. Rinse well and pat dry with paper towels. Rub with melted butter, salt, freshly ground black pepper, and a little cayenne. Place it on a buttered metal sizzle platter (or broiling pan) skin side down, and broil for eight to ten minutes, or until lightly browned. (These young fish are so thin, you don't have to turn them over. The hot pan cooks the underside.) Drizzle with a little butter, sprinkle with paprika and chopped parsley, and serve on the hot sizzle platter with lemon wedges. If you choose, you can serve it with the Maitre d'hotel butter or the anchovy butter given in the previous recipe.

STUFFED WHOLE SPECKLED TROUT
(Serves 4)

4 1-lb trout
1 cup shrimp, boiled, peeled, and chopped
1 cup crabmeat
2 scallions with 3″ of their green leaves,
** thinly sliced**
1 small rib celery, minced
½ small green pepper, minced
2 tbsp chopped fresh parsley
2 cloves garlic, minced
¼ stick butter
2 eggs, beaten
¼ 8-oz loaf French bread
1 tsp Worcestershire sauce
¼ tsp Tabasco
¼ cup dry white wine
** salt and freshly ground black pepper**
** sherry**

Keep the heads and tails on for good looks—the speckled trout is a very beautiful fish. Scale and clean the trout, remove their backbones, and rinse out their body cavities thoroughly. Dry them and set them aside.

Melt the butter in a skillet, add the scallions, green pepper, celery, parsley, and garlic, and cook until the vegetables are soft and translucent. Add the crabmeat and shrimp and mix well. Season with salt and black pepper. Moisten the bread until it's workable with the fingers, and make a paste of it. Beat the eggs, white wine, Worcestershire sauce, and Tabasco together, pour this mixture over the bread and work it in, and add all this to the shrimp-crab-

meat mixture. Stuff the trout with the dressing, and sew them up or close with small skewers. Bake in a preheated 400° oven until nicely browned, about 25 minutes. Place on preheated serving plates, drizzle with melted butter, sprinkle a few drops of sherry on each fish, and decorate with a generous number of parsley sprigs and lemon wedges. Serve at once, piping hot.

REDFISH ARE BIG AND BRASSY

The redfish is a favorite of both seafood fanciers and people who fish for sport. It is a member of the croaker and drum family and a cousin of the speckled trout. It is found all up and down the Atlantic and Gulf coasts from Massachusetts to Brownsville, Texas. On the Gulf coast it's called redfish and channel bass, but on the Atlantic seaboard it's called the red drum. Its iridescent reddish-bronze color gives it its name. There's always at least one conspicuous black spot (sometimes two or three) near the upper base of its tail. Legend has it that this was the fish Christ fed to the multitude, and the spot was where his thumb touched it, marking the species indelibly forever.

Redfish can grow to a very large size (the world record is eighty pounds) and they're fierce fighters and tackle smashers. That's why they're so eagerly sought after in sport fishing. Large redfish are called "bull reds," and the small fish are called "rat reds." Gulf coast redfish average five to six pounds in weight, but along the Carolina coast they range from fifteen to thirty pounds.

Fish under fifteen pounds are the best for eating and the little "rat reds" are especially good. When fishing, the conservation-minded will throw back any fish over fifteen pounds to maintain a spawning reserve. The smaller fish should be cut into fillets, the larger fish cut into steaks or baked whole. This is the fish that provides not only the Cajun dish famous in song and story, Redfish Courtbouillon (p. 54), but also that New Orleans favorite, Boiled Redfish Hollandaise.

Since speckled trout and redfish are close cousins—both are members of the croaker family—all the recipes given for speckled trout can be used for preparing redfish, sometimes with even better results. Because the redfish is frequently larger, it's especially adaptable for baking, stuffing, boiling, and stewing.

BOILED REDFISH HOLLANDAISE
(Serves 4)

One of the feature attractions at Arnaud's Restaurant is their Boiled Redfish Hollandaise. The owner, Mrs. Germaine Cazenave Wells, gave me the following recipe for it many years ago.

1 3-lb redfish
salt and freshly ground black pepper to taste

ARNAUD'S HOLLANDAISE SAUCE
6 egg yolks
1 tsp dry mustard
1½ oz tarragon vinegar
1 lb butter
salt and freshly ground white pepper to taste

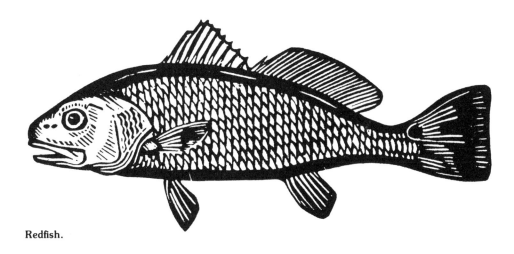

Redfish.

Melt the butter. Beat the egg yolks in a small saucepan, adding salt, white pepper, vinegar, and dry mustard. Keeping the saucepan over very low heat, continue beating and slowly add the melted butter. Keep the sauce warm while preparing the fish.

Fillet the redfish and cut the fillets in half to make four portions. Heat enough water to cover the fish in a flat pan. Gently boil the fish until they're done, that is, when the flesh flakes easily when tested with a fork. Remove the fillets, drain well, place on a warm serving platter, and cover with the Hollandaise sauce. Sprinkle with paprika, decorate with parsley sprigs or watercress, and serve at once.

BAKED STUFFED REDFISH

(Serves 8 to 12)

THE FISH
- **1 8-lb redfish**

THE STUFFING
- **1 cup crabmeat**
- **1 cup shrimp, boiled, peeled, and chopped**
- **1 stick butter**
- **1 green pepper, chopped**
- **1 large onion, chopped**
- **2 cloves garlic, minced**
- **½ cup chopped celery**
- **4 strips bacon, fried brown and crumbled**
- **1 tsp dry mustard**
- **1 tsp Worcestershire sauce**
- **½ tsp Tabasco**
- **½ tsp thyme**

- **½ cup sherry**
- **4 eggs, beaten**
- **¾ 8-oz loaf French bread**
  fish stock or chicken broth, as needed
  salt and freshly ground black pepper
  to taste

FOR THE BAKING
- **1 cup white wine**
- **1 cup olive oil**
- **1 cup (or more) fish stock or chicken broth**
- **3 medium onions, sliced**
- **3 tomatoes, sliced**
- **1 cup sliced fresh mushrooms**
- **2 tbsp flour**

MAKING THE STUFFING
Melt the butter in a large skillet, and cook the celery, green pepper, chopped onion, and garlic until soft and transparent. Add the Worcestershire sauce, dry mustard, sherry, Tabasco, thyme, and crumbled bacon, and cook for five minutes more. Add fish stock or chicken broth if the mixture is too dry. Tear the French bread into pieces, moisten with fish broth, and knead to a paste with the fingers. Add the beaten eggs and work them into the mixture. Mix in the shrimp and crabmeat. Season to taste with salt and black pepper.

PREPARING THE FISH
Clean and scale the redfish, leaving the head and tail on just for looks (or cut them off if there isn't room in your roasting pan). Remove the backbone in a strip from just behind the head to the front of the tail. This is done by severing each rib carefully where it joins the vertebrae and then undercutting the spine. Rub

the fish inside and out with melted butter, salt and black pepper, and a little cayenne.

BAKING THE FISH

Put the dressing into the belly cavity of the redfish and sew it up, or close with small skewers. Put the cup of olive oil, the cup of white wine, and a cup of fish stock or chicken broth in the bottom of a turkey roasting pan. Lay sliced onions and tomatoes on top of the fish and some more around it in the pan juice. Cover the pan and bake in a 350° oven for 45 minutes to an hour, basting it often to keep it from drying out. Add more stock if necessary. About 15 minutes before the fish is done, sprinkle the flour and sliced mushrooms into the juices around the fish. Leave the pan uncovered for the last 15 minutes. At the end spoon the pan juices and their ingredients over the top of the fish. If you don't have a large silver platter, cover a tray with bright aluminum foil, carefully remove the fish from the pan, and place it on the center of the tray. Decorate profusely with parsley sprigs, watercress, and lemon slices. Serve at once.

WHOLE BOILED REDFISH

(Serves 4)

In the old days they used to boil a whole redfish, and to keep it from falling apart, they sewed it up tightly in a clean piece of linen with a strap at each end for lifting it. (They rubbed it first with flour to keep it from sticking to the cloth.) The fish was lifted in its shroud into a roasting pan with enough gently boiling water to cover it. The water was flavored with vegetables, spices, and wine. Then when the fish was done (about thirty minutes) it was lifted out, the shroud was cut away, and there was the fish lying there, as beautiful as the moment it was caught. Try it yourself with the following ingredients and see.

1 redfish (6-8 lb) with head and tail on
1 large onion, sliced
2 ribs celery, chopped
2 bay leaves
½ lemon, sliced
1 tsp mixed pickling spices
2 cloves garlic, crushed
1 cup white wine

Use a large serving platter or a tray covered with foil. Make a bed of lettuce leaves, and lay the whole cooked fish on it. Cover with a blanket of Hollandaise sauce, Veronique sauce, or Marguery sauce (see index for these sauces). Decorate profusely with watercress, parsley, lemon wedges, radish roses, olives, and so on. Make it as handsome as it is delicious. Take a color photograph of it before you eat it. And of course serve a good wine with it, red or white.

BROILED REDFISH

(Serves 4)

4 8-12-oz redfish fillets (or 8 small ones)
½ stick butter, melted
    salt and freshly ground black pepper
    cayenne
    fresh lemon juice

JOE "KING" OLIVER

SUGARFOOT STOMP

Beside the river, beside the river,
Down in Dixieland,
Banjos are ringin', everybody's singin',
Everything is grand.
Just listen to that stomp down band
When they start dancin', stompin', and
    prancin'
The dance called Sugarfoot Stomp.
Old man River just seems to whisper:
Let your doggies romp,
High steppin' mammas
Keep shoutin' all night long:

Chorus
O Daddy, Sweet Daddy, rock your mamma
like a cradle.
Sweet Papa, I must let my doggies romp,
Do the dance with me they call the Sugar-
    foot Stomp.

Drawing by Emily Davis

Joe "King" Oliver (1885–1938) is one of the immortals of jazz. Not only a great cornetist and band leader, he was a creative composer and wrote many tunes that became jazz standards. Among them were *Dippermouth Blues, Sugarfoot Stomp, Snag It, West End Blues, Chimes Blues, Doctor Jazz, Canal Street Blues,* and *Jazzin' Baby Blues.*

He started playing around 1905 for parades, funerals, and parties, and by 1910 he was playing regularly in Storyville cabarets. They called him "the King" and the title stuck. He let Louis Armstrong sit in with his band when Louis was still a boy in short pants.

After Storyville closed, Oliver went to Chicago, and when he sent to New Orleans for young Louis Armstrong to play second cornet, King Oliver's Creole Jazz Band was the greatest in America. In the 1920s they recorded about thirty records that became classics, and old King Oliver records are now treasured by collectors. After his band broke up in 1927, Joe still made a few recordings for Victor and Brunswick with pick-up bands.

His fortunes went into a decline in the 1930s. His health failed, the sight in his one good eye was failing, and he lost his teeth—a disaster because a cornetist cannot play without teeth. He died in Savannah on April 10, 1938, penniless and forgotten. It was a sad ending for a man who had been one of the greatest Kings of Jazz.

Rub the redfish fillets with melted butter, and sprinkle with salt, black pepper, and a little cayenne. Butter individual metal sizzle platters, and place a fillet on each, skin side up. Broil for four or five minutes, flip each fillet over with a large spatula, and broil the other side. Squeeze a little lemon juice over it while it's broiling. The fish is done when it flakes easily when tested with a fork. Don't overcook. Spoon Maitre d'hotel butter over the fillets, and serve piping hot on the sizzle platters. (If you don't have sizzle platters, you can broil them on a flat broiler pan and transfer them when done to warm serving plates.) Anchovy butter is also delicious on redfish fillets, and of course, so is Hollandaise sauce.

REDFISH FILLETS WITH OYSTER SAUCE
(Serves 4)

- 4 redfish fillets or steaks
- 1 stick butter
- 3 scallions with 3 inches of their green leaves, thinly sliced
- 1 rib celery, chopped fine
- 1 clove garlic, minced
- 2 dozen oysters (about a pint) and their liquor
- 1 tbsp chopped fresh parsley
- ½ cup light cream
- ¼ cup dry white wine
- ¼ tsp cayenne
- salt and freshly ground black pepper to taste

Melt a half stick of butter and cook the scallions, celery, garlic, and parsley until soft. Add the oyster liquor and allow it to evaporate a little. Add the cream and white wine, and stir them in rapidly. Cook until the sauce thickens a little. Add the oysters and cook until they are plump and their edges curl. Set this sauce aside and keep it hot. Melt the other half stick of butter, place it on four individual metal sizzle platters or in a broiler pan, rub the redfish fillets with salt, black pepper, and cayenne, and broil the redfish fillets for four to five minutes on each side (or until done, that is, when it flakes easily when tested with a fork). Pour the oyster sauce over the fish just before serving. Sprinkle with paprika and chopped parsley.

A SNAPPY FISH, THE RED SNAPPER

This bright red beauty is the one Gulf of Mexico fish that's well known all over the country, both because it's in very good supply and because it's a very, very tasty fish. Baked Red Snapper à la Creole is one of the most universally popular fish dishes in America. If it weren't for this dish, many people in far places would never have heard the word "Creole." The fish goes under several different names—Pensacola Snapper, after the city where it was first caught commercially; Mexican Snapper, because it's so abundant on the reefs of the Gulf of Campeche; Colorado; and Acara Aya.

A few years ago I was sipping beer with friends at a small beachside bar in the ghost town of Sisal, Yucatan. As a considerate "gift of the house," our host brought us a big four-pound baked fish to go with our beer. We squeezed lime juice over it and ate it with our bare hands, as is the custom in Yucatan bars. It was truly one of the most delicious fish I had ever tasted, and when I asked our host what it was, he said, "Acara Aya, the most popular fish in Mexico." But he couldn't give us the gringo name for it. When I got back to Merida, I looked it up in the dictionary. It meant red snapper, a fish I'd been eating all my life.

Red snappers hang out around deep-water reefs fifty miles or more out in the blue Gulf. They feed close to the bottom in water from 100 to 400 feet deep. The oil rigs out in the Gulf off the coast of Louisiana have turned out to be ideal "reefs," and the snappers congregate around them in thick schools. A group of friends and I used to charter a boat and go out there to catch king mackerel, but when the kings weren't around, we'd fish near the bottom for the snappers. It's so easy to hook snappers that you could almost say they're eager to be caught, but it can almost work your arm off reeling up fish after fish from a depth of 200 feet. At the end of a trip we sometimes had more than 500 pounds of snappers on ice, which brought in enough to pay the expenses of the voyage, including several cases of beer.

In the old days the typical long-range fishing schooner working out of Pensacola carried a crew of nine men. Fishing with handlines, those men could catch up to 4,000 pounds in an hour, or 8,000-10,000 pounds a day,

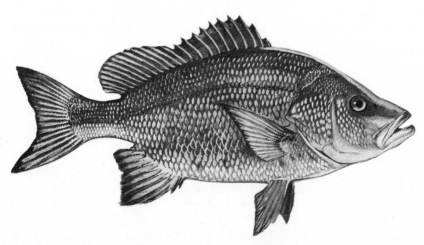

Red snapper, *Lutjanus blackfordi*. (Drawing by Duane Raver, Jr., courtesy of Louisiana Wildlife and Fisheries Commission)

depending on the depth of the water and wind and tide conditions. Such a plenitude of fish explains why the delicious red snapper has always been available in fish markets all over the country. It's a great blessing that its quality is equal to its quantity.

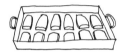

BAKED RED SNAPPER A LA CREOLE I
(Serves 12)

Baked red snapper à la Creole is the classic method of cooking this fish, and it's one of the most delicious of all Creole fish dishes. The term *à la Creole* usually means "with tomato sauce," but there are as many kinds of Creole tomato sauces as there are Creole cooks. It's an impromptu improvisational thing. Some of the sauces are very complex, and others are relatively simple. There are recipes here for both types, and you can take your choice. Or as we've suggested before, freewheel it and invent your own. A little added cognac or whatever never hurt anybody.

THE FISH
12 8-oz red snapper fillets or steaks

CREOLE TOMATO SAUCE
1 32-oz can plum-type tomatoes
1 6-oz can tomato paste
6 scallions with 3″ of their green leaves, chopped

2 medium onions, chopped
2 cloves garlic, minced
1 green pepper, chopped
2 ribs celery, chopped
½ cup fresh chopped parsley
1 dozen stuffed olives, sliced
2 tbsp capers
2 sticks butter
4 tbsp flour
1 cup red wine
2 cups fish stock (or water)
2 tbsp lemon juice
1 tbsp sugar
1 tbsp Worcestershire sauce
¼ tsp ground cumin
½ tsp basil
½ tsp thyme
¼ tsp cayenne
salt and freshly ground black pepper

Melt the butter in a large skillet or Dutch oven, add the flour, and stir over low heat for 10 minutes to make a light roux. Add the onions, scallions, green pepper, celery, parsley, and garlic, and cook until the vegetables are soft and transparent. Drain and chop the tomatoes, saving the juice. Add the tomatoes and juice to the pan. Add all the other ingredients except the fish, and mix well. Bring to the boil, lower the heat, and simmer for 1½ to 2 hours; stir it now and then, scraping the bottom of the pan to keep it from sticking and scorching. Add more salt if necessary. The sauce should be semifluid, so it may be necessary to add some hot water.

Grease the bottom of a large flat baking pan, and lay the red snapper fillets or steaks on it. Pour the sauce over them. Bake in a pre-heated 350° oven for 20 to 25 minutes, or until the fish flakes when tested with a fork. When they're done, lift the fish pieces out with a large spatula, place on warm serving plates, and cover with a blanket of the sauce. Serve a large bowl of steaming hot rice on the side. And a bouncy red wine.

BAKED RED SNAPPER A LA CREOLE II
(Serves 4)

Here's a somewhat simpler version of the same dish.

4 8-oz red snapper fillets or steaks
1 16-oz can of tomatoes
½ 6-oz can tomato paste
2 scallions with 3″ of their green leaves, chopped
1 medium onion, chopped
½ green pepper, chopped
1 clove garlic, minced
2 tbsp fresh chopped parsley
1 rib celery, chopped
2 bay leaves
2 lemon slices
1 tsp chili powder
1 stick butter
2 tbsp flour
   salt and freshly ground black pepper

Melt the butter, add the flour, and stir until blended. Add the tomatoes, tomato paste, scallions, onion, green pepper, garlic, parsley, and celery. Add the bay leaves, lemon slices, chili powder, salt, and black pepper. Cook and stir until the vegetables are soft and transparent. Add enough hot water to make the

sauce semifluid, and let it boil gently for 20 minutes. Remove the bay leaves and lemon slices. Preheat the oven to 350°. Place the fish fillets in a greased oven pan, cover with the sauce, and bake for 20 to 25 minutes, or until the fish flakes easily when tested with a fork. Lift the fish out with a spatula, and place on preheated serving plates, and cover with the sauce. Decorate with lemon slices, sliced stuffed olives, and parsley sprigs, and serve at once.

BAKED STUFFED WHOLE RED SNAPPER

You'll need a red snapper weighing from ten to twelve pounds and a stuffing of your choice, perhaps the oyster dressing or the shrimp-crab-meat dressing, both of which are given in this book.

In haute cuisine one of the chef's goals in preparing a handsome fish like a red snapper is to preserve its beauty, so that when it's brought to the table it looks pristinely fresh and alive, as if it had just come out of the water, with sparkling eye, glistening scales, fins and tail intact—all the result of trickery and sleight of hand by the chef.

Here's how some of the skullduggery is accomplished. First, the eye must sparkle so take a small sharp knife, carefully remove the eyeball from its socket, and place it in a teacup in the refrigerator. Leave the head on. The tail and fins must stay on, so wrap them with foil to keep them from burning and falling off.

Then rub the scales generously with oil to keep them glistening. And finally, stuff the fish and sew up the stomach slot as inconspicuously as possible.

Line a large baking pan or turkey roasting pan with heavy-duty foil. Add a cup of olive oil and a cup of white wine. Lay the fish in the pan. Cover it loosely with a piece of foil. Preheat the oven to 350° and bake the fish for 45 minutes to an hour or more, depending on its size. Brush it frequently with oil to keep it from drying out.

If you don't have a large silver platter, cover a large tray with aluminum foil. Make a bed of watercress, romaine, or escarole on the platter, and then carefully remove the fish from the pan and place it on this bed in a natural position. Remove the foil from the tail and fins. Run to the refrigerator and get the sparkling eye and replace it in its socket. Decorate the rim of the tray with lemon slices, watercress, parsley, and whatever other greenery you like. Call in the photographers and reporters, and ask the jazz band to strike up something hot.

After the oohs and ahhs are over with and you're ready to eat, peel the skin and scales off the snapper, slice it up into individual portions, and give each guest plenty of stuffing. It's such a festive dish that a good dry Champagne is called for.

BROILED RED SNAPPER

The ideal way to cook the fillets of freshly caught young red snappers is to broil them in butter. The meat is sweet, very white, and light-flavored—delicate enough to please the palate of the most exacting connoisseur. No sauces are required, but of course, you can gild the lily if you want to. If the fillets are small and thin, allow two per serving. If they're thick and weigh eight ounces or more (a 12-ounce fillet is ideal) allow one per serving.

Broil the fillets in individual metal sizzle platters or in a flat metal broiler pan. Rub each with melted butter, salt, freshly ground black pepper, and a little cayenne. Butter the platter or pan, and place the fillets in it. If they're thin, place them skin side up, and broil them for eight to ten minutes without turning (the hot metal cooks the bottom part). If they're thick, place them on the sizzle platter skin side up, broil for five minutes, flip them with a large spatula, and broil four minutes more. Serve them at once on the sizzle platters, sprinkled with paprika and decorated with watercress or parsley sprigs and lemon wedges.

BROILED RED SNAPPERS WITH SMALL BUSTER CRABS

Sometimes buster crabs are small, about the size of a silver dollar, and they are a delicacy much sought after by gastronomes. They combine beautifully with pompano, red snapper, or other high-quality fish. Broil the red snapper steaks as instructed above, and while they're cooking, lightly flour the little busters and cook them gently in butter with a little lemon juice added. Brown them very lightly on both sides. To serve, place two little busters atop each serving of red snapper, and pour over it

Béarnaise sauce or Maître d'hotel butter. As the great Escoffier said, "The best dishes are simple dishes," and this is one of the very best.

BROILED RED SNAPPERS WITH LUMP CRABMEAT

Broil the red snapper fillets or steaks as instructed above, and while they're cooking, melt butter in a skillet, and add lemon juice and the lump crabmeat. Don't stir or the lumps will fall apart. Just heat it through. Place the crab lumps on top of the fillets, and pour on the pan juices. Or you can use Maître d'hotel butter, Béarnaise sauce, or Hollandaise sauce.

NOTE: Always remember that crabmeat is pre-cooked—that is, it's picked from boiled crabs. Therefore you must always be careful not to overcook it when it's used in a sauce of this type.

BARBECUED RED SNAPPER
(Serves 6 to 8)

This is a good dish for outdoor summer cook-outs when the barbecue pit or grill is going full blast, but it can also be successful in wintertime if you make judicious use of your oven and broiler.

2 red snappers, 2-3 lb each
1 stick butter (or more)
1 medium onion, grated

2 tbsp fresh chopped parsley
2 tbsp Worcestershire sauce
1 tbsp Tabasco
2 lemons, sliced
salt and freshly ground black pepper

Keep the fish whole, heads and tails on. Rub them inside and out with salt and pepper. Lay them on a sheet of heavy-duty foil. Melt the butter in a skillet and add the onion, parsley, Worcestershire, Tabasco, and lemon slices. Stir well and cook slowly for two or three minutes until the flavors are blended. Pour the sauce over the fish. Take another piece of foil the same size as the bottom one and place it on top. Roll and crimp the edges of the foil tightly so that the package is hermetically sealed with no chance of leakage. Place the package on a barbecue grill (preferably with a hood, but it's not absolutely necessary). Turn the package every 20 minutes, taking care not to tear the foil. Cook for an hour to an hour and a half, depending on the size of the fish. At the end of this time, remove the fish from the foil, and place them on the well-greased grill. (At this point one of those small mesh-wire flip-over grills is ideal.) Grill for 10 minutes on each side, basting with the sauce.

NOTE: To achieve a smoky flavor, soak wood chips (hickory preferred) in water for an hour, drain them, and place them on the charcoal. This method produces maximum smoke and prevents their flaming up. If they do flame up, however, add more wet chips. (If you're cooking indoors, you'll have to fudge a little and add liquid smoke to your sauce.)

As with all barbecuing, there are lots of tricky variables involved—weather, humidity, intensity of heat, type of grill, to name several. You may have to practice until you get it down pat.

OUR FLOUNDER IS A FINE FLUKE

Flounder is one of the most popular fish in New Orleans restaurants, especially with visitors from the North who are anxious to try our famous "fillet of sole" or whole stuffed flounder. The flesh of the flounder is delicious no matter how it's cooked—sautéed, fried, broiled, or poached—plain or with elaborate sauces. Its flavor rivals that of the famous Dover sole of Europe, and for that reason it's called "fillet of sole" in many restaurants.

Our Southern flounder is really a fluke because it has a large mouth and its eyes grow on the left side, whereas the true flounder, which is found in New England, has a smaller mouth and eyes on the right side. The flounder undergoes a strange metamorphosis. It starts life in the normal manner of fishes swimming around upright, but at the age of about three months its skull twists around under its scalp, depositing both eyes on the same side, and from then on the flounder swims on its side. The eyes are stemlike, and the fish loves to bury itself in the sand with only its eyes exposed, waiting for prey to pass along. This fish is a past master at the art of camouflage and can change its color and texture to match the color of any surface it may be lying on—gravel, sand, mud, or whatever.

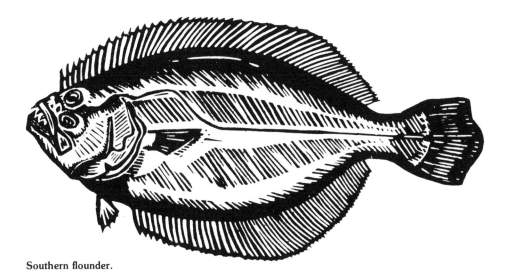

Southern flounder.

A flounder laid on a checkerboard can duplicate the black and white squares underneath it almost instantly!

Flounders are caught year-round, but they're more plentiful during spring and summer. Typically they weigh from one to three pounds and measure from twelve to twenty inches, but fish weighing up to twenty pounds are not unknown. The world's record is thirty pounds.

Most of the commercial catch of flounders is made by the shrimp boats. Most people who fish for sport catch flounders while "playing the field," that is, fishing for anything that will bite, but some specialists know the fish's habits well enough to pursue it deliberately. The flounder can be caught anywhere, but it has some general preferences that make seeking it out possible. For instance, it likes to lie around in deep water at the tail end of sandbars, where the current eddies will swirl shrimp, minnows, and other food to it. The flounder also likes brackish salt-water creeks and bayous with steep mossy banks and deep holes and bends. At night it works right up to the beach line or into marsh grass where the water is only a few inches deep.

This nightime love of shallow water has led to a unique kind of flounder fishing on the beaches of the Gulf islands and along the long continuous beach of the Mississippi Gulf coast. Armed with a broom handle spear and a Coleman lantern, the fisherman wades along in the shallow water next to the beach line. He spots the flounder by looking for its eyes and the very slight outline or shadow its body casts in the sand. Then he spears the fish and strings it up. The "stringer" is a long strong cord tied to the fisherman's belt, which drags along in the water behind. Sometimes there may be as many as 20 fish on the line.

If you can't catch your own flounders, you can always depend on your supermarket. Frozen flounder fillets are among the most commonly available fish in supermarkets all over the country, and they're almost as good as the fresh product.

CREOLE SPICED FLOUNDER FILLETS
(Serves 4 to 6)

Walter Stauffer McIlhenny, the president of the Tabasco Company, furnished us with this recipe for spicy hot flounder fillets. The recipe calls for a barbecue grill or hot coals or an open hearth or campfire, but if none of these are available, you can do it almost as well in the broiler of your oven.

2 lb fresh flounder fillets
½ cup vegetable oil
½ cup water
⅓ cup lemon juice
⅓ cup Worcestershire sauce
¼ cup grated onion
2 tbsp brown sugar
2 tbsp salt
1 tsp Creole mustard (or powdered mustard)
1 clove garlic, minced
1 tsp Tabasco sauce
paprika

Have the fillets cleaned and ready. Combine all the sauce ingredients except the paprika, and simmer for five minutes, stirring occasionally. Cool. Place the fillets in a single layer in a shallow baking dish. Pour the sauce over the fish and let it marinate for 30 minutes, turning once. Remove the fish, reserving the sauce for basting. Place the fish in well-greased, hinged wire grills, and sprinkle generously with paprika. Cook about four inches from moderately hot coals for five minutes. Baste with sauce, sprinkle with paprika, turn, and cook for five to eight minutes longer. If the fillets are very thin, reduce your cooking time accordingly. Serve piping hot with cold beer as a fine accompaniment.

OF FATE, TIME, AND STUFFED FLOUNDERS

Stuffed whole flounder is one of New Orleans's most popular dishes. The custom of stuffing the flukes probably originated in the nineteenth century at one of the lakeshore seafood palaces at Milneburg or West End. These were year-round resorts, but in the summertime the Lake Pontchartrain crabs and flounders were especially plentiful, and the citoyens of New Orleans would drive out in their carriages to consume them.

The late Joe Astorias was chef at the Roosevelt Hotel, and his handiwork was well known to local gastronomes. When he and his wife, Marguerite, opened their own restaurant, the Paradise Point on the Mississippi Gulf coast, they made stuffed flounders one of their specialties, and gourmets from Alaska to Zanzibar came to try it. Many of them swore that it was one of the greatest seafood dishes under the sun.

The Paradise Point is of hallowed memory for many people. The Gulf coast was wide open in those days, and there was a small casino in the back room of the restaurant, where a person could join in an innocent crap game or play a little roulette. But it was the stuffed flounder that packed them in.

Joe Astorias passed away several years ago, and then hurricane "Camille" came along and blasted the Gulf coast. There's nothing left but a bare concrete slab on the beach site where the Paradise Point Restaurant stood, a bleak memento mori of a good eating establishment. But Joe's monument was his cookery, and his recipes have survived him. His widow, Marguerite, a well-known artist herself, has given me his recipe for stuffed flounder, and I'm passing it on to you.

STUFFED FLOUNDERS
(Serves 6)

6 large whole flounders, 1-1½ lb each
2 cups crabmeat
1 medium onion, chopped fine
½ cup chopped celery
½ green pepper, diced fine
4 cloves garlic, minced
1 tbsp prepared mustard
1 tbsp Worcestershire sauce
dash of Tabasco
4 eggs
¼ loaf French bread
1 tbsp butter
1 tbsp sauterne
salt and freshly ground black pepper

Bone the six flounders by cutting an "X" lengthwise and crossing the body (see illustration). Fold back the free corners, and lift out the backbone.

Cook the celery, onion, garlic, and green pepper in butter until brown. Moisten the bread until it's workable with the fingers. Beat the Worcestershire, Tabasco, sauterne, and mustard into the eggs until thoroughly mixed. Pour this mixture over the bread, add the cooked vegetables, the crabmeat, salt, and black pepper, and mix well. Stuff the mixture lightly into the open flounders. Bake at 400° until nicely done and golden brown, about 25 minutes. Just before serving, sprinkle a few drops of sherry over each fish. Garnish with parsley sprigs and lemon wedges.

NOTE: Where fresh crabmeat is not available, chopped shrimp, lobster meat, chopped scallops, or chopped hardshell clams make an excellent substitute. These seafoods may be used separately or combined in making the stuffing. Use your imagination!

OYSTER-STUFFED FLOUNDER
(Serves 4)

4 whole flounders, 1-1½ lb each
4 dozen oysters and their liquor
    (about 2 pints)
3 scallions with 2" of their green leaves,
    thinly sliced
2 tbsp fresh parsley, chopped
½ cup fresh mushrooms, chopped

2 slices bacon, fried brown and crumbled
½ stick butter
1 tbsp cornstarch
    salt and freshly ground black pepper

Melt the butter in a skillet, add the cornstarch, and blend well. Add the scallions, parsley, mushrooms, and bacon, and cook until the vegetables are soft and transparent. Cut the oysters into quarters (smaller if they're large) and add them along with their liquor (if no liquor is available, use a half cup or more of fish stock or bouillon). Cook until the oyster meats are lightly firmed. This stuffing does not have to be as firm as the other dressings. It's more of a sauce with no bread crumbs.

Split the flounders as for Stuffed Flounders II, stuff with the oysters, and bake as instructed in that recipe.

This lighter dish than the others calls for a Chablis, the traditional wine for oysters. It should be slightly chilled.

STUFFED FLOUNDER FILLETS

If whole fresh flounders aren't available, you can substitute flounder fillets, which are now available frozen in every supermarket in the land. Don't be put off when you see them lying there in the freezer. They have lots of culinary possibilities.

Make any of the stuffings described in the previous recipes. Thaw the flounder fillets. Lay them on a flat surface, place a small cylinder of stuffing at the end of each fillet, roll it up, and if necessary, pin the outer end with a

BESSIE SMITH

MAKE ME A PALLET ON YOUR FLOOR

Make me a pallet on your floor,
Make me a pallet on your floor,
Make me a pallet, baby, a pallet on your
floor,
So when your good gal comes,
She will never know.

Make it very soft and low,
Make it, babe, very soft and low,
Make it, baby, near your kitchen door,
So when your good gal comes,
She will never know.

I'll get up in the morning
And cook you a red hot meal.
I'll get up in the morning
And cook you a red hot meal
To show you I 'preciate, baby,
What you done for me
When you make me a pallet on your floor.

Make it soft and low,
Make it, baby, soft and low.
If you feel like laying down, babe,
With me on the floor,
When your good gal comes home,
She will never know.

Drawing by Emily Davis

Reprinted with permission of Pookie Tree Publishing
Company, New York, New York.

Bessie Smith (1895–1937) was the acknowledged queen of the blues singers. At 17 she learned how to belt them out from Ma Rainey, the mother of blues singing. Bessie had a robust, rich, earthy voice. She organized one of the tent shows that were a main source of entertainment in small southern towns in the days before movies, radio, and TV.

Starting in 1923, Bessie made dozens of records, many of them best sellers. She starred in the movie *St. Louis Blues* in 1929, and she frequently sang over the radio.

In the mid '30s she started belting the bottle, and her career hit the skids. She was killed in a car wreck in Mississippi—a tragic loss, because she could have been saved if any good ambulances and hospitals had been available.

toothpick or small skewer. If the fillets are very small and thin, four rolls make an individual serving, but if they're large, two rolls will do. Place the fillets on buttered sizzle platters (or in a pan) and bake for 15 minutes in a preheated 350° oven, or just until the tops of the rolls begin to brown. When they're done, drizzle the rolls with melted butter, sprinkle on a few drops of sherry, garnish with lemon wedges, chopped parsley, and paprika, and serve piping hot. Stuffed flounder fillets are very good when served in this simple manner, but if you want to get elaborate, you can cover the rolls with a blanket of Hollandaise sauce, Marguery sauce, Mornay sauce, or Maitre d'hotel butter.

NOTE: This stuffing method goes well with fillets of any lean white-fleshed fish, such as speckled trout, redfish, red snapper, haddock, cod, or ocean perch.

BAKED FLOUNDER ROLLS A LA VICTOR

One of the best seafood cooks I've ever known was a fisherman on a three-man fishing dragger. He was such a good cook that the other two members of the crew elected him chef with lifetime tenure. Victor Pacellini is now captain of the boat, but he still likes to do the cooking himself. Several of my favorite recipes came from Victor's supply of know-how. Always down to earth, he doesn't beat

around the bush. Here's how he describes making flounder rolls.

When you're on the boat and the net comes up, take some live flipping flounders right out of the net. Scale them but don't skin them. Cut off the fillets, and cut each fillet lengthwise down the middle into two pieces. Starting with the small end, roll them loosely around the index finger, and pin the roll together with a toothpick. Fill the center holes with a bread stuffing of your own invention. (Fried onions and shrimp? Crumbled bacon? Diced fried salt pork?) Line a baking pan with aluminum foil, grease it with butter, and lay the flounder rolls on it. Brush them generously with lemon-butter sauce.

Cover them with another sheet of aluminum foil, and bake in a preheated 350° oven for 15 to 20 minutes. (*Tip from Victor:* The bottom sheet of aluminum foil should always be made kind of crinkly, not smoothed out completely. If it's smooth and slick, the fish may stick to it.)

VICTOR'S FLOUNDER FILLETS A LA BUTTERMILK

Cover the bottom of a baking pan with crinkly foil, butter the foil, and lay flounder fillets skin side down on it. Take a brush and slop well-salted buttermilk on top of the fillets and around them. Sprinkle with chopped green onion leaves, salt, and freshly ground black pepper. Cook in a preheated 350° oven for 10 to 15 minutes, basting now and then with the pan juices. Serve on preheated plates with the juice spooned over them.

FLOUNDER FILLETS WITH SALT PORK A LA VICTOR

Rub some large, thick flounder fillets with a layer of salt and let them sit in the refrigerator overnight. Next day wash them well, and dry with paper towels. Sprinkle moderately with salt and plenty of freshly ground black pepper. Melt some margarine, chop some onions, and lightly brown them in the skillet on a fast hot fire. (Margarine works best here because it has a high smoke point and will not burn or scorch.)

Set the onions aside and fry some diced salt pork cubes until they're three-quarters done. Cover the bottom of a baking pan with crinkly foil, grease it, and lay the fillets on it skin side down. Sprinkle with onions and pork cubes. Preheat the oven to 350° and bake the fillets for 10 to 15 minutes. Remove the pan from the oven and sprinkle the fillets with Parmesan cheese. Cook for five minutes more, or until the cheese and pork cubes become brown. Place fillets on hot plates and serve immediately.

FLOUNDER FILLETS PAN-FRIED IN BATTER
(Serves 4)

  4 large (or 8 small) flounder fillets
  corn flour
  milk
  butter
  salt and freshly ground black pepper

Melt the butter in a skillet. Rub the fillets with salt and pepper. Dip them in milk, then in yellow corn flour. Shake off the excess flour, and lay them in the skillet. Cook gently. Shake the skillet now and then to keep the fillets loose and prevent them from sticking to the bottom. Flounder fillets are often very thin and fragile and must be handled with extreme care. If a fillet sticks to the skillet, it may fall apart when you run the spatula under it to flip it over. (A Teflon skillet is a godsend for this particular job.) After the fillets have turned light golden brown on the bottom, take a large spatula and carefully lift each one up, flip it over, and brown the other side. More than any other fish, flounder fillets absolutely must not be overcooked.

Place the fillets on heated serving plates, sprinkle with melted butter, paprika, and chopped parsley, or watercress. Provide lemon wedges. Pan-fried flounder fillets require no sauce except the butter and lemon juice. Simplicity is the great virtue of this dish.

GOUJONETTES OF FLOUNDER
(Serves 4)

Mr. Warren Le Ruth, the owner-chef of Le Ruth's Restaurant in Gretna, gave me this recipe for cooking flounder fillets. They're called goujonettes, meaning "little fish," because the flounder fillets are cut into strips shaped like small fish. They do look handsome when placed on a platter. They make great hors d'oeuvres for a party.

1½ lb flounder fillets, cut into strips—"little
    fish"
3 eggs, beaten
    flour
    bread crumbs
1 stick butter
    lemon juice
    salad oil

Heat the oil to 365°. Dip the "little fishes" in
flour, then eggs, and then bread crumbs. Fry
in deep oil until golden·brown. Drain well.
Place on warm serving plates and keep hot.
Cook the butter in a small saucepan until
chestnut brown, and add lemon juice. Pour
over the "little fishes." Serve piping hot.

FLOUNDER FILLETS EN PAPILLOTE
(Serves 6)

Wrapping food to preserve its juices has been
practiced since ancient time with such diverse
materials as palm leaves, banana leaves, grape
leaves, cabbage, and so on. Cooking fish in
parchment bags reached its heyday in France
with such practitioners as Escoffier, Prosper
Montagné, and others. It's a high-toned practice, but there's no reason to be afraid of it. It's
nothing but a seafood sauce and fish fillets
wrapped and baked. Modern aluminum foil
can be used instead of parchment, but it lacks
the glamour of the old method.

12 medium flounder fillets, 4-6 oz each
4 chopped scallions with 2″ of their
    green leaves

6 fresh mushrooms, chopped
1 tbsp fresh chopped parsley
¼ cup dry white wine
2 egg yolks, beaten
½ cup cream
1 cup cooked shrimp, chopped (or whole
    "titi" shrimp)
1 cup crabmeat
2 cups fish stock (or bouillon)
½ stick butter
2 tbsp flour
    pinch of cayenne
    pinch of nutmeg
    salt and freshly ground black pepper to
    taste

Heat the fish stock almost to the boil in a flat
poaching pan. Poach the fillets until they're
half done, about four or five minutes. Remove
the fillets and keep them warm. Reserve the
stock. Melt the butter in a skillet, add the flour,
and blend well. Add the scallions and parsley,
and cook until they're soft and transparent.
Add the mushrooms. Add one cup of the fish
stock (more if needed) and cook slowly, stirring constantly, until it thickens a little. Add the
cayenne, nutmeg, salt, and black pepper. Add
the wine, cream, shrimp, and crabmeat, and
stir them in gently so as not to tear up the
crabmeat. Cook over low heat for five minutes
longer. Remove from the fire, let the mixture
cool a moment, and then stir in the egg yolks.

Place a fillet in the center of a piece of
buttered aluminum foil. Spoon on a good layer
of the sauce and place another fillet on top.
Lift the edges of the foil, crimp them, and roll
them down. Then crimp and roll up the ends.
Punch a few small holes in the foil to allow
steam to escape. Bake in a preheated 400°

oven for 20 to 25 minutes. Serve them in the sacks so your guests can have the fun of opening them.

NOTE: Redfish, red snapper, and other types of firm, lean fish fillets may be cooked in this manner, but if you want to try one of New Orleans's most regal dishes, try Pompano en Papillote.

FILLETS OF SOLE BONNE FEMME
(Serves 4)

Call me a chauvinist, but our American flounders are as good as Dover sole any day, maybe even better. The yellowtail flounder, gray sole, lemon sole, and our own southern flounder make for superb dining. If you want to call all these flounders "fillet of sole," go ahead. They're worthy of the name.

Fillet of Sole Bonne Femme is the favorite method of cooking Dover sole in France. It's a very old method, and it was very popular in New Orleans in antebellum days, especially in the dining rooms of such luxury hotels as the St. Charles, where "les Americains" liked to dine, and the St. Louis in the French Quarter, that habitat of the rich Creole aristocrats.

Bonne Femme, of course, means "good mistress" or "good wife"—whichever she happens to be—but in culinary terms it means "with mushrooms."

4 large (or 8 small) flounder fillets
14 fresh mushrooms, sliced (about 1½ cups)

3 scallions with 1″ of their green leaves, thinly sliced
1 tsp fresh parsley, chopped
½ cup dry white wine
½ cup fish stock (or bouillon)
½ cup white bechamel sauce
1 tbsp butter
1 tsp lemon juice
salt and freshly ground black pepper to taste
cayenne

Place the mushrooms, scallions, and parsley in the bottom of a well-buttered ovenproof glass dish. Season the flounder fillets with salt, black pepper, and a smidgin of cayenne, and lay them on top of the mushrooms. Preheat the oven to 400°. Pour the wine and fish stock over the fillets, and cover loosely with a piece of aluminum foil. Cook for 10 minutes, or until the fish flakes when tested with a fork. Don't overcook. Carefully lift the fillets out with a spatula, and place them on warm serving plates. Put the mushrooms and scallions on top of the fillets, leaving the juices in the baking dish, place the dish on top of the stove, add the white sauce, lemon juice, and butter, and stir until the mixture is heated thoroughly and the butter is melted. Pour the sauce over the fillets, quickly glaze under the broiler flame, and serve at once. A high-quality white Bordeaux is recommended.

NOTE: This is an excellent method of cooking the fillets of any lean, firm-fleshed fish: speckled trout, redfish, red snapper, haddock, ocean perch, turbot, and others. The same is true for all of the fillet cooking methods that follow.

FILLETS OF SOLE A LA NANTUA
(Serves 4)

The lowly Louisiana mudbug crashes into the domain of haute cuisine when it is made into a Nantua sauce. Nantua means "with crawfish tails" or "with crawfish puréed." The sauce goes beautifully with flounder fillets.

> 4 large (or 8 small) flounder fillets
> 1 cup fish stock (or bouillon)
> 1 cup bechamel sauce
> ½ cup heavy cream
> ¼ cup dry white wine
> 1 cup crawfish tails, boiled, peeled, and deveined
> 1 tbsp fresh parsley, chopped
> 1 tbsp sherry
> salt and freshly ground black pepper to taste

Place the flounder fillets in a well-buttered flat poaching pan. Pour the fish stock and the white wine over them. Heat to just this side of the boiling point, and poach for 10 to 15 minutes, depending on the thickness of the fillets. The fish is done when it flakes easily when tested with a fork. Remove the fillets with a large spatula, place them on preheated serving plates, and keep them warm. Turn the heat high and boil down the juices in the pan until reduced by one half. Lower the heat and add the bechamel sauce, cream, crawfish tails, parsley, and sherry. Heat until it thickens a little, blend well, and pour the sauce over the fillets. Run under the broiler flame a moment to glaze the sauce. Garnish with watercress or parsley and serve at once.

NOTE: If you substitute chopped boiled shrimp (or whole "titi" shrimp) for crawfish in this recipe you'll have "Sole aux Crevettes," a delicious dish.

FILLETS OF SOLE DUGLERE
(Serves 4)

This dish was invented by the great chef Dugléré of the Café Anglais in Paris. Dugléré has come to mean "with tomatoes"—a doubtful glory for a great cook.

> 4 8-oz (or 8 smaller) fillets of flounder
> 1 small onion, grated
> ¼ stick butter
> 1 tbsp cornstarch
> ½ cup fish stock
> ½ cup dry white wine
> 1 large Creole tomato, peeled and chopped (or ½ 16-oz can tomatoes, chopped)
> ½ small green pepper, finely chopped
> 1 tbsp fresh chopped parsley
> salt and freshly ground black pepper to taste

Melt the butter in a skillet, add the cornstarch, and blend well for a minute or two, stirring constantly. Add the onion, green pepper, and chopped parsley, and cook until the vegetables are wilted. Add the tomato and cook for a few minutes more. Add the fish stock and white wine, and blend well. Season to taste with salt and black pepper. Roll the sole fillets and pin them with toothpicks. Place them in the skillet, cover, and cook gently for eight minutes. Turn the rolls over, cover, and cook for seven minutes more. Place the fillets on preheated serving plates, and ladle the sauce in the skillet over them. Garnish with watercress or parsley sprigs, and serve at once.

NOTE: This is a good way to cook fillets of trout, redfish, red snapper, or any other lean, white, firm-fleshed fish.

FILLETS OF SOLE A LA MARTINI
(Serves 4)

One of my restaurant patrons, an inveterate martini guzzler, always drank three or four before dinner. When he finally asked me to prepare a fish so that it tasted like martinis, I agreed that I'd cook him an irresistible fillet of sole à la Martini if he'd stop drinking them before dinner. (It is my confirmed opinion that the custom of drinking martinis before dinner should be abandoned. They paralyze the taste buds and make the finest dishes almost tasteless.) He agreed, and I cooked him up the following concoction. When the dish was brought out, my bartender, Mark Dittrick, realizing that he had lost a customer, grumbled, "One man's fish is another man's poisson." I hope to use that maxim for my epitaph.

4 8-oz (or 8 smaller) fillets of flounder
2 cups dry vermouth
2 tbsp gin

6 juniper berries, if you can find them
(optional)
½ stick butter
3 tbsp flour
1 cup cream
1 tbsp chopped fresh parsley
salt and freshly ground black pepper

Put the dry vermouth in a flat poaching pan, add the gin and juniper berries, and season with salt and pepper. Boil until the alcohol has evaporated from the liquid, just two or three minutes. Turn the heat low (it must not boil from here on) and poach the flounder fillets for 10 to 15 minutes, depending on the thickness of the fillets. They're done when the flesh flakes easily when tested with a fork. Remove the fillets, drain them well, set them aside, and keep them hot. Save the poaching liquid.

Melt the butter in a skillet, add the flour, and stir until well blended and the flour has cooked enough to lose its "floury" taste. Add one cup of the poaching liquid very slowly, blending it in. Add the cream slowly. Don't let the sauce boil. Stir over very low heat until it thickens. Add the chopped parsley. Place the fish fillets on preheated serving plates, and put a blanket of the sauce over them. Sprinkle with paprika and serve at once.

FILLETS OF SOLE FLORENTINE
(Serves 4)

In making this dish you should prepare the Mornay sauce and the spinach first, keep them warm, and have them ready.

4 large (or 8 small) flounder fillets
1 bunch fresh spinach (or 2 pkg frozen)
¾ stick butter
   Parmesan cheese
   salt and freshly ground black pepper

MORNAY SAUCE
½ stick butter
¼ cup flour
1 cup fish stock (or bouillon)
2 egg yolks
¼ cup grated Swiss cheese
1 cup cream
   salt and freshly ground black pepper

Melt a half stick of butter in a skillet, add the flour, and cook slowly until thoroughly blended and free of lumps. Add the fish stock and mix it in. Add the Swiss cheese and stir until it's melted. Beat the cream and the egg yolks together and add them. Cook over very low heat, stirring constantly, not allowing it to boil, for 10 minutes more (or until it thickens). Season with salt and pepper. Set aside and keep it warm.

Wash the spinach and leave a little water clinging to it. Melt a quarter stick of the butter in a saucepan, add the moist spinach, cover the pan, and steam it until done, stirring now and then. Don't overcook it. Set aside and keep it warm.

Melt the remaining half stick of butter in a skillet, and gently cook the flounder fillets, turning once with a spatula.

Drain the spinach well and place a bed of it on each of four preheated serving plates. Lay the fillets on the spinach, cover each with a blanket of Mornay sauce, and sprinkle with Parmesan cheese. Run them under the broiler

flame for a moment to glaze the sauce and melt the Parmesan slightly.

FILLETS OF SOLE MORNAY

Prepare exactly as instructed above for Fillets Florentine, but omit the spinach.

FILLETS OF SOLE MARGUERY

Use the recipes given for Trout Marguery.

FILLETS OF SOLE VERONIQUE

Use the recipes for Trout Fillets Veronique.

POMPANO IS A PATRICIAN

The pompano is as delicious as the less criminal forms of sin.
Mark Twain, on tasting his first pompano

Ask a widely traveled seafood connoisseur what are the two most delicious fish in the world, and the chances are pretty good that he'll name the red mullet of the Mediterranean and the pompano of the Gulf of Mexico. Chefs and aficionados of the art of seafood cookery will probably agree. Curiously enough, the flavor of the two fish is almost identical—firm, rich flesh, slightly redolent of the salty deep blue sea. Let Europe have its red mullet. The pompano is undeniably the tastiest fish in America, unequaled by anything that swims in either salt water or fresh water, and that includes salmon, brook trout, and all the rest. That's a big mouthful, but I'll stand by it.

Pompano.

It's a beautiful creature, too. It has a thin, shallow body and a forked tail, and it's silvery blue to bluish green on top, with iridescent silvery sides and a bottom flecked with golden yellow. A single fish can weigh up to ten pounds but typically the weight ranges from a half pound to three pounds. They're small, but ounce for ounce they're the fiercest fighters of all the game fish, and a whole school of pompano anglers has grown up. They fish with light tackle, and with a ten-pound test monofilament line to give the valiant little gladiator a sporting chance. The pompano has no teeth, but it nibbles at the bait—it's the biggest bait stealer in the world. A fisherman has to keep the line taut, and he must learn to recognize this nibbling action as a sign to set the hook.

The early Spanish explorers dubbed the fish pompano, which means "grape leaf." Pompano range all the way from Massachusetts to Brazil. They're found around the Bahamas, off the Carolina coast, near Florida and the West Indies, and especially in the Gulf of Mexico and the Caribbean Sea. They're most plentiful in January and February. A strange phenomenon takes place on the Carolina coast in the early spring. Large schools of round silvery baby pompano ride the crests of incoming waves that toss them up on the beach. They lie there flipping on the sand, looking for all the world like a bunch of bright silver dollars jumping up and down. The next wave that comes in takes them back out to sea. The little fish seem to actually enjoy this sport since they do it over and over.

Pompano were once very difficult to find. They appeared only over oyster reefs and the outer beaches of the Gulf islands. Today, however, Louisiana is the top pompano fishing area of the world, and the reason for the change is interesting. Since the first offshore oil drilling platform was built in 1947, more than 3,000 of them have been constructed. Like a reef or a wreck, the underpinnings of these platforms attract the small microorganisms on which fish feed, and this in turn attracts the fish. It was discovered very early that pompano were attracted to the rigs in vast numbers, and now Louisiana has some great pompano fishing spots—more than 3,000 in fact.

More pompano are eaten in New Orleans than in any other place on the globe. The great restaurants vie with one another to see who can prepare the fish in the most attractive and delicious manner. Brennan's puts almonds and lump crabmeat on top of the fish. Antoine's invented Pompano en Papillote, now one of that restaurant's most popular features. Drago's Lakeside and other restaurants broil it to perfection. Take your choice of the recipes below. You can't go wrong with a fish this good.

BROILED WHOLE POMPANO

(Serves 1)

Pompano is such a delicious fish that the best way to cook it and maintain its delicate flavor is to broil it whole with its beautiful head and tail on. Take a pompano weighing a pound to a pound and a half, and rub it with melted butter, salt, freshly ground black pepper, and a little cayenne. Cut two or three gashes with a sharp knife on each side of the pompano. Place it on a well-buttered individual metal sizzle platter (or in a broiler pan), and put it under the broiler flame for eight to ten minutes. Turn it over and broil the other side. It's done when the flesh flakes when tested with a fork. Serve it right on the sizzle platter (or on a preheated serving plate) decorated with watercress or parsley sprigs and lemon wedges.

It calls for a great wine, such as Chassagne-Montrachet or another really fine white Burgundy.

BROILED POMPANO FILLETS

Next to the broiled whole pompano, broiled fillets are best. Rub the fillets with melted butter, salt, freshly ground black pepper, and a little cayenne, place skin side up on buttered sizzle platters (or a broiler pan), and broil for three or four minutes. Flip with a spatula and broil the other side. The cooking time depends on the thickness of the fillets, but be careful not to over-

cook them. The fillets are done when the flesh flakes easily when tested with a fork. Serve piping hot right on the sizzle platters. (If you used a broiler pan, lift the fillets with a spatula, and place them on preheated serving plates.) Garnish with watercress or parsley and lemon wedges. Again we call for Chassagne-Montrachet. Lacking that, crack out a dusty old bottle of Clos Vougeot, or if you can't get that, a good red Chambertin will go well. Pompano is a rich fish.

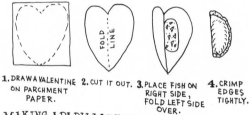

1. DRAW A VALENTINE ON PARCHMENT PAPER. 2. CUT IT OUT. 3. PLACE FISH ON RIGHT SIDE, FOLD LEFT SIDE OVER. 4. CRIMP EDGES TIGHTLY.

MAKING A PAPILLOTE FOR POMPANO

POMPANO EN PAPILLOTE

(Serves 4)

This is New Orleans's most regal and ostentatious seafood dish. Mr. Jules Alciatore of Antoine's perfected it in 1901 in honor of the visit to New Orleans of Santos-Dumont, the famous Brazilian balloonist, who was a hero of the Charles A. Lindbergh type in his day. What Mr. Jules did was to cut the conventional parchment paper (the papillote) in such a way that the final result resembled a balloon—well, sort of. And Santos-Dumont was tickled pink. We are not sure of Mr. Jules's exact recipe, but here's one way of doing it.

4 8-oz. (or 8 smaller) pompano fillets
4 chopped scallions with 2″ of their green leaves

1 tbsp chopped fresh parsley
¼ cup dry white wine
2 egg yolks, beaten
½ cup cream
1 cup cooked shrimp, sliced into quarters
   (or whole "titi" shrimp)
1 cup crabmeat
2 cups fish stock (or bouillon)
½ stick butter
2 tbsp flour
   pinch of cayenne
   pinch of nutmeg
   salt and freshly ground black pepper to
   taste

Ask your fishmonger to save you the heads, tails, bones, and trimmings of your pompano after the fillets have been removed (or the heads and bones of any other white-fleshed fish). Prepare enough fish stock (p. 55) so that you have the two cups you need.

Heat the fish stock in a flat pan almost to the boiling point, lower the heat, and poach the fillets until they're half done, about four or five minutes. Remove the fillets and set aside. Melt the butter in a skillet, add the flour, and blend well, removing all lumps. Add the scallions and parsley, and cook until they're soft and transparent. Add the fish stock and cook, stirring constantly until it thickens a little. Add the cayenne, nutmeg, salt, and black pepper. Beat the wine, cream, and egg yolks together, and add to the skillet. Keep the heat low and don't boil. Add the shrimp and crabmeat, stirring them in gently so as not to tear up the crabmeat. Cook over low heat for five minutes longer. Set the sauce aside.

Cut four 11″ × 14″ pieces of parchment paper into heart shapes (see illustration) and butter them well. (If you don't have parchment paper, you can use any white or brown paper, well buttered, or if you're ultramodern, you can use aluminum foil.) Fold the valentines down the middle. Place each fillet on a heart next to the folding line on the right side. Divide the sauce into four parts, and blanket the fillets with it. Fold the left side of the heart over, and bring its edge together with the right edge. Roll up the edges of the paper and crimp them tightly in a well-sealed packet. Preheat the oven to 400°. Place the packets on a buttered cookie sheet, and bake for 15 minutes or until the bags are lightly browned. Serve in the bags, with blaring of trumpets, dancing girls, dimmed lights, and Pol Roger Champagne.

NOTE: The "Young Turks" school of French chefs, who are antisauce, would say it's a disgrace to pile all that gunk on such a noble fish as a pompano. Paul Bocuse himself said as much on a recent visit to New Orleans. However, those fellers are Frenchmen, not Creoles, and traditional New Orleans cooks would never give up their beloved seafood sauces.

POMPANO FILLETS SAUTE MEUNIERE
(Serves 6)

Take three pompanos of about 2½ pounds each and fillet them. The fillets should weigh about a half pound each. Dip the six tenderloins in cold milk, then sprinkle with corn flour, and season with salt, freshly ground black pepper, and a little cayenne. Melt a half pound of butter in a large skillet, and cook the fish slowly, browning on both sides. Remove the fish and place on warm serving plates. Add the juice of 2 lemons to the frying butter. Raise the heat, and scrape the sides and bottom of the pan to release any brown particles clinging to it (this stuff is the soul of the meunière). Stir until the butter turns light brown, pour over the fish, and serve piping hot.

POMPANO FILLETS SAUTE MEUNIERE AMANDINE
(Serves 6)

  6 8-oz (or 12 smaller) pompano fillets
  ½ lb butter
    corn flour
    juice of 2 lemons
    milk
  ¼ lb sliced almonds
    cayenne
    salt and freshly ground black pepper to taste

Use only sliced almonds, not slivered. Cook the almonds gently in a little butter just until they're golden yellow. Set aside.

Soak the pompano fillets for a few minutes in cold milk, and then drain. Dip them in corn flour, and shake off the excess flour. Melt the butter in a large skillet. Place the fillets in the skillet, and cook very slowly, browning on both sides. Remove the fish, place it on warm serving plates, and keep it hot. Raise the heat high, add the lemon juice and almonds to the frying butter, and stir until the butter turns light brown and the almonds are a light golden

brown. Don't cook the almonds dark brown or they'll have an acrid flavor. Pour the sauce over the fish, and serve piping hot.

POMPANO AMANDINE AUX CRABES
(Serves 6)

This is one of the world's most ambrosial dishes, suitable fare for kings, queens, Creoles, Cajuns, and a few others. Where else but in New Orleans could you find such good fresh pompano and lump crabmeat? (You can make the dish in far-off places by using frozen products, but will it be as good? Not quite, but probably better than any other seafood dish in your old hometown.)

  1 lb lump crabmeat
  6 8-oz (or 12 smaller) pompano fillets
  3 sticks butter
    corn flour
    juice of 3 lemons
  ¼ lb sliced almonds
    cayenne
    salt and freshly ground black pepper

Melt one stick of butter in a skillet, and add the juice of one lemon. Add the lump crabmeat, but don't stir, or you'll tear it apart. Cook gently, just enough to heat it through. Set aside and keep warm.

Prepare the Pompano Amandine exactly as described in the previous recipe. When the finished fillets and almonds are on the serving plates, divide the lump crabmeat into four parts and place the lumps in a ring around the fillets on each plate.

Serve a Blanchot Chablis Grand Cru with this dish—if you can find it!

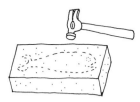

POMPANO A LA ROCK SALT

This very old fish cooking method must have originated down near Avery Island, where the salt mines provide plenty of rock salt and the nearby Gulf of Mexico provides plenty of pompano. You'll need a tin loaf pan about twelve inches long by six inches wide by four inches deep and plenty of rock salt. You can use ice cream salt or Morton's coarse kosher salt.

Wash a nice fat fresh pompano. Leave the guts in and the head and tail on. (If the fish is too long for the pan, cut off the tail.) Put an inch layer of salt in the pan, and lay the pompano on it. Add more salt to the pan until it's an inch above the fish so that the fish is completely encased. Sprinkle water generously over the salt until it's soaked. The water will solidify the salt. Bake in a preheated 400° oven until all the water has evaporated and the salt is hard as a brick. Turn it out on a platter, and deliver it to the table with a hammer. The diner has to break the block open to get at the beautiful fish inside. The flavor is out of this world. Contrary to what you'd expect, it is not too salty—it's just right.

This method of cookery also works well with Spanish mackerel or any other fat-fleshed fish.

NOTE: It's sometimes an accepted practice to cook a fish that's absolutely fresh with the innards left in. When the fish is cooked well done, the stomach can be peeled right out. As with red mullet, ortolans, woodcocks, and others, the stomach contributes something to the ultimate flavor.

CHOCTAW POMPANO A LA MUD

My Choctaw Indian friend Nick Ducré, who taught me all about gumbo filé, also taught me how the Bayou Lacombe Indians on the North shore of Lake Pontchartrain used to coat a pompano with mud and bake it in the coals of the campfire. Here's a modernized version of his method.

Rub a whole pompano with oil, salt, and pepper, and wrap it in a tight layer of dampened paper towels. Get some firm clay that's free of sand, moisten it just enough to make it thick and malleable, and cover the fish all around with a one-inch layer of the mud. Place the package on the coals of the campfire and cover with more hot coals. Let it bake for a couple of hours or more, or until the clay is hard as a brick. Bring it to the table and crack the clay open with a hammer. Remove the paper towels, and devour the fish with glee and a few war whoops. Wash it down with slugs of usquebaugh. This definitely ain't a dish for the dainty, but it's unbelievably delicious.

The Indians used this method for cooking all sorts of fresh-water and salt-water fishes, but just as we do, they treasured the pompano over all other fishes.

"KID THOMAS" VALENTINE

Kid Thomas playing on the balcony steps of the "Sky-scraper." (Photo by Johnny Donnels)

AFTER YOU'VE GONE

Now won't you listen, dearie, while I say,
How could you tell me that you're going
    away?
Don't say that we must part,
Don't break my aching heart.
You know I've loved you truly many years,
Loved you night and day.
How can you leave me, can't you see my
    tears?
Listen while I say:

Chorus
After you've gone
And left me crying,
After you've gone
There's no denying,
You'll feel blue, you'll feel sad,
You'll miss the dearest pal you've ever had.
There'll come a time, now don't forget it,
There'll come a time when you'll regret it.
Someday when you grow lonely,
Your heart will break like mine
And you'll want me only,
After you've gone, after you've gone away.

Kid Thomas, now 82 years old and still blowing strong, is the greatest living exponent of the hot New Orleans trumpet. He and his Algiers Stompers Band pack them in twice a week at Preservation Hall. Kid Thomas is one musician who has steadfastly refused to migrate North. He organized his first band in the early 1920s, and for over 30 years they kept West Bank night clubs jumping. Those working class clubs demanded their jazz hot and in the gutbucket style, and that's the way Kid Thomas gave it to them. The band could play current popular tunes as well as traditional jazz—a versatility that kept them working in the dance halls so long. In the 1950s they were transplanted to Preservation Hall, which is a concert hall. Kid Thomas says he misses seeing those people dancing to his music.

Kid Thomas and his band have scored triumphs all over the world. The Kid says, "Rio was my favorite place. Man, down there they get up and dance and shout. That's the way I like it."

THE SHEEPSHEAD IS WARY AND SLY—AND GOOD EATING

Sheepshead is a delicious fish. Its firm white flesh tastes so much like crabmeat that some restaurants have been known to dilute their lump crabmeat cocktails with sheepshead in order to make a little profit. Boiled and baked sheepshead were very popular items in luxury restaurants in the old days. The irregularity of supply was probably responsible for the decline of sheepshead. Although it's available year-round it's a difficult fish to catch. The fisherman has to study its feeding habits in the same manner as he does with the pompano.

A beautiful fish, the sheepshead has the boldest markings of any Gulf of Mexico fish—silvery colored with six or seven bold black stripes. Its markings suggest a convict, and in fact, it is sometimes called the convict fish. The name sheepshead comes from the fact that it has big flat buck teeth like those of a sheep. It can swim right up and bite the barnacles off a post or piling, and it has crushing molar back teeth to chew them with. Knowing that barnacles are the sheepshead's favorite food, the fishermen drop their lines near bridges, railroad trestles, wrecks, and underwater obstructions, where barnacles are plentiful. The fish is very wary and sly, and like a pompano, it can nibble bait off a hook like a kid eating a popsickle off a stick. The fisherman must be able to detect this nibbling and set his hook at just the right moment. Sometimes the fisherman can also be wily and sly. Knowing that the sheepshead loves shellfish, he'll wrap a small oyster

Sheepshead.

in a piece of hairnet and bait the hook with it. If there's a sheepshead around, it will usually grab the oyster. Also good as bait are hermit crabs, fiddler crabs, shrimp, and chopped hard-shell crabs—almost anything that comes out of a shell.

BOILED SHEEPSHEAD
(Serves 4)

In olden days boiled sheepshead was a popular item in the dining rooms of luxury hotels and high-toned restaurants. For some strange reason it is no longer served in restaurants, but it is still a delicious fish, and if you can catch your own or buy it at a fish market, boil it as instructed below, and you'll have a Lucullan banquet.

A turkey roasting pan is ideal for this operation.

1 whole sheepshead, 4-6 lb
1 large onion, sliced
2 ribs celery, chopped coarsely with the leaves
½ lemon, sliced
2 bay leaves
1 cup parsley sprigs
1 tsp mixed pickling spices
2 cloves garlic, crushed
1 cup white wine
 salt and freshly ground black pepper
 water to cover the fish
 Hollandaise sauce

Heat the water in the pan, and add all ingredients listed except the fish and Hollandaise, bring to a rapid boil, and boil for 15 minutes to make a rich liquor.

Leave the head and tail on the fish. Wrap it in double cheesecloth, leaving a flap at each end for lifting it in and out of the pan. These flaps should hang out of the ends of the pan. Lower the fish into the liquor in the pan. Remember that it should be completely covered, so add water if needed. Bring to the boil, then lower the heat to a gentle boil, and cook for 20 to 30 minutes, depending on the size of the fish.

Remove the fish from the water, drain and unwrap. Transfer it carefully to a silver platter or a tray covered with bright foil. Remove the skin from the topside of the fish. Remove the eyeball and replace it with a slice of pimento-stuffed olive. Place a blanket of Hollandaise sauce on top of the fish. All around the fish, decorate with watercress, parsley sprigs, and lemon wedges. It should be a real objet d'art. And when you bring it triumphantly to the table, just listen to your guests say ooh and ahh.

NOTE: One good way to boil fish is to wrap them loosely in heavy-duty aluminum foil and roll and crimp the edges. Punch a lot of holes in each side so the broth can circulate in and out. Of course you can buy yourself a real fish-poaching pan with a rack inside, and your problem is solved immediately.

BAKED SHEEPSHEAD
(Serves 4)

1 sheepshead, 4-6 lb
2 onions, chopped

1 green pepper, diced
2 cloves garlic, minced
6 fresh mushrooms, sliced
1 16-oz can plum tomatoes, chopped,
    and their juice
½ tsp ground cumin
½ tsp thyme
½ cup white wine
4 tbsp olive oil (for frying)
½ cup olive oil (for baking)
2 tbsp flour
1 onion, sliced thin
1 tomato, sliced thin
    salt and freshly ground black pepper to
    taste
    cayenne
    melted butter

Heat the olive oil in a skillet, add the flour, and blend well. Add the chopped onions, green pepper, garlic, and mushrooms, and cook until the vegetables are transparent. Stir in the cumin and thyme. Add the chopped tomatoes and cook slowly for 20 minutes more. Rub the fish inside and out with melted butter, salt, black pepper, and a little cayenne. Leave the head and tail on the fish for looks (but if it's too big for your pan, it's perfectly all right to remove them). Lay the fish in a baking pan with ½ cup olive oil and ½ cup water. Sprinkle the wine over it, and ladle on the tomato sauce. Spread thin slices of onion and tomato over the fish. Bake in a preheated

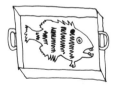

350° oven for 30 to 40 minutes, depending on the size of the fish. Baste it now and then with the sauce. The fish is done when the flesh flakes easily when tested with a fork. Decorate profusely with parsley sprigs and lemon slices, and take it to the table right in the baking pan.

SHEEPSHEAD CHOWDER
(Serves 4)

3 lb sheepshead fillets
¼ lb salt pork
4 potatoes, diced
4 onions, chopped
1 quart milk (or 1 pint cream
    and 1 pint milk)
1 quart fish stock
2 tbsp butter
2 tbsp flour
    salt and freshly ground black pepper

A well-made fish chowder is better than a New England clam chowder, and the sheepshead is an ideal fish to make it with. One of the secrets of making a good fish chowder is to use fish stock instead of plain water. When you buy your sheepshead fillets, ask at the fish market for the heads, tails, bones, and trimmings, and use them to make a good fish stock, enough for the one quart needed here.

Have a soup pot ready. Fry the diced pork in a skillet with a little water, and remove the pieces when they are opaque white and firm but not browned. Add to the pot. Put the onions in the pan and cook until golden brown. Drain off the fat, and put the onions in the pot. Put the potatoes and fish stock in the pot. Cook slowly until the potatoes are done. Rub the butter and the flour together thoroughly, and add to the pot. Cut the sheepshead fillets into one-inch pieces, and add them. Bring to the boil, lower the heat, and cook for about 15 minutes more.

Add the milk or milk-cream mixture just before serving. Then heat the chowder through gently, being careful not to let it boil. Add salt and pepper to taste. Ladle the chowder into large preheated soup bowls. Float a little dab of butter on top of each bowl, and sprinkle with chopped chives or chopped green scallion leaves and a small dash of paprika. Serve with pilot crackers or beaten biscuits. A bowl of this husky chowder is a meal in itself.

NOTE: Any firm-fleshed lean fish can be used for making fish chowder, and you can use several varieties in one chowder.

FISH HEAD CHOWDER

(Serves 4 hungry fishermen)

Fishermen know a lot of good tricks that you'd never learn at the Cordon Bleu. (Don't ever forget that Bouillabaisse was originally a humble fishermen's dish.) Here's how my friend Victor Pacellini, cook on a fishing boat, makes fish head chowder.

> **Some big fish heads (8-10 lb) from sheepshead, redfish, cobia, king mackerel, etc.**

½ lb salt pork, diced and fried light brown
4 large onions, fried in the pork fat
4 large potatoes, diced
1 pint milk
1 pint cream
½ stick butter
**   salt and pepper**

Place the fish heads in a big pot. Fry the salt pork and add it to the pot. Save the grease, fry the onions in it, and add them to the pot. Add the potatoes. Add water—a gallon or more, enough to cover everything by an inch. Boil for an hour. Remove the fish heads and let them drain. Remove the "cheeks" (the large lumps of flesh just under the eyes and in front of the gills) and add them to the pot. Add the milk and cream, and heat through. Slice up the butter and drop it in. Add salt and pepper to taste. Serve in large bowls with plenty of crackers.

SPANISH "MACK" IS A JIM DANDY

Spanish mackerel is another of those fishes that love the warm water of the Gulf of Mexico best of all. It ranges in schools from New York to Brazil. It's usually a blue water creature, a fish of the open sea, but in the summertime it sometimes comes in close to shore and affords great sport for pier and rockpile fishermen. It weighs from two to twenty-five pounds, and on light tackle it offers plenty of sport, leaping into the air and frantically trying to throw the hook.

The Spanish mackerel is one of the world's most beautiful fish. The coloring of its back is

Spanish mackerel.

rich blue or green with iridescent tones of gold and purple, and its belly is bright silver. Along its sides are irregular rows of golden spots. The Spanish mackerel is shaped like a torpedo or guided missile, and it's just about as fast when it's in a hurry to get somewhere.

As food, Spanish mackerel ranks with pompano, speckled trout, and flounder, right at the top among the epicurean favorites. It's good no matter how you cook it—broiled, baked, fried, marinated, or smoked. In the old days Spanish mackerel was a great favorite in New Orleans restaurants, but irregularity of supply has caused it to be dropped from most menus. If you're lucky you'll be able to find it in the fish markets. Buy it quick, take it home, and cook it according to any of the methods given here.

BROILED SPANISH MACKEREL

A freshly caught Spanish mackerel is one of the tastiest of all fishes. Its meat is sweet, light, and delicate enough to please the palate of the most exacting connoisseur. It's only when one has been out of the water too long that it develops a strong flavor. Small fish can be broiled whole, but the larger fish should be filleted and the fillets broiled.

To broil a whole small Spanish mackerel, you'll usually have to cut off the tail to make it fit the sizzle platter (and you may even have to cut off the head). Split a Spanish mackerel down the back from the head to the tail, but don't cut all the way through. Flip it open like the pages of a book, clean out the entrails, and with an old toothbrush clean out the black stomach lining and the blood next to the backbone. Take a small knife and cut under the backbone and remove it. Brush the fish lightly with melted butter inside and out, and sprinkle with salt, freshly ground black pepper, and a little cayenne. Place on a buttered metal sizzle platter (or broiling pan) skin side down, and broil for eight to ten minutes. (Spanish mackerel are usually so thin you do not have to turn them over, because the hot pan cooks the bottom side.) Garnish with parsley sprigs and lemon wedges and serve the fish on its hot sizzle platter. If you used a broiler pan, transfer the fish to a hot serving plate with a large spatula.

Fillets from larger fish should be broiled in the same manner. If the fillets are thick, they should be broiled skin side up at first and then flipped over.

Spanish mackerel is a rich fat fish, and a good red Bordeaux or Burgundy goes well with it.

SPANISH MACKEREL A LA CREOLE
(Serves 1)

Split a Spanish mackerel and broil it as instructed in the preceding recipe. When it's done, cover it with a blanket of hot Creole tomato sauce (p. 189), and serve it on the hot sizzle platter. If cooked in a broiler pan, remove it to a preheated serving plate and put the sauce on top. Fillets from large Spanish mackerel should be cooked the same way.

This is also a good way to cook small whole bluefish or bluefish fillets. The Creole sauce counterbalances the rich oiliness of these fishes in a truly metaphysical manner.

CAJUN SPANISH MACKEREL AU GRATIN
(Serves 1)

This is a dish for hungry people. At first it seems to be overdoing things, but the various flavors blend symphonically.

Split and clean a Spanish mackerel as instructed in the recipes above, and lay it on a well-buttered sizzle platter (or broiler pan). Cover with a good blanket of Creole tomato sauce. Cover the blanket of tomato sauce with thin slices of sharp cheese. Place three or four slices of fresh tomato in a row on top of the cheese. Bake for 15 to 20 minutes in a preheated 350° oven. Garnish with green onions and slices of green peppers, and serve piping hot to someone who's really hungry.

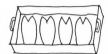

MME. FANNY FIELDS'S BAKED SPANISH MACKEREL
(Serves 6)

A lady of Canadian French descent taught me many good tricks of fish cookery. She had the un-French name of Mrs. Fanny Fields, and she was one of the greatest whizzes in the kitchen that I've ever known. Whenever a local seafood restaurant felt that its cooks were slipping, they'd call in "Aunt Fanny" for consultation, and she'd shake up that kitchen from top to bottom and teach those cooks a few things. Here's the way she baked Spanish mackerel.

6 small Spanish mackerel (or the fillets from larger fish)
2 large onions, sliced and made into rings
6-8 fresh tomatoes, sliced very thin (or a 32-oz can of plum-type tomatoes, chopped)
salt and freshly ground black pepper

Grease well the bottom of a large baking pan or cookie sheet. Cut the heads and tails off the Spanish mackerel, split them down the back, spread them, and clean them. Lay them in the pan skin side down. Spread the tomatoes and onion rings over them. Sprinkle with salt and pepper. Bake in a preheated 350° oven for 15 to 20 minutes, a little longer if the mackerel are thick. Lift the fish out with a large spatula, place on preheated serving plates with the onion rings and tomatoes on top, and serve at once. This dish loses its good taste and attractiveness if allowed to dry out. Very simple but delicious!

DRY MARINADE

VICTOR'S MARINATED SPANISH MACKEREL

You cannot soak a Spanish mackerel in a liquid marinade as you would some other fishes, because the meat would get soggy and fall apart. But you can still jazz it up in the following manner. Lay a split Spanish mackerel or some fillets on a plate, sprinkle it with onion powder, garlic powder, a little powdered cumin, rosemary, salt, and freshly ground black pepper, and rub it in. Then sprinkle on some vinegar and rub that in. Do this three or four times over a six-hour period, cutting down on the condiments each time so that at the end you're just using vinegar, and very lightly at that. Fry the cured fish in a skillet in bacon grease or lard. Don't use vegetable oil, margarine, or butter, because the vinegar and spices would cause it to break down and curdle. Eat enough of these and you'll burst out singing some Cajun folk songs.

NOTE: Although you can't marinate fresh Spanish mackerel, you *can* marinate fried Spanish mackerel as explained in the next recipe.

HOLY MACKEREL!
(A red hot Spanish mackerel hors d'oeuvre)

You can make one of the world's best hors d'oeuvres out of Spanish mackerel. I call the things Holy Mackerel because, to me at least, the flavor approaches the sublime, and the heat makes you exclaim "Holy Mackerel!" It's great fun to sit at a bar all afternoon guzzling beer and munching on these fiery fish sticks. A hostess who serves them at a cocktail bash will receive high praise. Of course, if the guests don't like hot peppers, they may want to run her out of town, but when these hors d'oeuvres are served to drinkers who love hot peppers, they'll disappear fast.

3 lb thick Spanish mackerel fillets
1½ cups flour
1 cup beer
1 tsp salt
1 tsp baking powder
¼ tsp freshly ground black pepper
2 tbsp butter, melted

Put all ingredients except the fish in a mixing bowl and mix well but don't stir. Let the batter rest a half hour before using.

Rinse the fillets and dry them with paper towels. Cut them into finger-sized strips four to five inches long. Dip them in the batter, and fry them in deep hot fat until they're well browned. Drain on paper towels and cool.

Now I might as well tell you that the Holy Mackerel sticks should be firm and chewy, and to get that firm effect requires hocus pocus. Put the fried fish sticks in a pan or glass dish, and leave them in the refrigerator for 24 hours. At the end of that period they will be hard and firm.

HOLY MACKEREL MARINADE
12 Trappey's (or another brand) red hot pickled peppers, chopped fine
2 tsp crushed red pepper seeds
6 cloves garlic, finely minced
1 medium onion, chopped
1 cup tomato sauce

1 cup vinegar
1 cup water
¼ cup olive oil
1 tbsp mixed pickling spices
¼ tsp ground cumin
½ tsp salt
1 tsp sugar
   freshly ground black pepper

Combine all ingredients and mix well. Place the fried hardened fish sticks in a flat glass bowl or enamel pan and pour the marinade over them. Turn them over now and then, working from the bottom so that all the sticks will be in the marinade for a while. Let them soak for an hour. Don't marinate them too long or they'll get soft again. Keep a close eye on them. Remove them from the marinade, drain on paper towels, and arrange on an attractive silver platter. Serve them only to your best friends—they're too damn good for casual acquaintances. They should be hot, spicy, garlicky, and tart—a whole symphony of tastes. Serve with them beer, wine, martinis, Sazeracs, Bloody Marys, or whatever.

NOTE: This kind of legerdemain can be practiced with any kind of fish sticks, but those from fat fish are the best. It works especially well with small whole fish, such as smelts, fresh sardines, baby "tinker" mackerels, and baby butterfish.

SPANISH MACKEREL WITH ONIONS AND OLIVES

(Serves 2)

2 1½-lb Spanish mackerel (or fillets from a larger fish)

1 cup chopped onions
1 cup chopped green olives
   melted butter
   black Greek olives, radishes, lemon wedges, capers, onion rings, parsley

Split the Spanish mackerel (as instructed at the beginning of this section), clean them, and remove the backbone. Butter individual metal sizzle platters (or a broiling pan) and lay the fish on them, skin side down. Brush with melted butter, and sprinkle on the chopped onions and olives. Bake in a preheated 350° oven for 15 to 20 minutes, depending on the thickness of the fish. It's done when it flakes easily when tested with a fork. If you're using sizzle platters, serve the fish right on the platters. If you use a broiling pan, transfer them to preheated serving plates. Decorate with Greek olives, radish roses, lemon wedges, capers, watercress, parsley sprigs, and whatever else you like. Make as attractive as possible, and serve piping hot with a bouncy red wine.

SPANISH MACKEREL WITH ANCHOVY AND ROSEMARY

(Serves 2)

Rosemary is for remembrance. And rosemary is for Spanish mackerel—there's a great affinity between the two.

   Split and clean two small Spanish mackerel, or use fillets from a larger fish. Place the fish on buttered sizzle platters or in a flat pan. Brush with melted butter. Cut anchovy fillets in quarter-inch pieces and dot the fish with them. Sprinkle with dried rosemary leaves. Bake in a preheated 350° oven for 15 minutes, or until the flesh flakes when tested with a fork. Garnish with lemon wedges, watercress, and parsley sprigs, and serve piping hot.

GOOSEBERRIES

SPANISH MACKEREL WITH GOOSEBERRY SAUCE
(Serves 2)

The classical French method of serving the Boston or common mackerel is with green gooseberry sauce (in France they're called mackerel berries). The method works as well or even better with our Spanish mackerel from the Gulf of Mexico. You can very often find this sauce in gourmet food shops and specialty stores. When most folks see it on the shelves, however, they can't even guess what it's best used with.

Split and clean two mackerel (or use fillets from a larger fish). Broil on metal sizzle platters or flat broiler pans. Heat the gooseberry sauce, spread it over the mackerel, and serve at once.

Serve a full-bodied wine, either white or red—take your choice.

THE KING'S ALIVE! LONG LIVE THE KING!

The king mackerel is one of the most popular gamefish of offshore Louisiana waters, and as a bonus it's one of the best eating fishes. The tarpon is the silver king of all Louisiana sport fishes, but it's seasonal, scarce, and no good as a food fish. The kingfish is almost always out there hanging around the oil rigs, waiting for you to come and fight it. Bait your hook with a dead menhaden, cast about 30 feet from the boat, and if the king is there at all, it will hit your bait like a streak of lightning. When it realizes it's hooked, it can really stage some theatrics. It can jump all the way over your boat and scare the wits out of you.

Knowing that the king's teeth are sharp as a razor, many an angler, when this fish starts

King mackerel.

jumping in the air, instinctively starts looking for a tree to climb, but there aren't any trees to climb out there, so you have to turn around and fight it out. Kings usually weigh from fifteen to twenty-five pounds, but they're sometimes much larger, and one can weigh up to seventy-five pounds. They're as everlastingly game as a gamecock and explosive as a stick of dynamite. When a kingfish finds it cannot throw the hook by leaping around, it will sometimes take long angling dives that can almost drag you out of the boat. Your arms can be weary enough almost to drop off before you finally get it gaffed and into the boat. It's dangerous even then, however. It will flash its evil eye at you, and when you try to remove your hook, its sharp teeth can take your thumb off as quickly as a hamburger grinder.

As the name denotes, the king mackerel is the king-sized cousin of the highly respected Spanish mackerel and, like its cousin, is gourmet fare. Antebellum menus from the St. Charles Hotel and the St. Louis Hotel show that boiled kingfish was a very popular dish among the seafood epicures of that day. Boiled or otherwise, kingfish would probably be very popular today if the supply was more regular. They are usually dressed into steaks, which are sometimes available in the fish markets. The steaks can be cooked in a wide variety of tasty ways.

NOTE: In addition to the recipes given below for king mackerel, the fish can be cooked by any of the methods given for Spanish mackerel.

"GALVANIZED" KING MACKEREL STEAKS
(Serves 4)

"Galvanizing" is a fisherman's term for marination. The process works especially well with king mackerel steaks.

> **4 king mackerel steaks, about 1½″ thick**
> **2 cups Creole tomato sauce**
>   **"galvanizing" marinade**

THE GALVANIZING MARINADE
  1 cup vinegar
  1 cup water
  1 medium onion, chopped
  6 cloves garlic, minced
  2 bay leaves, crushed
  1 tbsp mixed pickling spice
  ¼ tsp thyme
  ¼ tsp basil
  ¼ tsp cumin
  6 peppercorns, crushed
  ½ tsp salt

Place all ingredients in a glass bowl or enamel pan, and stir to mix well. Place the fish steaks in the marinade, and let them soak for an hour, turning them over now and then. While they're soaking, you can make the Creole tomato sauce (p. 189).

Remove the steaks from the marinade, brush off all the herbs and spices, and dry them with paper towels.

Grease metal sizzle platters or a broiler pan with lard (the marinade would curdle butter or margarine). Broil the steaks for eight minutes on each side. They are done when the flesh flakes easily when tested with a fork. Cover each steak with hot Creole tomato sauce. Garnish with parsley sprigs and serve at once. New boiled potatoes are good as accompaniment.

BROILED KING MACKEREL STEAKS

This is the best method of cooking king mackerel steaks—simple and unadorned but delicious. The steaks should be an inch to an inch and a half thick. Rub them well with melted butter, lemon or lime juice, salt, freshly ground black pepper, and a little cayenne. Place them on buttered metal sizzle platters or broiler pans. Broil four inches from the flame for six to eight minutes on each side, basting frequently to keep them from drying out. The fish is done when it is lightly browned, flakes easily, and is opaque clear through. Open it with a fork, and if the meat inside is still transparent, it needs more cooking. When serving, garnish the sizzle platters with sprigs of parsley and lemon wedges.

BAKED KING MACKEREL STEAKS
(Serves 4)

2 lb king mackerel steaks, skinned and sliced thin (about ½″)
3 medium onions, sliced and made into rings

½ cup olive oil
½ cup dry white wine
    cayenne
    lemon or lime juice
4 cloves garlic, put through a press
    salt and freshly ground black pepper

Rub the steaks with lemon or lime juice, salt, black pepper, a little cayenne, and garlic. Place the olive oil in a baking pan, spread the onion rings on the bottom of the pan, and place the fish pieces on the onions. Sprinkle the wine over the top. Bake in a preheated 350° oven, basting frequently, for 20 to 25 minutes, or until the fish is tender and flakes easily with a fork. Place the fish on a hot serving platter, and cover with the onion rings and pan juices. Decorate with parsley sprigs and lemon wedges. Serve piping hot with a bouncy red wine.

NOTE: This is a good method for preparing steaks of swordfish, halibut, and fresh tuna.

CHICK PEAS
(GARBANZOS)
(CECI)

KING MACKEREL WITH TOMATOES, ONIONS, AND CHICK-PEAS
(Serves 4 to 6)

2 lb king mackerel steaks
3 tbsp olive oil
1 16-oz can garbanzos (chick-peas)
3 medium onions, sliced and made into rings
8 pimento-stuffed olives, sliced

I CAN'T GIVE YOU ANYTHING BUT LOVE

"Duet" by Kenneth Burke

Gee but it's tough to be broke, kid,
It's not a joke kid, it's a curse,
My luck is changing, it's gotten
From simply rotten, to something worse.
Who knows, someday I'll win, too,
I'll begin to reach my prime,
Now though I see what our end is,
All I can spend is just my time.

Chorus
I can't give you anything but love, baby,
That's the only thing I've plenty of, baby,
Dream awhile,

Scheme awhile,
We're sure to find
Happiness and I guess
All those things you've always pined for.
Gee, I'd like to see you lookin' swell, baby,
Diamond bracelets Woolworth's doesn't sell,
  baby,
'Till that lucky day you know darned well,
  baby,
I can't give you anything but love.

1 **16-oz can plum-type tomatoes, chopped**
3 **cloves garlic, minced**
2 **tbsp fresh chopped parsley**
  salt and freshly ground black pepper
  bread crumbs
  butter

Cut the steaks into two-inch squares, removing the skin and bones. Rub the pieces with salt and pepper, and set aside.

Heat the olive oil in a skillet, add the onion rings, parsley, olives, and garlic, and cook for five minutes until the onions are wilted. Add the chick-peas, chopped tomatoes, and their juice, and simmer for 15 minutes. Place one half of the sauce in the bottom of a buttered ovenproof casserole dish. Place the fish pieces on the sauce and cover with the remaining sauce. Sprinkle with bread crumbs, dot with butter, and bake in a preheated 375° oven for 20 to 25 minutes.

COBIA IS NOT A "LEMON"

The cobia is both a gamefish and an eating fish. It can grow up to 100 pounds, but the average in the Gulf is fifteen to twenty pounds. They're courageous fighters and they never give up until you've got them gaffed and in the boat. Many fishermen call the cobia lemonfish, but it's definitely not a "lemon."

It's a strange fish, a loner usually, although three or four sometimes travel together. It has some odd habits that make it different from its deepsea brethren. It likes to hang around under objects that float in the water, such as floating debris, flotsam and jetsam, driftwood logs, buoys, and channel markers. If you see an old orange crate floating out in the Gulf, stop your boat and investigate, because as likely as not there'll be a big cobia swimming around under it. When it sees you coming, it will swim right out to meet your boat, dorsal fin cleaving the water like a shark. When the fish gets close to the boat, toss your baited hook or lure overboard, and the cobia will sidle up and smell the bait. Just as it does so, give the line a sharp jerk, and the cobia may get excited and pounce on the hook. It will then take off for the wild blue yonder, stripping your line off the reel in spite of the star drag. You'll have to fight a wearying battle before you get that fish into the boat.

After a cobia is caught, the head should be removed and the fish hung up by the tail for bleeding. The meat will then be clear white. For cooking it should be cut into steaks. Many seafood gourmets consider cobia steaks the equal of swordfish, salmon, and halibut. Because the meat has the flavor and texture of lobster, it is often cooked Newburg style as in one of the following recipes. The day will come when the fine restaurants discover cobia, and then this delicious fish will be more widely available to the public.

BROILED COBIA STEAKS
(Serves 4)

Many seafood fanciers think cobia steaks are so good that they need no adornment other than butter and lemon juice.

Rub four cobia steaks with melted butter, salt, freshly ground black pepper, and a little

Cobia.

cayenne. Lay them on buttered metal sizzle platters (or in a broiler pan) and broil for five minutes. Flip them over with a spatula and broil five minutes more. A little longer cooking time may be required if the steaks are very thick. To test the steak for doneness, lift the flesh with a fork and look inside. If it's opaque white clear through, it's done, but if the flesh is still transparent on the inside, it needs more cooking. Brush with melted butter and sprinkle with chopped parsley and a dash of paprika. Serve right on the sizzle platter with lemon wedges. (If you used a broiler pan, transfer steaks to preheated serving plates.)

COBIA STEAKS WITH SOUR CREAM-MINT SAUCE

(Serves 4)

Broil the steaks as in the preceding recipe. While they're broiling, make a sour cream sauce as follows:

To a pint of heavy sour cream, add a half cup of grated onion and a quarter cup of chopped fresh mint leaves, and season to taste with salt and freshly ground black pepper. Mix well and place a blanket of the sauce on each broiled fish steak. Shove it under the broiler flame until the sauce is heated through.

This unbelievably delicious sauce is one of the best of all sauces for broiled fish steaks.

NOTE: This sauce goes beautifully with the steaks of red snapper, redfish, striped bass, haddock, and other lean, firm, white-fleshed fish.

COBIA STEAKS A LA CREOLE-NEWBURG

(Serves 4)

- **2 lb cobia steaks**
- **3 oz Monterey Jack cheese, cubed (or other American cheese)**
- **2 slices chopped pimiento**
- **6 fresh mushrooms, sliced**
- **½ tsp Creole mustard**
- **¼ cup sherry**
- **⅓ stick butter**
- **2 tbsp flour**
- **1 cup milk**
- **1 cup cream**
- **1 bay leaf**
- **1 lemon slice**
  salt and freshly ground black pepper to taste

Heat salted water in a saucepan with the bay leaf and slice of lemon. Boil the cobia steaks gently for 10 minutes. Drain.

Melt the butter in a saucepan, remove from heat and add the flour, blending well until free of lumps. Add the milk little by little, stirring constantly. Add the cream. Return to fire, add the cheese cubes, and stir to make a smooth mixture as the cheese dissolves. Add the mustard, sherry, pimiento, mushrooms, and cobia steaks broken into bite size chunks. Season to taste with salt and black pepper. Serve with steamed rice on the side.

COBIA WITH CREOLE TOMATO SAUCE
(Serves 4)

2 lb cobia fillets
½ cup olive oil
2 cloves garlic, minced
2 cups Creole tomato sauce
2 tbsp pimientos, chopped
6 olives, sliced
2 tbsp sherry
   dash of Tabasco
   milk
   flour
   bread crumbs
   Parmesan cheese
   salt and freshly ground black pepper to taste

Cut the cobia fillets into two-inch squares. Heat the olive oil in a skillet until a haze forms over it. Dip the cobia pieces in milk and then in flour, and fry in the oil until brown on both sides. Drain and set aside, keeping them warm. Mix the Creole tomato sauce with the garlic, pimientos, olives, sherry, Tabasco, salt, and black pepper, and stir well. Place half the mixture in an earthenware casserole or oven-proof baking dish. Place the fried cobia squares on the sauce and cover with the remainder of the sauce. Sprinkle with bread crumbs mixed with Parmesan cheese, and bake in a pre-heated 350° oven until the top is golden brown.

NOTE: This is also a good method of cooking Spanish mackerel and king mackerel.

THE ART OF SMOKING MULLET

Smoked mullet is one of the most delicious seafood treats to come out of the Deep South. I state unequivocally that it's as good as smoked salmon (lox, the sweetheart of the bagel) and smoked whitefish, both of which sell for enormous prices in delicatessens. Good smoked mullet sells for high prices, too—that is, when there's any left to sell. Most smokers eat it all up themselves because it's too damn good to sell to strangers.

If you're one of those do-it-yourself people, it's very easy to build yourself a fish smoker. An old refrigerator works perfectly. Just cut out the bottom, install a metal firebox, and cut a hole in the top for a vent. If you have a backyard barbecue pit, all you have to do is build a plywood box to fit on top of it. Or you can make a smoker out of an old barrel or a metal oil drum. The possibilities are practically unlimited. Any hollow object that will hold smoke inside it can be made into a "smoke-house." There are small portable fish smokers on the market, but they're generally too small and flimsy to do a good job. After you've built your smokehouse, get yourself about three dozen good mullet and proceed as follows:

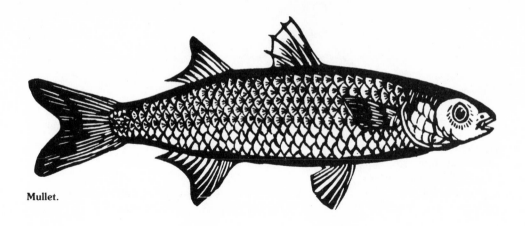

Mullet.

Cut off their heads, but leave on the hard bony plate just below the gills, called the "collarbone." Take an old toothbrush and clean out all the intestines, membranes, black stomach lining, and so on. With a small sharp knife, cut under the backbone and remove it. Wash the fish thoroughly under a running faucet, put them in a container of clean water, and let them soak for a half hour to leach out any remaining blood. Next make a solution of brine in the ratio of a pound of salt to a quart of water. Let the fish soak in the brine for from one to three hours, depending on how fat they are. This procedure "conditions" them. Next remove them from the brine, rinse thoroughly, and dry with paper towels. Lay them on chicken wire mesh racks in a breezy fly-free location for an hour or two until both sides are dry. A wet soggy fish does not smoke well, and the flesh turns greyish instead of the rich golden color you want.

Start the fire under the "smokehouse" an hour before beginning to smoke, so that any moisture present inside will evaporate. Mount the fish on smoking sticks or rods, or lay them on wire mesh smoking trays. Make sure that no two fish are touching each other. Place the sticks or trays in position inside the "smokehouse."

For smoking fish, the nut woods are best, such as hickory, pecan, or oak. Either eucalyptus or sweet bay is excellent, but dried palmetto roots are best of all. You'll need hardwood sawdust to keep the fire "smothered" and to produce smoke. If you can't get suitable wood, an excellent shortcut is to use a charcoal fire and cover it with hickory chips that have been soaked in water for an hour. If the fire flares up, throw on more wet chips or sawdust. Never use pine wood or sawdust, because it gives a resinous taste to the fish.

Keep a close watch on your fire, and never let it go out or flare up. Smoking for six hours is usually long enough if the fire isn't too hot, but a slow smoke for eight to twelve hours is even better. Time adjustments come with practice. The fish are done when they have a rich golden color. They should not be allowed to blacken like barbecued steer.

If smoked properly, the fish should keep for about ten days at room temperature, but it's better to play safe and keep them refrigerated, wrapped in waxed paper or foil to keep them from drying out. They'll keep indefinitely in the freezer.

When ready to eat, brush them lightly with the sauce given below and brown them a little under the broiler flame. Oh, what fun it is to sit in a small bar all afternoon with a group of congenial friends, eating smoked mullet and washing them down with voluminous quantities of good cold beer.

1. Off with their heads.

2. Split them down the back.

3. Spread them.

4. Wash them well.

5. Soak in clean water for a half hour.

6. Soak them in brine for 1 to 3 hours, then rinse them thoroughly. Brine formula: a pound of salt to a quart of water.

7. Dry them out on a chicken wire rack in a breezy location.

8. Rack them up on steel rods or

9. Lay them flat on wire mesh trays.

10. Smoke them!

How to prepare mullet (or any other fish) for smoking.

THE SAUCE FOR SMOKED MULLET

Mix well together a 16-oz can of tomato sauce, a clove of garlic put through a press, the juice of half a lemon, a quarter teaspoon of Tabasco, and freshly ground black pepper (the fish already has a salty tang from the brine). Brush the sauce on the smoked mullet, and brown lightly under the broiler flame.

NOTE: Fat-fleshed fish are generally the best for smoking—for example, Spanish mackerel, king mackerel, bonito, yellow fin tuna, shad, and pompano. In other parts of the country, you can use salmon, whitefish, common mackerel, herrings, alewives, sardines, tuna, or fresh anchovies. Although haddock is a lean fish, it also can be smoked and is then called finnan haddie. Oysters and shrimp are unbelievably good when smoked.

NOTE: The "smokehouse" makes an excellent baking oven when charcoal or a wood fire producing flames heats the oven to a temperature of 200° or 225°. Make a medium density of smoke. You can use whole mullet, whole red snapper, redfish, black drum, or any other baking fish. Place them in a baking pan with your favorite sauce, and baste now and then while they're cooking. A meat thermometer is a valuable aid here. A whole fish is done when the center of the fish has a temperature of 140°. Decorate the pan with watercress or parsley, and take it right to the table. Your guests will be amazed at the delicious smoky flavor of your baked fish.

CHARCOAL-BROILED MULLET

Mullet are ideal for charcoal broiling on an outdoor barbecue grill or hibachi, because their built-in oil prevents them from drying up. Place them directly on the greased grill, or you can use a hinged double wire grill, well greased, which makes it possible to flip all the fish over at one time. No sauce is needed. The broiled mullet's flavor is so good it doesn't need jazzing up.

Leave the heads and tails on for looks. Starting at the front of the head, split the fish down the back to the tail. Spread it open and clean out the insides and the abdominal lining with an old toothbrush. With a small sharp knife, cut under the backbone and remove it. Wash the fish. Bury them in coarse salt and let them "cure" for an hour. Dig them out and rinse off most of the salt but not all of it, because you want the fish to have a salty tang. Dry them with paper towels. Rub them with olive oil, place on the grill (or in the hinged grill), and cook about four inches above the hot coals, browning lightly on both sides. Eat them with your bare hands without any trimmings. Wash them down with cold beer or a bouncy red wine.

OVEN-BROILED MULLET

You can almost duplicate charcoal broiling indoors by broiling the mullet in the oven. Prepare the fish as instructed in the preceding recipe and lay them skin side up on a cookie sheet or broiler pan. Broil for five minutes, then flip them over, and broil four minutes more. Place on preheated serving plates and garnish with parsley or watercress and lemon wedges.

BROILED BLUEFISH
(Serves 4)

Scale and fillet a very fresh five-pound bluefish, and cut the fillets in half to make four pieces. The fish is so oily that you don't need to use butter or fat. Lay the fillets on metal sizzle platters or in a broiler pan, skin side up, and place them four inches below the flame. After the skin has browned, turn the fish over with a large spatula and broil the other side. The second phase takes less time because the fish is already hot and partially cooked by the broiler plate. Serve with lemon wedges. This simple unadorned piece of fish is considered by many gourmets to be the supreme piscatorial dining treat.

BAKED BLUEFISH STUFFED WITH OYSTERS
(Serves 4)

1 5-lb bluefish
3 dozen oysters (about 1½ pints) and their liquor
2 tbsp chopped fresh parsley

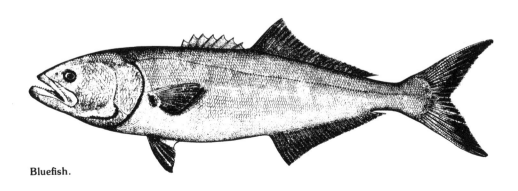

Bluefish.

freshly ground black pepper
½ cup dry white wine
4 slices French bread
1 egg yolk
melted butter

Clean and scale the bluefish, leaving the head and tail on. Cut the abdominal cavity back to the tail to make a stuffing space. Poach the oysters in their liquor and the white wine, adding a little freshly ground black pepper (the liquor furnishes the salt). Cook until they are firm and their edges are curled. Drain off the broth and use it to wet down and knead the French bread to a paste. Knead in the parsley, beat the egg yolk, and add it to the paste. Mix the oysters with the paste gently so as not to tear them up. Add salt and more black pepper, if necessary. Stuff the bluefish with the mixture and sew it up (or fasten the edges with small skewers). Lay the fish on greased aluminum foil in a baking pan, and bake in a preheated oven at 350° for 30 minutes, or until it's browned and cooked through. Brush it a couple of times with melted butter during the baking to keep it from drying out. Lay the whole fish out on a platter on a bed of watercress, escarole, or romaine lettuce. Serve Creole tomato sauce in a side dish, and a Graves wine lightly chilled.

CATFISH, DARLING OF DIXIE

The darling dish of Southern country folks is catfish and hushpuppies. Around about July, when the crops are laid by, the men in the family will usually get restless and decide to go catfishing. In my neck of the woods they called it "hand fishing"—no hooks, nets, or anything. When I was a small kid, my uncles used to take me hand fishing with them, and it was a very exciting business. We would wade along in the water of a canal or bayou, and my uncles would feel along the bank under the water surface, looking for the catfish holes. When one of them found a hole, he'd stick his hand in and sometimes pull out a big catfish weighing ten to twenty pounds.

Channel catfish, *Ictalurus lacustris*. (Drawing by Duane Raver, Jr., courtesy of Louisiana Wildlife and Fisheries Commission)

Sometimes he'd pull out a big fat water moccasin by mistake, and then everyone would scatter fast. My uncles weren't afraid of the snakes because of a belief that snakes can't bite underwater. By midafternoon we'd have filled several croaker sacks with more than a hundred pounds of catfish, and we'd take them home. That night there would be a big fishfry, and neighbors and kinfolks from all over would come to join in the feasting and fun.

The favorite catfish in South Louisiana is the blue cat or channel catfish. They sometimes grow to enormous size. They can be caught on trot lines, a series of baited hooks strung out on a long main line, or in long traps called trammel nets. Pass Manchac, a short stream about forty miles above New Orleans, connects Lake Maurepas with Lake Pontchartrain. The catfish from Pass Manchac are just about the best in the world. Middendorf's, a restaurant at Pass Manchac, has become famous for its fried catfish and hushpuppies.

The small brown bullhead catfish are also delicious, and many rice farmers are now raising them commercially in flooded rice fields. The supply of catfish is never sufficient to meet the demand, and it's the highest-priced fish on the market except for pompano.

For frying, small catfish should be skinned and filleted. Large catfish should be skinned and cut into steaks or squares about a half-inch thick.

FRIED CATFISH

Clean the catfish and cut it into fillets, steaks, or squares. Wash the fish well and dry it with paper towels. Sprinkle with salt, black pepper, and cayenne. Roll the fish pieces in cornmeal. Heat an inch of lard in a deep heavy skillet to 375° (a wooden kitchen match will ignite when dropped into it). Fry the pieces in the hot fat, turning once, until well browned. Drain well on paper towels, and keep the first pieces hot until all of them have been fried. Serve with hushpuppies.

HUSHPUPPIES

Hushpuppies, the sweetheart of fried catfish (or any other deep-fried fish), are said to have gotten their name in antebellum days. In the summertime the slaves cooked their meals over an outdoor fire. Overcome by ravenous hunger and by the delicious smells rising from the skillet, the family dog would walk around crying and whining. The cook would toss him one of these delicious tid-bits and say, "Hush, puppy!" Hushpuppies may be spoon-dropped, patted into small cakes, or rolled into balls. The spoon-dropped type seem to be the crispiest and tastiest. You can fry them in the same fat the fish were cooked in.

1 cup cornmeal
1 cup flour
1 medium onion, finely chopped
6 scallions with 2″ of their green leaves, finely chopped
2 tsp baking powder
2 tsp salt
½ tsp freshly ground black pepper
1 egg
½ cup (or more) buttermilk

Put the first seven ingredients in a mixing bowl and mix well. Add the egg and mix it in. Add enough buttermilk to make a thick heavy paste. Drop tablespoons of the mixture into

Black drum.

hot fat, and fry until they're done all the way through. Drain well and keep the first batches warm while the later ones are being fried.

CATFISH FRIED WITH SESAME SEEDS

This is a Soul Food dish that goes way back to antebellum days when the slaves cooked with the sesame (benne) seeds that they had brought with them from Africa.

4 lb catfish fillets
flour
beaten eggs
1 cup cornmeal
1 cup sesame seeds
salt and freshly ground black pepper
cayenne

Mix the cornmeal and the sesame seeds together. Rub the catfish fillets with salt, pepper, and a little cayenne. Dip them in the flour, then in beaten eggs, then in the cornmeal mixture. Heat an inch of lard in a heavy iron skillet, and fry the catfish until golden brown, turning the pieces over once.

You can serve hushpuppies if you wish, but the sesame seeds have such a good rich flavor that the puppies are not really necessary.

A CREOLE COOKS A CREOLE FISH

My friend Gilbert Fortier is a Creole from way back—too far back for it to matter to him. His great-grandfather, Valcour Aimé, was the largest sugar planter in Louisiana in the days befo' de wah. Aimé's mansion in St. James Parish was called "Petit Versailles" and had extensive botanical gardens modeled after the original in France. Gilbert's grandfather, Alcée Fortier, who grew up at Petit Versailles, later became a scholar on things Creole and Cajun. His *History of Louisiana* is a landmark. Gilbert himself, not to be outdone, has written a couple of scurrilous little volumes of "Creoleo" history (asked what that term means, he says, "Looks like butter but it ain't"). These books are fast sellers in junk bookshops.

Gilbert is an avid fisherman and a seafood gourmet with several original Creole recipes to his credit. His lasting claim to fame will probably be his delicious way of cooking a black drum, a fish that most other fishermen throw back.

BLACK DRUM A LA FORTIER
(Serves 2)

1 3-lb black drum, about 10″ long
¼ cup olive oil
¼ cup vinegar
1 tbsp minced onion
1 scallion with 3″ of its green leaves, finely chopped
1 tsp finely chopped parsley
1 tbsp finely chopped green pepper
2 cloves garlic, put through a garlic press
½ tsp mixed pickling spices
½ tsp freshly ground black pepper
½ tsp salt

Scale and eviscerate the black drum. Wash it well inside and out. Rub it well inside and out with salt, freshly ground black pepper, and a

Yellowfin tuna.

little cayenne. Cut three shallow gashes on each side of the fish. Set it aside.

Mix all the remaining ingredients to make the marinade. Put the marinade in an empty Wishbone Salad Dressing bottle, and it will look just like the real thing (advt.). Shake the bottle vigorously to amalgamate all the elements. Take a big piece of heavy-duty foil, and make a "pocket" big enough to hold the fish, rolling and crimping the sides tightly but leaving the top open. Slide the fish into the bag. Holding the bag upright, pour in half the marinade on one side of the fish and the other half on the other side. Roll up the top and crimp it tightly to make the package as airtight as possible. Preheat the oven to 375° and bake the package for 30 minutes. Remove the fish, arrange it attractively on a silver platter, and pour the marinade over it. Decorate with watercress, parsley, and lemon wedges, and serve at once.

Gilbert says that when you boil a black drum, its flesh has exactly the same texture and flavor as lump crabmeat. You can serve it as mock crabmeat cocktails, or you can use it in place of crabmeat in making stuffings and dressings.

And Gilbert is not alone in his admiration of this fish. When the eminent French chef Paul Bocuse gave a seafood cooking demonstration in New Orleans recently, he chose—from among our scores of delicious fish—the lowly black drum.

FRESH TUNA, EPICURE'S DELIGHT

There are large schools of yellowfin tunas a hundred or more miles out in the Gulf of Mexico, but they're fished mostly by cannery boats or a few sports fishermen who are willing to go that far out. They're never sold in fish markets or restaurants, and this is tragic because a fresh tuna steak properly prepared is a true epicurean delight. Ask a Japanese gourmet. Fresh tuna sells for $10 a pound in Tokyo. In New England, Japanese buyers hang around the fish wharves, buy all the giant bluefin tunas the boats bring in, and ship them to Japan by air express. Bluefin tunas weigh up to 700 pounds each, and that's a lot of valuable fish. The yellowfin tunas of the Gulf, a smaller species weighing up to a hundred pounds, are the famed albacores, whose meat is lighter and tastier meat than that of other tuna species. Fresh tuna steaks should be salt-cured to bring them off their high horse, and then they should be marinated by a process fishermen call "galvanizing." If you're ever lucky enough to get your hands on some fresh tuna steaks here's how to do it.

"GALVANIZED" FRESH TUNA STEAKS A LA CREOLE

(Serves 4)

- **4 fresh tuna steaks, 1 lb each and 1½″ thick**
- **4 Idaho potatoes, boiled, peeled, and quartered**
  "galvanizing" marinade
- **4 cups Creole tomato sauce**
  salt

MARINADE
- **2 cups vinegar**
- **2 cups water**

LENA FROM PALESTEENA

LENA FROM PALESTEENA

In the Bronx of New York City
Lives a girl, she's not so pretty,
Lena is her name,
Such a clever girl is Lena,
How she plays a concertina,
Really it's a shame.
She's such a good musician,
She got a swell position
To go across the sea to entertain,
And so they shipped poor Lena
Way out to Palesteena,
But now I hear that she don't look the same
They say that:

Chorus
Lena is the Queen of Palesteena,
Just because they like her concertina,
She plays it day and night,
She plays with all her might,
She never gets it right,
But how they love it,
Want more of it,
I heard her play once or twice,
O! Murder! Still it was nice.
She was fat but she got leaner
Pushing on her concertina
Down old Palesteena way.

Photo courtesy of the Special Collections Division, Tulane University Library.

Ever since Little Egypt shook her fanny to fame at the Chicago World's Fair in 1892, Americans have been fascinated by Hootchykootchy "Oriental" type music. A whole series of tunes of this type worked their way into the mainstream of jazz music in the 1920s — *Dardanella, Lena from Palesteena, Egyptian Ella, The Sheik of Araby,* and others. When the Original Dixieland Jazz Band from New Orleans cut a record of *Dardanella,* it became the most popular tune in America, and everybody was whistling or singing it. When Rudolph Valentino snuck into that pretty girl's tent and silently sang *The Sheik of Araby* (the words were printed in subtitles), the pit orchestras in the theatres backed him up to the hilt, and the audiences sang along with Valentino and the orchestras.

1 large onion, chopped
8 cloves garlic, minced
4 bay leaves, crushed
2 tsp mixed pickling spices
½ tsp thyme
½ tsp basil
½ tsp cumin
1 dozen peppercorns, crushed
1 tsp salt

Leach the tuna steaks in cold salted water for two hours to remove any blood. Remove from the water and dry with paper towels. Pour a half inch of salt into a pan, lay the tuna steaks on it, cover them with another half inch of salt, and place them in the refrigerator to "cure" overnight. The next day, rinse off all the salt. Set the tuna aside and make the marinade.

Place all the marinade ingredients in a large glass bowl or enamel pan, and stir to mix well. Place the tuna steaks in the marinade, and let them soak for an hour, turning them over now and then. While the tunas are marinating, make the Creole tomato sauce. Remove the steaks from the marinade, brush off the spices, and dry with paper towels. Place the tuna steaks in the bottom of a well-greased oven-proof dish or enamel pan. Pour the tomato sauce over them, and add the quartered potatoes to the sauce around the fish. Bake in a preheated 350° oven for 30 minutes, or until the flesh flakes easily when tested with a fork. Serve on preheated plates with the sauce ladled over the fish and the potatoes placed around it. Or you can place the steaks on metal sizzle platters and broil for eight to ten minutes on each side. Heat the tomato sauce and the quartered potatoes together, place a thick blanket of the sauce on each tuna steak,

and place the potato quarters around the fish. This is one of the best uses for the famous Creole tomato sauce.

BROILED FRESH YELLOWFIN TUNA STEAKS

Fresh yellowfin tuna steaks are delicious when simply broiled. Leach four tuna steaks, 1½ inches thick, in strongly salted water for two hours. Rinse them with fresh water and dry with paper towels. Place on buttered sizzle platters (or in a broiler pan), and broil on each side for eight minutes or until the flesh flakes when tested with a fork. Serve with Maître d'hotel butter.

A VERY OLD FISH

Like the sturgeon, the garfish is a monster that can trace its ancestry back to the Paleozoic epoch, 300 million years ago. It was a million years old when the first dinosaurs came along, did their act, and then became extinct. It has the strongest armor of any fish, with tough scales locked together so tight that you can't spear the garfish with a harpoon or shoot it with a .22 rifle. Everything bounces off. Its teeth are so sharp and its mouth so hard that you can't catch it with an ordinary hook and line. The way to get a garfish is with a sort of lasso made of piano wire and baited with a fish head. When the garfish begins to gnaw at the fish head, you tighten the noose over its nose and top jaw and then drag him out of the

Garfish. (Drawing by Duane Raver, Jr., courtesy of Louisiana Wildlife and Fisheries Commission)

water—a real chore if it weighs 50 to 100 pounds.

To get at the meat of the garfish, you chop open its underside (which is a little softer than the top) with a sharp hatchet. Then you open it up and scrape out the meat with a spoon. The meat is tender and of an unbelievably delicate flavor, great for making fish cakes.

BILL SPAHR'S GARFISH CAKES

Bill Spahr owns a restaurant and fishing camp at Des Allemands, a village in the middle of a swamp about fifty miles west of New Orleans. Right in his backyard he has a big lake teeming with fish, alligators, and gars. I always stop by there for lunch and a few beers when I'm passing through. Here's one of the specialties of the house, Garfish Cakes.

  4 lb scraped raw garfish meat
  5 Irish potatoes, boiled, peeled, and mashed
  6 scallions with their leaves, chopped
  1 large onion, chopped
  ½ green pepper, diced
  3 cloves garlic, minced
  2 eggs, beaten
    Tabasco to taste
    salt and pepper to taste

Mix the ingredients well and pat into cakes 2½ inches wide by a half inch thick. Dip the cakes into flour, and fry until brown in deep hot fat.

Man, this tastes as good as virgin sturgeon!

HOMAGE TO THE LOWLY SQUID

I make no apologies for the ugly squid—it doesn't need them. In the hands of a skillful cook this octopus-faced monstrosity is one of the greatest of seafood delicacies. Among Mediterranean peoples, Latin-Americans, Chinese, and Japanese, the squid is highly prized.

There are a great many squid in the Gulf of Mexico, and they're caught, mostly by accident, by shrimp boats and fishing draggers. In New Orleans the fish markets patronized by Italians, Spaniards, Cubans, and Latin-Americans sell large quantities of squid, but they're strictly for home consumption, and you'll hardly ever find them on a restaurant menu. The one exception that I know of is Drago's Lakeside Restaurant, an excellent Yugoslavian restaurant in Metairie, which lists a delicious baked stuffed squid among its Dalmatian spe-

cialties. I'm still waiting for someone to start selling squid stew and fried squid ring appetizers.

To clean a squid, pull off the head and tentacles, and then cut off and separate from the tentacles the eyeballs and the hard mouth part, or "beak." Discard eyes and beak, but save the tentacles, which are the best part. Turn the cylinderlike body wrongside out, wash off the entrails, and remove the cellophanelike backbone called the "pen." Now you're ready for some gourmet cooking.

CREOLE SQUID STEW
(Serves 8 to 10)

3 **dozen squid and their tentacles, cleaned and diced**
   diced potatoes equal in volume to the squid

1 **quart red wine**
1 **quart fish stock or hot water (more if necessary)**
1 **16-oz can tomatoes, chopped, and their juice**
1 **6-oz can tomato paste**
1 **large onion, chopped**
6 **cloves garlic, minced**
3 **tbsp olive oil**
2 **tbsp Worcestershire sauce**
¼ **tsp ground allspice**
¼ **tsp ground cumin**
   salt to taste
   cayenne, enough to make it hot as hellfire

Cook the onions and garlic in the olive oil until they're soft, and then dump them into a stew pot. Put all the squid, vegetables, liquids, and condiments into the pot, bring to the boil, lower the heat, and then simmer for 1, 2, 3, 4, or 5 hours, depending on the amount of time you have on your hands. Stir it now and then, and scrape the bottom of the pot to pre-

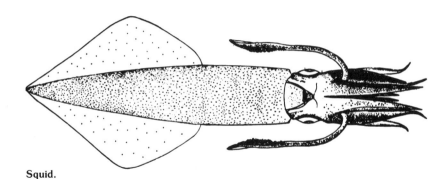

Squid.

vent sticking. Adjust the salt. Serve in large soup bowls with hot French bread. Some of your guests, having it for the first time, will probably say it tastes like boiled tennis shoes, but don't let 'em kid you, it's one of the world's great stews.

FRIED SQUID RINGS

Everybody has eaten French fried onion rings, but few people have had the joy of eating fried squid rings. The squid's body is a perfect cylinder and can be cut into perfect circles. Pull off the heads and clean out the body cavity. Slice the body into circles a quarter inch wide. Dip the rings in flour, then in beaten eggs, then in bread crumbs, and fry in deep hot fat (375°). Keep all the rings separate from one another or they'll stick together. Cut off the tentacles just in front of the eyes, and dip and fry these, too. They're the best part. Fried squid rings and tentacles make delicious and uniquely different hors d'oeuvres for a cocktail party. Whole baby squid about three inches long don't need to be cleaned. They're fried and eaten whole, feathers and all, and they're so good that your guests will keep hollering for more and more.

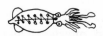

DELUXE STUFFED SQUID
(Serves 6 or more)

2 dozen large squid
1 lb raw shrimp, peeled and chopped

6 strips bacon
2 medium onions, chopped
4 scallions with 2″ of their green leaves, chopped
2 tbsp chopped fresh parsley
1 rib celery, minced
2 cloves garlic, minced
2 cups bread crumbs
salt and freshly ground black pepper
chicken broth, bouillon, or water
butter, melted
sherry
cayenne

For use in the stuffing, clean two of the squid, and dice finely the meat of the body and tentacles. Fry the bacon until crisp and brown, and then drain and crumble it. Pour off half the bacon fat in the skillet. In the remainder, cook the onions, scallions, celery, garlic, and parsley until the vegetables are soft and transparent. Add the diced squid meats, chopped shrimp, and crumbled bacon, and cook for 10 minutes longer, stirring constantly. Season with salt and black pepper. Add the bread crumbs, and wet the mixture with enough chicken broth, bouillon, or water to make a heavy paste of it. This is your stuffing. Set it aside.

Cleaning a squid to prepare it for stuffing is a tricky business, because you want to keep the head and tentacles on so that the squid will look whole and pristinely alive after it's cooked. Split the body carefully, and clean out the innards and cellophanelike backbone. Remove the beaklike mouth part just below the eyes. Rinse the body thoroughly.

Stuff the squid bodies, filling them only two-thirds full. The dressing will expand and the squid will shrink, so if you overload them, they'll burst while cooking. Take a needle and strong thread and sew them up in the best surgical manner, working from the tail upward, and when you reach the top, put a couple of loops through the head to keep it from falling off. Lay each squid on a square of heavy-duty foil. Sprinkle with a tablespoon of melted butter, a teaspoon of sherry, salt, black pepper, and a little cayenne. Lift the edges of the foil, roll them up, and crimp them tightly. Then roll up and crimp the ends.

When finished, you'll have tightly sealed cylinders with squid inside. Bake them in a preheated 400° oven for 30 minutes, or a little longer if the squid are very large. Take them to the table in the wrappings, and serve each guest two or three squid, according to his capacity.

VICTOR PACELLINI'S STUFFED SQUID

(Serves 6)

12 squid
12 slices bacon
 1 lb chicken livers
 1 16-oz can tomato sauce
 1 cup white wine
    salt and freshly ground black pepper

Fry the bacon in a skillet until it's three-quarters done but still limp. Remove the bacon from the pan and set it aside. Cook the chicken livers in the bacon fat in the skillet until they're three-quarters done. Season with salt and black pepper. Remove the livers, drain on paper towels, and chop them coarsely.

Clean the squid as instructed in the recipe for Deluxe Stuffed Squid, keeping the heads on.

For each squid take a strip of bacon and line the bottom of the body cavity with it. Cover with chopped chicken livers until two-thirds full, and sew up. Place the squid in a well-greased baking pan, the side with the bacon facing up. Sprinkle with the tomato puree and white wine. Bake in a 350° oven for 30 to 45 minutes, or until the squid are browned and tender. Baste them frequently with the pan juices to keep them from drying up. When you eat a squid prepared this way, cut it crosswise in slices so you'll have a little piece of bacon with each bite.

ED GIOBBI'S STUFFED SQUID ITALIAN STYLE

(Serves 2 to 4)

My friend Ed Giobbi, who is already a famous painter, is getting to be even more famous as an Italian cook. His *Italian Family Cookbook* has been a best-seller among cookbooks for several years. He gave me his recipe for Italian style stuffed squid.

 4 large squid

THE STUFFING
 6 slices bread, moistened and kneaded
 2 cloves garlic, minced
 1 tbsp fresh flat-leaf parsley, chopped
 2 tbsp high-grade olive oil
 1 tbsp Parmesan cheese
    chopped tentacles and wings of the squid

THE SAUCE
½ cup olive oil
1 tbsp chopped flat-leaf parsley
1 clove garlic, sliced
2 cups plum-type tomatoes
½ tsp oregano
1 cup green peas
steamed rice
salt and freshly ground black pepper
red pepper, crushed

To clean the squid, remove the heads and wings, carefully turn the tubes inside out, and scrape and wash them. Remove the cellophanelike backbone, and turn them right side out again. Cut off the eyes and the beaklike mouth part from the tentacles. Chop the wings and tentacles.

To make the stuffing, mix the bread, garlic, parsley, olive oil, and Parmesan cheese together with the chopped tentacles and wings. Stuff the squid with the mixture, and sew or skewer

the opening to keep the stuffing from oozing out.

Heat the half cup of olive oil in a skillet, and cook the stuffed squid, adding salt, black pepper, crushed red pepper, garlic, and parsley. Continue to cook over moderate heat until the squid begin to brown. Then add the tomatoes and oregano, cover the pan, and simmer very slowly for 30 minutes, or until the squid are tender. Add the peas and cook another 10 minutes. Serve on hot plates with steamed rice on the side.

Chapter 9

Delicious Denizens of the Swamp: Frogs, Turtles, Alligators

THE BULLFROG, BASSO PROFUNDO OF THE SWAMP

The frog, called *grenouille* by the French and *ouaouaron* by the Cajuns, is one of Louisiana's best gifts to the world of haute cuisine. That Cajun word is an Algonquin Indian term, and it's pure onomatopoeia, an effort to duplicate the bullfrog's love song. If you've never heard the chorus of a swamp full of bullfrogs on a spring night, you've really missed something. The melody has the cacophony and decibels of a Lexington Avenue subway train. It can be very frightening to the uninitiated, and it used to scare hell out of me when I was a very small kid living on the edge of a swamp.

Going frog gigging is a springtime nocturnal sport down in the bayou country. The frog gigger wades along in the bayou, creek, or pond, close to the bank. (Some froggers work in pairs in a boat, one rowing close to the bank while the other sits in the bow catching the frogs.) When the hunter throws a spotlight on a frog sitting on the bank, the frog is usually too startled to move, and the frog catcher gigs it. Some hunters catch them with their bare hands. When the hunting is good, a whole sackful can be caught before daylight.

Bullfrog farms are now well-paying operations throughout the southern part of Louisiana. That's why they're now available in supermarkets all over the country, at prices

241

Frog. (Courtesy of Louisiana Wildlife and Fisheries Commission)

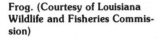

that are very reasonable compared with the sky-high prices of the old days. Frogs are highly perishable, and all the frogs' legs available on the market are frozen.

Only the large hind legs of the frog are eaten. When they're parboiled for three minutes and soaked in milk for an hour, the flavor is improved. The meat of frogs' legs is dry and must be cooked carefully so that the natural juices won't evaporate. The flavor is somewhat like quail or pheasant (some say chicken, but it's on a higher plane than chicken). Four pairs of small frogs' legs or two or three pairs of the larger ones make an individual serving. Frogs' legs are best when cooked in butter—slowly so that the butter doesn't burn. When you're cooking large quantities, it's a good idea to combine butter and margarine in equal parts. The margarine inhibits the burning of the butter.

FROGS' LEGS SAUCE PIQUANTE

(Serves 4)

This is the favorite Cajun way of cooking frogs' legs, and the Creoles have happily adopted it.

"Piquante" is a euphemistic Cajun term meaning "hot as hell." If you don't like hot pepper, leave out the cayenne in the sauce, but then it won't be authentically Cajun.

16 pairs small (or 8-12 pairs large) frogs'
    legs
    milk
    corn flour
1 stick butter
1 stick margarine
4 fresh tomatoes, broiled (optional)

SAUCE PIQUANTE FOR FROGS' LEGS
1 stick butter
3 tbsp flour
1 medium onion, chopped
4 cloves garlic, minced
½ green pepper, chopped
1 rib celery, finely chopped
2 scallions with 3″ of their green leaves,
    thinly sliced
2 tbsp fresh chopped parsley
1 16-oz can tomatoes, chopped, and their
    juice
1 tsp cayenne (or less)
3 cups bouillon (or water)
    salt and freshly ground black pepper

To make the sauce, melt the butter and add the flour. Cook very slowly, stirring constantly, for about 15 minutes to make a light roux. Add the onion, garlic, green pepper, celery, scallions, and parsley, and cook until the vegetables are soft and transparent. Add the water or bouillon. Add the tomatoes and their juice, the cayenne, salt, and black pepper. Simmer over low heat for an hour, adding more water or bouillon if necessary.

While the sauce is simmering, cook the frogs' legs. Melt the butter and margarine in a skillet. Dip the frogs' legs in milk and then in corn flour, shaking off the excess flour. Cook the frogs' legs gently in the butter until golden brown on one side. Then carefully turn them over and brown the other side. Remove the first pairs of legs from the skillet and keep them warm until all have been cooked. Place all the frogs' legs in the sauce and cook for five to ten minutes, just until the whole mixture is good and hot.

Use preheated round serving plates. Arrange the frogs' legs on the plate like the spokes of a wheel, and cover them with the sauce piquante. Although optional, a fresh tomato with its top sliced off and broiled or baked with a cap of Parmesan cheese makes a nice hub for each "wheel" of frogs' legs to rotate around.

FROGS' LEGS SAUTE MEUNIERE
(Serves 3 or 4)

12 pairs small (or 6-8 pairs large)
   frogs' legs
   corn flour
   milk

2 sticks butter
   juice of 2 lemons
   salt and freshly ground black pepper
   cayenne

Parboil the frogs' legs for three minutes, and then soak them in milk for an hour. Melt the butter in a skillet. Remove the frogs' legs from the milk, and sprinkle with salt, black pepper, and a little cayenne. Dip in flour, and shake off the excess flour. Place them in the skillet and cook them gently, browning both sides. Place the frogs' legs on warm serving plates. Add the lemon juice to the butter in the skillet, raise the heat high, and scrape the sides and bottom of the skillet to dissolve any browned particles clinging to it. Cook until the butter lightly browns. Pour the meunière sauce over the frogs' legs, sprinkle generously with chopped parsley, and serve at once, piping hot.

FRIED FROGS' LEGS
(Serves 3 or 4)

12 pairs small (or 6-8 pairs large)
   frogs' legs
   corn flour
   bread crumbs
1 stick butter
   juice of 1 lemon
   milk
3 beaten eggs
   cayenne
   salt and freshly ground black pepper

Separate the pairs of frogs' legs into single pieces like small chicken drumsticks. Dip the legs in milk, then in flour, then in eggs, and then in bread crumbs that have been seasoned with salt and pepper. Fry in deep hot fat (365°) until golden brown. Keep them hot. Melt the butter in a skillet, and cook it until light brown. Add the lemon juice. Pour this over the frogs' legs and serve at once, piping hot.

Small frogs' legs cooked in this way make excellent hot hors d'oeuvres for a cocktail party.

FROGS' LEGS FORESTIERE

(Serves 4)

As noted earlier, those rich old sugar planters down on Bayou Teche liked to distill home-made rum out of their cane juice, and they liked to use it in their cookery. Also fond of rum were the Dominican and Caribbean refugees who flocked to New Orleans at the beginning of the nineteenth century.

12 pairs small (or 6-8 pairs large)
    frogs' legs
 2 sticks butter
 2 tbsp flour
 1 small green pepper, chopped
 3 scallions with 2″ of their green leaves,
    finely sliced
 2 cups fresh mushrooms, sliced
    juice of 1 lemon
 2 tbsp fresh chopped parsley
 1 cup rum

 1 oz rum
    salt and freshly ground black pepper
    cayenne

Divide the paired legs into single legs like chicken drumsticks. Parboil them for three minutes, and let them cool. Mix the cup of rum with a cup of water in a glass dish. Add salt and pepper, and marinate the frogs' legs in this liquid for an hour. Remove, drain, and dry them. Rub them with salt, black pepper, and a little cayenne. Cook them in the butter until they're golden brown on both sides, and set aside. Add the flour to the butter in the skillet, and blend it in well. Add the green pepper, scallions, mushrooms, parsley, and the jigger of rum, and cook until the vegetables are soft. Add the lemon juice, and season with salt and black pepper. If the sauce is too thick, add a little hot water. Place the frogs' legs in the sauce and cook just until they're heated through. Arrange on warm serving plates, and pour the sauce over them.

ALL ABOUT TURTLES

Next to Seafood Gumbo, Creole Turtle Soup is the most popular stew in New Orleans, and deservedly so, because it's one of the most delicious dishes in the whole bright lexicon of Creole-Cajun cooking. It epitomizes all the virtues and uses of the cuisine: the roux; the slowly cooked vegetables; the long, slow simmer; the aromatic herbs and spices; and the wine. It's all there in this one dish. None of your pale, thin bouillons that pass for turtle soup in Eastern and Continental restaurants!

Diamondback terrapin at home in the salt marshes. (Courtesy of Louisiana Wildlife and Fisheries Commission)

Catching a diamondback terrapin.

Creole Turtle Soup is a thick, heady stew with lots of meat in it, and it has such a medley of beautifully blended condiments that when you sniff the steam rising from a hot bowl of it, your head swims, and your taste buds go crazy with anticipation.

You'll find Creole Turtle Soup on the menu of every first-class restaurant in New Orleans, right there on the soup list next to the Creole Gumbo, and many restauranteurs tell me it outsells the gumbo. Like gumbo, it takes a lot of work. The soup chef, who is one of the most important members of the kitchen staff of a large New Orleans restaurant, works full time at it, and the other cooks pay obeisance and stay out of the way.

The diamondback terrapin is the choicest species in Louisiana for making turtle soup. A salt water turtle, it grows in brackish water in salt marshes in the southern part of the state. We now have turtle farms that raise the

The snapping turtle of the swamps. (Courtesy of Louisiana Wildlife and Fisheries Commission)

diamondbacks on a commercial basis. It's good to buy a live turtle in the shell, because then you get the eggs, if any, and the calipash and callipee, which are the choicest part of the turtle.

The next choices are the green sea turtle and the loggerhead turtle from far out in the Gulf of Mexico, the South Atlantic, and the Caribbean, especially around the West Indies. These turtles are sometimes giants weighing

several hundred pounds each. Their meat is delicious, and it's the type most often found frozen and canned. (Canned turtle meat makes an excellent substitute when you can't find it fresh or frozen.)

But the darling of Cajuns and Creoles is the fresh-water turtle. Because blacks are especially fond of turtle stew, you can often find turtle meat in the markets in black neighborhoods when you can't find it anywhere else. "Fresh Cowan Turtles Today" is a familiar sign in the window. Fresh-water turtles thrive in swamps, sloughs, marshes, bayous, bogs, and ponds, where you can often spot them sunning themselves on a log. The Cowan turtle and the snapping turtle are the most popular species among turtle fanciers. The snapper is a fierce devil, and there's a superstition that if he grabs hold of you with his powerful jaws, he won't let go 'til the sun sets, or it thunders. Other popular turtles are the mud "turkle," the leatherback or soft-shell turtle, wood turtle, painted turtle, and the yellow-bellied and red-bellied turtles. And while we're at it, let's not forget Lewis Carroll's mock turtle.

Making homemade turtle soup or stew is truly a fine art, and for those who want to give it a try, here are the details.

PREPARATION OF TURTLES

As noted, it's best to use live turtles, but dressing and preparing them is a diabolical and macabre business. If you're fainthearted, you should skip the following paragraphs and just buy some frozen or canned turtle meat at a good fish market or gourmet specialty store.

Fill a tub with water and add enough salt to make it very salty. Let the turtle swim around for an hour or two to purge itself and to soften and wash off any collected mud and dirt. Sharpen an axe, a hatchet, or a butcher's cleaver, and have it ready.

Remove the turtle from the tub, lay it on its back on a chopping block or heavy plank, and stand very quietly beside it with your axe poised in the air. Curiosity will get the best of

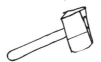

the turtle, and when it sticks its head all the way out of the shell to find out where it's at, bring the axe down quickly on its neck. It's as simple as that. (You needn't have any guilt feelings, because it doesn't hurt the turtle. Besides, it's all done for the sake of gourmandise!) Then you plunge the body and the head back in the tub of water and leave them there for a half hour, until they've shed all their blood. At the end of the half hour, change the water in the tub, scrub the turtle immaculately clean with a stiff brush, and rinse it well.

Turtles should be parboiled in enough unsalted water to cover them. A small ten-pound turtle should be done in 45 minutes, but a twenty-pound turtle may take an hour or more. The turtle is ready when the flesh of the feet and legs becomes soft when you press it. Skin the head, legs, and feet, and pull out the toe nails. The bottom shell is called the plastron and the top shell the carapace. Cut the bottom and top shells apart with a very sharp knife. The ligament joining them together is sometimes very tough and resilient. Lift the top shell off very carefully. It's very important not to break the gall bladder, the plum-shaped object attached to the liver. Cut it off and discard it, and don't let any of its contents leak out. Remove the liver, dice it, and set it aside in the refrigerator. Remove the eggs, if any are present, and refrigerate them. Discard the entrails, the heart, and the tough white muscles. Some connoisseurs save the small lower intestine, clean it well, mince it, and mix it with the other meats. It's like chitterlings. Remove all the meat from the bones of the body, head, and legs. Save the bones to put in the stock. And now for something very important: The calipash and the calipee are the choicest por-

GEORGE LEWIS

LITTLE COQUETTE

*Tell me why you keep fooling, Little
   Coquette,
Making fun of the ones who love you?
Breaking hearts you are ruling, Little
   Coquette,
True hearts tenderly dreaming of you?
Someday you'll fall in love
As I fell in love with you,
Honey, maybe, someone you love
Will just be fooling,
And when you're all alone
With only regret,
You'll know, Little Coquette,
I loved you.*

Lyrics by Gus Kahn, music by Carmen Lombardo and
Johnny Green. Copyright 1928, renewed 1956, Leo Feist
Inc., New York, N.Y. Used by permission.

This must be the saddest little song ever written. In the late 1920s it made strong men cry in their Prohibition beer and bathtub gin to listen to it. The tune stuck in the mind and inner ear for days on end, and you couldn't throw it out, come hell or high water. It has stuck in the author's mind for 49 years and is still one of his all-time favorites.

However, the song signaled something else, the approaching end of the golden age of jazz. The name of a Lombardo among its composers shows that the era of swing was beginning, with its big bands, saxophones, sweet sentimentality, written music, and arrangements. The next twenty years would belong to the big swing bands of Guy Lombardo, Coon-Sanders, Benny Goodman, Glenn Miller, Fred Waring, and others. Almost forgotten except by a few jazz purists were the small combos, the gutbucket ensembles, the wild improvisations. And then in the 1950s, BANG! A rebirth occurred. The small hot bands came back with improvisation and creative jazz. In New Orleans the old-time jazz bands sprang to life again, playing for a startled younger generation that had never heard their sound. It caught on, there was a genuine renaissance, and today traditional New Orleans jazz is more popular than it ever was before. The city has come to recognize its treasured heritage. Kid Thomas says, "I'm only 82. I hope to stay around blowing till doomsday."

Clarinetist Extraordinary

Drawing by Johnny Donnels

Until his death at the age of 68 in 1968, George Lewis was the greatest New Orleans clarinet player. He led his own band, and he also frequently played with Kid Thomas and his Algiers Stompers at Preservation Hall. In three consecutive years—1963, 1964, and 1965—he led his band on tours of Japan, converting thousands of Japanese to New Orleans jazz. George was the last of a long line of famous New Orleans clarinetists that included Alphonse Picou, "Big Eye Louis" Nelson Delisle, Sidney Bechet, Papa Celestin, and Johnny Dodds. Naturally his favorite tunes were *High Society* and *Muskrat Ramble*.

tions of the turtle, and they must not be thrown away by mistake. The calipash is the dull-greenish fatty substance inside the upper shell, or carapace. The calipee is the light yellow fatty substance attached to the bottom shell, or plastron. Scrape this substance off the shells, and save it along with the other meat. No soup or stew is complete without it. The connoisseur can tell when he's eating turtle soup instead of beef stew by looking for the lumps of calipash and calipee in it.

Set aside and refrigerate the quantity of turtle meat, liver, and calipash you need for your current soup or stew, and freeze the rest. Turtle meat is perishable and will quickly spoil if left lying around.

The shells aren't used in Creole turtle soup or stews, but they're indispensable for making clear turtle soup (see recipe for Green Turtle Soup au Sherry). Chop the shells up with a hatchet, place the pieces in a plastic bag, and keep it in the freezer until needed.

Now that the preliminaries are over, you're ready to go to town!

CREOLE TURTLE SOUP
(Serves 10 to 12)

3 lb turtle meat, including any available
    calipash, calipee, eggs, and turtle bones
2 quarts hot water
2 quarts beef broth (or 4 16-oz cans)
1 stick butter
4 tbsp flour

2 large onions, chopped fine
1 green pepper, chopped fine
2 ribs celery, minced
2 tbsp chopped fresh parsley
4 cloves garlic, minced
1 16-oz can tomatoes, drained and finely
    minced, and their juice
1 lemon, sliced (for the pot)
2 lemons, thinly sliced (for garnish)
1 tbsp Worcestershire sauce
½ tsp cayenne
¼ tsp ground allspice
¼ tsp ground cloves
¼ tsp marjoram
½ tsp thyme
½ tsp basil
2 bay leaves
½ cup sherry
    chopped parsley and 3 hard-boiled eggs,
    chopped for garnish
    salt and freshly ground black pepper

In a large, heavy pot make a roux with the butter and flour, cooking slowly and stirring constantly until it's a reddish russet brown, about 20 to 30 minutes. Add the onions, green pepper, celery, chopped parsley, and garlic, and cook and stir until the vegetables are soft and translucent. Dice the turtle meat into half-inch cubes. Add the meat. Add the calipash, calipee, and bones, if any, to the pot. Add the beef broth, hot water, and the bay leaves. Bring to the boil, then lower the heat, partially cover, and simmer for two hours. Remove the bay leaves. Add the allspice, cloves, basil, thyme, marjoram, cayenne, lemon slices, and Worcestershire sauce, and mix well. Partially cover the pot and simmer for at least two more hours, preferably as much as four hours more. Stir it now and then, scraping the bottom of the pot with a metal kitchen spoon. If a brown residue shows up on the tip of the spoon, you're scorching it, so slow down and put an asbestos pad under it. A half hour before it's done, add the sherry and turtle eggs, if any. Remove the lemon slices and turtle bones. Season to taste with salt and freshly ground black pepper.

Ladle from the bottom upward into pre-heated soup bowls, sprinkle chopped hard-cooked eggs and chopped parsley on top of each bowl, and float a thin slice of fresh lemon on each. Ah beauty!

CAJUN SWAMP TURTLE SOUP
(Serves 12 to 14)

THE STOCK
- 3 lb fresh-water swamp turtle meat
  turtle bones, if any
- 6 quarts hot water
- 2 large onions, coarsely chopped
- 3 ribs celery with green leaves, coarsely chopped
- 1 cup parsley sprigs
- 4 cloves garlic, minced
- 2 bay leaves
- ½ tsp ground cloves
- ½ tsp ground allspice
- ½ tsp thyme
- ½ tsp cayenne
  salt and freshly ground black pepper to taste

THE SOUP
- calipash and calipee, if any
- 2 large Creole tomatoes, peeled (or a 16-oz can)
- 1 8-oz can tomato sauce
- 4 scallions with 3″ of their green leaves
- ½ lb country ham (or boiled ham)
- 1 stick butter
- 4 tbsp flour
  juice of 1 lemon
- 1 tbsp Worcestershire sauce
- ½ tsp grated lemon peel
- ½ cup sherry
- 4 hard-boiled eggs
  finely chopped green onion leaves (scallions)
  thin lemon slices
  sherry

MAKING THE STOCK
Put the turtle meat and bones in a heavy soup pot with six quarts of water, and add all the other ingredients in the stock list. Bring to the boil, lower the heat to a slow boil, and cook for two hours. Put an asbestos pad under the pot to keep it from sticking and scorching. Stir now and then, scraping the bottom of the pot to make sure it's not burning. If it gets too thick, add more water or beef broth to the pot. Strain the stock through triple cheesecloth. Save the meat and cut it into half-inch dice for the soup. Discard the vegetables and bones.

If the country ham is raw, cook the slices very slowly in a covered iron skillet, browning on both sides, about 20 minutes. Put it through the fine blade of a grinder. The ham gives a terrific punch to the soup. Grind the scallions and the tomatoes as well.

Melt the stick of butter in a skillet, add the

flour, and cook very slowly, stirring constantly, for 20 to 30 minutes to make a reddish russet-brown roux. Add the ground scallions, tomatoes, and ham to the roux, and cook for five minutes.

Clean the soup pot the stock was made in. Add the stock and the roux mixture to the pot, and mix well. Add the diced turtle meat and calipash-calipee, if any. Add the tomato sauce, sherry, grated lemon peel, and Worcestershire sauce. Bring to the boil, lower the heat, and simmer for an hour. Place an asbestos pad under the pot to prevent sticking and scorching. Stir now and then, scraping the bottom of the pot. If it gets too thick, add hot water or beef broth. It should be of the consistency of a light gravy. At the end, stir in the lemon juice. Adjust the salt. It should be salty and savoury.

Put a tablespoon of sherry in each preheated soup bowl before ladling in the soup. Sprinkle chopped hard-boiled eggs and finely chopped green onion leaves (scallions) over the top of each bowl, and float a thin lemon slice in the center.

SWAMP TURTLE SOUP AU RHUM

As you may recall from an earlier section, the old-time sugar planters made a potent dark rum called "tafia," which worked its way into plantation cookery. It gave an especially good tang to swamp turtle soup. In the recipe above, after the scallions, tomatoes, and ham have cooked in the roux for five minutes, make a small "well" in the corner of the skillet,

and add two ounces of dark rum. When it becomes heated, flame it and burn off the alcohol, and then mix it in well with the other ingredients in the skillet.

GREEN SEA TURTLE SOUP AU SHERRY
(Serves 10 to 12)

This is the soup in which you use the chopped turtle shells, as mentioned in the section on the preparation of turtles. However, if you don't have the shells, forget them and go ahead with your soup. The calipash and calipee should also be used if you have any, but they're not absolutely necessary.

- 3 lb green sea (or other) turtle meat, diced
  calipash and calipee, if available
- 4-5 lb turtle shells, chopped (optional)
- 2 quarts beef broth
- 2 quarts hot water
- 1 16-oz can plum-type tomatoes, chopped, and their juice
- 1 8-oz can tomato sauce
- 3 medium onions, chopped
- ½ cup fresh chopped parsley
- 4 scallions with their green leaves, sliced
- 1 green pepper, diced
- 2 cloves garlic, minced
- ½ tsp thyme
- ½ tsp ground allspice
- ¼ tsp cayenne
- 3 egg whites, beaten

juice of ½ lemon
salt and freshly ground black pepper
sherry

Place all the ingredients except the calipash-
calipee, sherry, salt, and lemon juice in a large
pot with a thick bottom. Bring to the boil,
lower the heat, partially cover, and simmer for
six hours, stirring now and then and scraping
the bottom of the pot to keep it from sticking.
Add more stock or water if necessary to keep
it fluid. At the end, strain it twice through
quadruple cheesecloth. Place a small amount
of the strained stock in a saucepan, and boil
the calipash-calipee for an hour. Set aside to
be added to the soup at the end. Save enough
of the turtle meat to have three or four small
cubes for each bowl at the end. To further
clarify the liquid, place it in a clean pot over
high heat, and add the beaten whites of three
eggs. Continue stirring vigorously until it boils,
then lower the heat, and boil slowly for a half
hour. Strain through quadruple cheesecloth
again. (If you have time, you can clarify it further by letting it sit in the refrigerator overnight
so that any sediment will sink to the bottom.)
Add the lemon juice. Add the calipash-calipee,
if any. Adjust the salt. Add one cup of high-
quality imported dry sherry for each quart of
soup. This may sound excessive, but it's
actually less than many French and English
cooks use. A fine old Madeira would be even
better than sherry, but good old Madeira is getting so scarce that it's better to drink it than to
squander it on soup.

Heat the soup, place the reserved cubes of
turtle meat in the bottom of each preheated
soup bowl, and ladle in the soup. Float a thin
lemon slice on each bowl, both for looks and
for aroma.

CAJUN TURTLE STEW PIQUANTE
(Serves a whole crowd of cousines)

This is the favorite Cajun way of cooking their
beloved swamp turtles. It's very much like the
swamp turtle soup, but it's thicker, meatier,
and h-h-hotter!

5 lb fresh swamp turtle meat, cut in ½″
cubes
2 cups flour seasoned with salt, black
pepper, and cayenne
1 gallon hot water (or more)
1 cup plain flour
2 sticks butter
3 large onions, chopped
6 ribs celery, chopped
6 cloves garlic, minced
2 green peppers, chopped
10 scallions with their green leaves, sliced
1 cup chopped fresh parsley
1 32-oz can plum-type tomatoes, chopped,
and their juice
1 6-oz can tomato paste
½ lemon, sliced
6 Trappey's (or other brand) red hot
pickled peppers, minced
2 bay leaves
½ tsp ground allspice
½ tsp ground cloves
½ tsp thyme
1 tbsp cayenne
6 hard-boiled eggs, chopped
2 cups sherry
lemon slices, chopped green onion
leaves, steamed rice

Melt the butter in the bottom of a heavy pot, add the cup of plain flour, and cook over low heat for 20 to 30 minutes to make a reddish russet brown roux. Add the scallions, celery, garlic, green pepper, onions, and parsley to the roux, and cook until the vegetables are soft. Add some water if it gets too dry. Add the chopped tomatoes, their juice, and the tomato paste. Add a gallon or more of water, enough to cover all the materials in the pot by two inches. Add the sliced lemon, hot pickled peppers, bay leaves, allspice, cloves, thyme, and cayenne. Bring to the boil, and then reduce to a slow boil. Place an asbestos pad under the pot to prevent scorching. Cook for an hour, stirring frequently and scraping the bottom of the pot to keep it from sticking.

While the vegetables are cooking heat a half inch of lard in a large skillet. Place the seasoned flour in a brown paper bag and shake the turtle meat cubes in it. Lift the cubes out and shake off the excess flour. Fry them in the hot lard until they're lightly browned on all sides, and set aside.

After the vegetables in the pot have cooked for an hour, add the turtle meat. The liquid in the pot should be about an inch above the materials in the pot, so add more water or beef broth if necessary. Bring to the boil, then turn the heat low, and simmer for an hour more. Keep the asbestos pad under the pot. Remember that this is a very thick, heavy stew, and it will scorch sure as hell if you don't keep a close watch on it. Stir frequently with a metal kitchen spoon, scraping the bottom of the pot thoroughly with the tip of the spoon to keep it from sticking. If the spoon comes up with a dark brown residue on its tip, you're scorching it, so lower the heat a little. Midway

of the final hour, add the sherry and chopped eggs. Serve in preheated soup bowls, sprinkle the top of each bowl with finely chopped green onion leaves, and float a thin slice of lemon in the middle. Have a big bowl of steaming rice on the table for those who want it with their stew.

BRAISED TURTLE STEAKS
(Serves 4)

   4 turtle steaks, 4″ long and 1″ thick
   4 tbsp lard
   4 Trappey's (or other brand) red hot pickled peppers
   1 16-oz can tomatoes, chopped, and their juice
   ¼ tsp ground cloves
   ¼ tsp thyme
   salt and freshly ground black pepper
   2 tbsp flour
   steamed rice

Melt two tablespoons of lard in a heavy skillet, put the steaks in the skillet, lower the heat, and cook them slowly, browning on both sides (about half an hour). Add the peppers, tomatoes, cloves, and thyme. Add a half cup of water, cover the skillet, and let the meat braise until the water is nearly evaporated. Scrape the bottom of the pan, turn the steaks over, and add more water. Continue to cook the steaks slowly, turning them now and then, and adding water often to keep the pan from drying out and the steaks from burning. Cook in this manner for two hours, or until the steaks are tender. About 20 minutes before the end, start cooking your rice. Toward the end, sprinkle the steaks with salt and black pepper. Place them on warm serving plates and keep them warm. Add two tablespoons each of lard and flour to the braising residues in the skillet, and stir to blend well. Add a cup and a half of hot water, raise the heat, and stir to blend well, scraping the sides and bottom of the skillet to release any browned particles. Season to taste with salt and black pepper. Serve in a gravy boat to be spooned over the steaks and steamed rice.

ALLIGATORS, ANCIENT EATING

Like the first families of Virginia, the DAR, and the Mayflower descendants, the alligator can be very proud of his lineage. He can trace his ancestry back to the Jurassic period of the Mesozoic epoch, that is, back about 175 million years. That was when the reptiles began to diversify into creatures like dinosaurs and ruled the earth for some 75 million years—quite a

span when one considers that Homo sapiens has been around only a million years or so. Therefore you should feel very humble when you eat an alligator, because the alligator fed on your ancestors when they were still crawling around in the ooze.

Yes, yes, yes, alligators are edible, and they're very tasty fare when Cajun and Creole cooks go to work on them with their hokus pokus. About 20 years ago the alligators of Louisiana had been hunted almost to extinction for their hides, which were used in making expensive wallets and shoes. But after a moratorium on hunting for several years, the alligator is coming back strong and can be legally hunted again in some areas. I predict the day will come when fillet of alligator will be served with pride in first-class gourmet restaurants, and frozen alligator meat will be available in the supermarkets. Be prepared!

I haven't spent enough time in the swamps to become an authority on alligator cookery, but my friend Marian "Pie" Pendley, the food editor of *Louisiana Conservationist* magazine, has a lot of friends down in Cameron Parish, where the alligators grow in abundance. These friends, some of them the wives of alligator hunters, have supplied her with recipes that are "straight from the horse's mouth," and she has passed them on to me. With some alligator meat a Cajun friend gave me, I kitchen-tested several of the recipes in my "laboratory," and I can vouch for the fact that they're very tasty. An alligator under five feet long makes the best eating, and the tail is the choicest part. An old "bull" alligator that's ten or twelve feet long is just too tough to negotiate, and if you could hear one of them bellow, you wouldn't want to eat him anyhow.

ALLIGATOR A LA CREOLE
(Serves 18)

  4 lb alligator meat, cut in very small
     pieces
  1 stick butter
1⅓ cups diced green pepper
1⅓ cups chopped onion
2½ cups diced celery
  ½ cup flour
  3 32-oz cans tomatoes (10 cups)
  2 tbsp brown sugar, packed
  3 bay leaves
  8 whole cloves
  2 tsp Worcestershire sauce
  ⅛ tsp Tabasco
  1 tbsp lemon juice
  ⅔ cup white wine
  7 cups raw rice
  ½ tsp black pepper
1½ tbsp salt

Melt the butter in an eight-quart heavy kettle. Add green pepper, onions, and celery, and cook until the vegetables are soft and transparent. Remove from the heat, add the flour, and blend thoroughly. Return to the fire and add the tomatoes gradually, squeezing them up and stirring constantly. Add the salt, pepper, sugar, bay leaves, and cloves, and bring to a boil. Add the alligator meat to the mixture, and bring to the boil again. Reduce the heat and simmer, uncovered, over low heat for 45 minutes, stirring occasionally. Start cooking your steamed rice 30 minutes before the end. Remove the stew from the heat, and stir in the Worcestershire sauce, Tabasco,

lemon juice, and white wine. Serve in preheated soup bowls over hot rice.

POT ROASTED STUFFED ALLIGATOR STEAKS
(Serves 4)

  4 alligator steaks, 1″ thick
  1 lb ground alligator meat
  ½ cup chopped green onions (scallions)
  ¼ cup fresh chopped parsley
  ½ cup oil
     salt and black pepper to taste
     water as needed

Mix the ground alligator meat with the green onions and parsley, and season to taste with salt and black pepper. Divide into four portions. Cut a slit lengthwise in the middle of each alligator steak to form a pocket. Stuff the seasoned ground meat into each pocket. Rub each stuffed steak with salt and black pepper. Heat the oil and fry the steaks brown on each side. Add one cup of water, a little at a time. Cover the pot tightly, and cook on low heat for about an hour. Add a little more water if necessary.

OVEN-BARBECUED ALLIGATOR
(Serves 8)

  6 lb alligator steaks
  ⅔ cup lemon juice
  ½ cup soy sauce

2 tbsp chopped parsley
1½ cups salad oil
8 drops Tabasco
⅛ tsp salt
1 tbsp garlic salt
¼ tsp black pepper
1 cup flour

Place the alligator steaks in a shallow glass dish or enamel pan. Combine the lemon juice, soy sauce, parsley, salad oil, Tabasco, salt, garlic salt, and black pepper, and mix well. Pour over the steaks and let them marinate for four hours, turning the pieces over occasionally. Drain the steaks, roll lightly in flour, and shake off the excess flour. Arrange the steaks in a shallow greased pan and bake in a moderate 350° oven for about an hour, or until tender. Serve at once on preheated serving plates.

FRIED ALLIGATOR TENDERLOINS
(Serves 6)

fresh alligator tenderloins
vinegar

salt, black pepper, and
cayenne to taste
2 cups cornmeal
½ cup flour
cooking oil or lard

Skin and tenderloin a fresh ten-pound alligator tail. Cut the flesh into two-inch pieces about an inch thick. Place the cut pieces in a flat glass dish or enamel pan. Pour on the pieces a small amount of vinegar. Add salt, black pepper, and cayenne to taste. Let the meat marinate for 30 minutes, turning the pieces over now and then. While the meat is soaking, put the cornmeal and flour in a brown paper bag. Shake the alligator pieces in the cornmeal mixture in the bag, and shake off the excess. Put about an inch of cooking oil or lard in a skillet, and heat to approximately 400°. Place enough pieces in the skillet just to cover the bottom. Fry them golden brown and serve them piping hot.

Shopping Mart

New Orleans has several seafood dealers who will ship seafood anywhere in the country by air express. You can order from them fresh or frozen shrimp (heads-on or heads-off); crabs (hardshell or softshell); crawfish; oysters in the shell by the sack, or shucked by the gallon; fresh or frozen whole fish or fillets: speckled trout, red snapper, redfish, pompano, freshwater catfish, and many other species. If you're giving a big party and want to serve boiled shrimp, boiled crabs, and boiled crawfish, Lama's and Battistella's will boil them for you before shipping. They have cooking vats constantly running, and the water has plenty of salt and spices in it.

Including the air express charges, what you pay for these great New Orleans seafoods will probably be ¼ to ½ lower than what you would have to pay for similar items in your hometown.

LAMA'S ST. ROCH MARKET, 2381 St. Claude Ave., New Orleans; phone (504) 944-9493. Ask for Tony Senior, Tony Junior, or Mrs. Lama. Lama's is one of the best seafood markets in the country. Its wholesale department supplies many other wholesale dealers. When the shrimp and crawfish seasons are in full swing, the great cooking vats at Lama's turn out hundreds of pounds per day of the delicious boiled crustaceans, always spicy and with plenty of salt. Tony Senior is an honorary member of the Guild of Chimney Sweepers because he always supplies them with perfect heads-on jumbo shrimp.

BATTISTELLA'S SEAFOOD CO., 910 Touro Street, New Orleans; phone (504) 949-2724. This is the dealer most famous for speed and skill in air expressing fresh or frozen seafood—shrimp, crabs, crawfish, oysters, and all sorts of fish. Battistella's supplies restaurants in California, Chicago, Philadelphia, and Baltimore. Maryland is famous for crabs, but they're sort of small and skinny, and the top restaurants of Baltimore and Philadelphia fly in fat Lake Pontchartrain crabs.

OLD SOUTH SEAFOODS, INC., 2330 Royal Street, New Orleans; phone (504) 944-7274. Lloyd Zehner and Richard Zehner, owners. They've been open only for a couple of years, but they've already built up a reputation for the quality of their oysters, shrimp, and soft-shell crabs. They are great sticklers for cleanliness and freshness, and the displays in their store are enough to drive a seafood gourmet mad with hunger. They'll ship anything fresh or frozen anywhere.

CENTRAL GROCERY CO., 923 Decatur Street, New Orleans, and PROGRESS GROCERY CO., 915 Decatur Street. These are two of the finest importers in America. They can supply you with real stringy-type saffron, gumbo filé, imported Parmesan, Romano, and other cheeses, dried codfish (bacala), stockfish, and a wide variety of canned seafood delicacies, such as octopus, squids in ink, and smoked oysters and clams. But most important for readers of this book, they can supply the Zatarain's, Yogi, or Rex crab and shrimp boil spices, required for boiling shrimp and crabs in the true New Orleans style.

LA CUISINE CLASSIQUE, 631 Royal Street, New Orleans, is a kitchenware supply shop that can supply many of the heavy cast iron, steel, and aluminum skillets, pots, Dutch ovens, etc., that are used in Creole and Cajun cookery.

LOUBAT'S, 510 Bienville Street, New Orleans, is one of the largest wholesale and retail restaurant and kitchenware supply houses in the nation. Loubat's can supply anything from the pot you cook it in to the dishes you serve it on.

CHARLES FAGET CO., 572 East Marlin Street, Gretna, Louisiana. This is an excellent source of crab peeling knives.

259

A Note on Fish Substitutions

Creole and Cajun methods of seafood cookery can be practiced anywhere in America today. Fast-freight shipping of fresh and frozen fish, shrimp, crabmeat, and oysters has made these products available in supermarkets everywhere in the country.

Fish are versatile, adaptable, and interchangeable. Generally speaking, lean white firm-fleshed fish can usually be substituted for one another in the recipes given in this book, and so can the darker-fleshed fat fish. In fact, you can even mix the fat and the lean together in many dishes. They sometimes offset one another perfectly. It's basic to the Creole-Cajun method to experiment, to make do (with a flourish) with whatever materials you have at hand. That's the joy of creative cookery!

Here is a table of lean and fat fish from all sections of the country; choose your fish, cook it in the Creole manner, and dine like a king!

LOCATION	LEAN FISH	FAT FISH
GULF COAST	Speckled trout, redfish, red snapper, flounder, fluke, sheepshead, cobia, spot, grouper, croaker, black drum, white trout, tripletail, dolphin, scamp, rockfish, scup (porgy)	Pompano, Spanish mackerel, bonito, king mackerel, bluefish, barracuda, mullet, yellowfin tuna, shad, eel, menhaden
ATLANTIC COAST	Haddock, cod, scrod, striped bass, flounder (all types), sole, hake, sea perch (rose fish), whiting, scup, wolffish (sea catfish), turbot, weakfish, goosefish, ling-cod, mud eel (monkey fish), black sea bass	Swordfish, pollock, bluefish, bluefin tuna, common mackerel, herring, sardine, anchovy, Atlantic salmon, butterfish, halibut, alewives, eel
PACIFIC COAST	All Pacific Coast versions of the species listed above	Black sea bass, pilchard, anchovy, salmon (all species), jack mackerel, yellow tail, albacore (tuna)
FRESH WATER	Black bass, all the breams, sunfish, yellow perch, white perch, crappie (sac-a-lait), catfish, pickerel, pike, carp, all the trouts, buffalo, gaspergou.	Lake herring, whitefish, shad, smelts, landlocked salmon

Bibliography

General

Herbert Asbury, *The French Quarter*, Knopf, New York, 1976.

Lyle Saxon and others, *Gumbo Ya Ya*, Federal Writers' Project, New Orleans, 1945.

Hartnett T. Kane, *Queen New Orleans*, William Morrow, New York.

Charles Edward Smith and Frederic Ramsey, Jr., eds., *Jazzmen*, Harcourt Brace Jovanovich, New York, 1977.

Cookbooks

The Original Picayune Creole Cook Book, The Times Picayune Co., New Orleans, 1971.

Gourmet's Guide, Creole Cookbook, Elaine Douglas Jones, Claitors, Baton Rouge, La.

Quelque Chose Piquante: Arcadian Meat and Fish Recipes, Mercedes Vidrine, Claitors, Baton Rouge, La., 1971.

Cajun Country Cookin', John and Glenna Uhler, Claitors, Baton Rouge, La., 1971.

Royal Recipes from the Cajun Country, John and Glenna Uhler, Claitors, Baton Rouge, La., 1969.

River Road Recipes, Junior League of Baton Rouge, Baton Rouge, La.

Talk About Good! Junior League of Lafayette, Lafayette, La.

American Cooking: Creole and Acadian, Peter S. Feibleman, Time-Life Books, New York, 1971.

The Plantation Cookbook, Junior League of New Orleans, Doubleday, New York, 1972.

The New Orleans Cookbook, Rima and Richard Collin, Knopf, New York, 1975.

Index